ENLIGHTENMENT, RIGHTS AND REVOLUTION SERIES

ISSUES OF SELF-DETERMINATION

ENLIGHTENMENT, RIGHTS AND REVOLUTION SERIES

ISSUES OF SELF-DETERMINATION

edited by
William Twining

Series Editors: Neil MacCormick, Zenon Bankowski

ABERDEEN UNIVERSITY PRESS
Member of Maxwell Macmillan Pergamon Publishing Corporation

First Published 1991
Aberdeen University Press
© Aberdeen University Press for the collected works 1991

British Library Cataloguing in Publication Data

Issues of self-determination.—(Enlightenment, rights and
   revolution series)
   1. National self-determination
   I. Twining, William *1934–* II. Series
   323.1

ISBN 0 08 040922 9

Typeset and printed by BPCC-AUP Aberdeen Ltd.

General Editors' Foreword

The Fourteenth World Congress of the International Association for Philosophy of Law and Social Philosophy (President: Professor Alice Erh-Soon Tay, University of Sydney, Australia) was held in August 1989. It was organised in Edinburgh, Scotland, in August 1989 on behalf of the UK Association for Legal and Social Philosophy (President: Professor Tom Campbell, University of Glasgow). There were over five hundred participants from some forty countries. It focused prophetically on the theme 'Enlightenment, Rights and Revolution'.

The sessions of the Congress produced a considerable number of papers discussing various aspects of the history of ideas and the theory of rights and of revolutions. Following on the volume of papers produced for the Congress's plenary sessions (*Enlightenment, Rights and Revolution*), it was decided to produce, under our general editorship, a series of volumes of selected papers from the Congress dealing in thematic form with some of the most pressing issues in legal and social philosophy and the history of ideas to emerge from the Congress. The present volume is the fourth of this series.

The Editorial Advisory Committee for these volumes comprises all those who presided over Plenary or Group Sessions of the Congress. Its Members are:

Aulis Aarnio, Helsinki; Robert Alexy, Kiel; André-Jean Arnaud, Oñati; Jose Faria, São Paulo; Åke Frändberg, Uppsala; Letizia Gianformaggio, Reykjavik; Roberta Kevelson, Reading, Pa.; Kalmán Kulcsár, Budapest; Nicola Lacey, Oxford; Jacques Lenoble, Louvain-la-Neuve; Adam Łopatka, Warsaw; Nicolás López Calera, Granada; Burns Machobane, Maseru; Rex Martin, Lawrence, Kans.; Alan Milne, Durham; Karl Mollnau, Berlin; Enrico Pattaro, Bologna; Hubert Rottleuthner, Berlin; Setsuko Sato, Yokohama; Roger Shiner, Edmonton; Ton-Kak Suh, Seoul; Raymond Wacks, Hong Kong; Ota Weinberger, Graz; Carl Wellman, St Louis, Mo.; Elizabeth Wolgast, Hayward, Cal.; Mitsukuni Yasaki, Seijo; Marek Zirk-Sadowski, Łòdz.

All of them gave us, immediately after the Congress, their impressions of papers presented in the various sessions, some indeed giving extremely thorough appraisals and comments. This was of great value, both to the general editors of the series and to the individual editors of particular volumes. We record our warm gratitude to them all, and to other colleagues who helped in the editorial process. Efrén Rivera-Rames kindly helped with reading the proofs of this volume. Anne Bankowska was an extremely thorough assistant editor. Sheila Macmillan as Congress Secretary, and Elizabeth Mackenzie, who succeeded her as our secretary in the Centre for Criminology and the Social and Philosophical Study of Law, both gave very great help. The series editors (and their helpers) acted with an unfailing promptness and efficiency and kept to a demanding schedule which enabled us to achieve the ambition of having all the texts ready for publication within a year of the Congress itself.

Finally we record particularly warm thanks to Colin Maclean, who has recently retired from his post as Managing Director of Aberdeen University Press. From the earliest stages of Congress planning and preparation he gave us wise advice and kind support. Without his enthusiasm and shrewdness, it would have been impossible to get so much of the proceedings of the Congress so speedily into print.

Zenon Bankowski
Neil MacCormick

The Volumes in the present series are:

1　*Enlightenment, Rights and Revolution*, edited by Neil MacCormick and Zenon Bankowski
2　*Women's Rights and the Rights of Man*, edited by André-Jean Arnaud and Elizabeth Kingdom
3　*Revolutions in Law and Legal Thought*, edited by Zenon Bankowski
4　*Issues of Self-Determination*, edited by William Twining
5　*Shaping Revolution*, edited by Elspeth Attwooll
6　*Revolution and Enlightenment in Europe*, edited by Timothy O'Hagan
7　*Law and Enlightenment in Britain*, edited by Tom Campbell

A further two volumes of Congress Proceedings, on themes concerning human rights, are being published as *Beihefte* of the *Archiv für Rechts- und Sozialphilosophie* for 1990 under the editorship of Werner Maihofer and Gerhard Sprenger.

Erratum to volumes 2 and 7 of this series:

We apologise most sincerely for the fact that certain names are missing from the editorial committee as listed in the Foreword and blurb in the above volumes. The full, and correct, list is as shown in volumes 3, 4, 5 and 6.

Contents

List of Contributors

RICHARD T DE GEORGE, University of Kansas

NEIL MACCORMICK, University of Edinburgh

JUHA RÄIKKÄ, University of Turku

M B RAMOSE, University of Zimbabwe

ISSA SHIVJI, University of Dar Es Salaam

DAVID GOSLING, Staffordshire Polytechnic

ANNA MICHALSKA, University of Poznan

R S BHALLA, University of Nairobi

IAN MACDUFF, Victoria University of Wellington

EFREN RIVERA-RAMOS, University of Puerto Rico

JOXERRAMON BENGOETXEA, University of the Basque Country

HUW THOMAS, Liverpool Polytechnic

Preface

Neil MacCormick and *William Twining*

Congress organisers and other intellectual entrepreneurs are almost inevitably tempted by the cult of the centenary, and the World Congress in Edinburgh was no exception. It was, after all, a Congress on 'Enlightenment, Rights and Revolutions'. Its organisers and participants, like those of dozens of other similar events, perhaps toyed with the idea of introducing into Congress name or paper title the numerical/historical series '1689, 1789, . . . 1989?' But whether they did or not, it is doubtful whether anybody engaged in forward planning in 1986 or 1987 could conceivably have had the faintest idea what a year of revolutions 1989 would in the end prove to be. Radical constitutional redefinitions of the politics of the Warsaw Pact countries swept through the second half of 1989 in a quite unpredicted though not absolutely unheralded way. By August, already a new order was shaping itself in Hungary, while in Poland the formation of the new Solidarity-based Government actually took place coincidentally with the IVR '89 Congress to whose Proceedings the present volume belongs. Even then, the prospects of serious change in East Germany, Czechoslovakia, or Rumania still seemed rather remote. Within the USSR, there had been stirrings in the Baltic republics and in the Caucasus, and the elections of 1989 had been interesting enough to show that perestroika was far from being a busted flush. In China, there had been signs of a new dawn in Tiananmen Square, but that had been brutally swept away by tanks and gunfire, and a new repression was already taking shape. Events in Southern Africa, the Middle East, Hong Kong and the Horn of Africa also marked 1989 a year of particular historical significance.

Perhaps it is a necessary, even a defining, feature of real scholarship that it runs a little behind the times. Certainly, the scholarship of the countries seized by 1989's wave of self-determination did not run towards anticipatory celebration of the theme at the Edinburgh Congress. With but a single exception, none of the papers offered on the theme 'Self-Determination and Decolonisation' in fact came from the countries whose revolutionary self-determinations political history will record as the most memorable events of 1989. On the other hand, the works here presented from scholars of the 'West' and of the 'Third World', although in some cases already showing an awareness of the stirrings in the Eastern part of Europe, focus mainly on other places and concerns.

The questions about decolonisation and self-determination remain in any event universal in form, for all the variety of their local manifestations. Thus it is the case that, at least as much by luck as by judgement, the present authors have as their field of inquiry what has turned out to be the hottest potato of our times. The year 1989 has perhaps been the year when 1919 came of age. For long enough, little credit has been given to Woodrow Wilson's insistence upon national self-determination as the governing principle for the new Europe determined by 'the War to end Wars'. No wonder, it may be said, since that war proved to be only a scene-setter for the next one. And this happened by very reason of the deep imperfections actually (or maybe even essentially) present in the implementation of the self-determination principle in 1919, redolent as the Versailles settlement was of victors' justice, and little enough as it did for the colonial peoples still subjected to the victorious imperial powers—to say nothing of the neo-colonialism implicit in the 'Mandate' system operating in the 'liberated' colonial possessions of the defeated.

What seems now to be afoot in Europe is a new exercise of self-determination, at any rate within the states carved out in 1919, and partially re-shaped at Yalta and Potsdam. Lithuania, Latvia and Estonia, incorporated into the USSR in 1941, are now again asserting their rights of self-determination, whether or not this can be sufficiently satisfied within a decentralising soviet system. The Caucasus is in ferment. Conversely, to the West, voices from Euskadi (the Basque Country), Wales and Scotland remind us that the existing structure of 'nation states' in Western Europe is at least contestable in its claim to the uncontroversial nationhood of the states in their entireties. It is no more than an open question whether or not the European Community will become the kind of framework envisaged by some of the present authors, hospitable to the recognition of many nationalities while inhospitable to (and making redundant) the older exclusivist, absolutist, and extremist forms of nationalism which to so great an extent in the past made one group's self-determination the death of another's.[1] At least, however, it seems possible that new political forms are emerging within which old questions about self-determination can at least get new answers. If so, these may well prove influential also for eastern Europe, whether or not through such devices as membership of or association with the European Community.

Meantime, in the years since 1945, the other great sphere of self-determination has been in the realm of decolonisation, and the ending—sometimes by bloody struggle, sometimes more peaceably, though never without some violence—of the old overseas colonial empires of the Europeans. This process has taken place more or less successfully everywhere, though for the time being it has not always or even usually had the long-term result of securing democratic institutions (certainly not by way of multi-party parliamentary democracy), apart from the glorious exception of India. According to one currently received view,[2] the only sphere within which the doctrine of self-determination is actually operative as a current doctrine of international law is that of decolonisation. This is in a way paradoxical, since so often the boundaries of former colonies, especially in Africa, fail to correspond with any sort of linguistic or tribal dividing lines, so that any sense of 'one nation' was almost inevitably lacking in the post-colonial period, and this in turn proved one ground or excuse for one-party rule in those cases where old tribe became new party, thereby threatening the unity and integrity of the ex-colonial independent state. And, as several contributors to this volume remind us, the process of decolonisation rarely ends with independence. So the strongest admitted sphere of self-determination is one in which it has been so far only at best partial in implementation.

We face therefore a real paradox: on the one hand, it seems as though the idea of, or demand for, self-determination is of vital significance in shaping the contemporary world. Yet it is at best imperfectly implemented where implemented at all, and always its implementation gives rise to severe controversy whenever the question arises as to who or what counts as a relevant unit for self-determination. It is then no wonder if much writing about the topic has been sceptical at best or even downright hostile. After all, no sooner had the boundary lines of the then new European states carved from the old Austro-Hungarian Empire been drawn than all were found to have national minorities within them, and what was sauce for the Czechoslovak or Rumanian goose could be equally claimed for the Sudeten German or the Transylvanian Hungarian. And the process continues. The commonest response has been to challenge the whole idea of the 'nation' or to deny the principle of 'self-determination' as a moral principle, or both.[3] Meanwhile the international lawyers have pursued their own controversies concerning the topic, chiefly in its decolonising modes; and steadily increasing manifestations of global interdependence continue to erode notions of sovereignty and of the nation state as the main unit of international relations.

This volume reflects the depth and the variety of the theoretical puzzles and practical problems surrounding the subject. It also reminds us of the variety of voices requiring to be heard. All but three of the papers included here were prepared in response to an open invitation to the international academic community to contribute to the exploration of this theme among others within the general rubric of the conference. Only one paper, by Huw Thomas, was first written with prior knowledge of the identity or views of the other contributors. Such an invitation to a World Congress risks achieving an even closer approximation to Babel than most other academic conferences. While contributors were invited to revise their papers in the light of discussions at the Congress and of the other papers, this has produced some dialogue, but few substantial changes. The outcome has been a greater homogeneity than we had reason to hope for and an equally pleasing diversity of perspectives and concerns. Both aspects of this dualism deserve a brief comment.

The authors of the papers, in order of appearance come from the American mid-west, Scotland, Finland, South Africa (working in Zimbabwe), Tanzania, England, Poland, India (working in Kenya), New Zealand, Puerto Rico, Spain and Wales. They include a theologian and two philosophers; the remainder are all academic lawyers, but they represent a variety of legal traditions, sub-disciplines and ideological perspectives, together with a general willingness to cross disciplinary boundaries. As is to be expected from a Congress on Social and Legal Philosophy, all of the papers are theoretical in the best sense of the term, but they proceed at a number of levels of generality, ranging from abstract analysis of conceptual issues to case-studies set in quite specific historical and legal contexts. As a group they can be considered as contributions to 'philosophy' in the broad usage of the Scottish Enlightenment rather than the narrower professional usage of some English contemporaries. In the same spirit they are all directly relevant to contemporary issues in the world of affairs. While it is probably true to say that all of the authors are broadly sympathetic to the values associated with 'self-determination', they espouse differing conceptions of that elusive notion with varying degrees of caution and enthusiasm.

In the first chapter Richard De George argues that the claimed right to collective self-determination 'is not a moral right, not a human right, not a political right'. Rather it is best understood as a myth, the value and effectiveness of which depends on how it is used. In sounding a cautionary, mildly sceptical note, De George presents a challenge which is taken up by several other contributors.

In Chapter Two, Neil MacCormick, a committed Scottish Nationalist, examines the reason for a widespread philosophical disenchantment with nationalism and argues for what he claims to be 'a moderate and liberal theory of nationalism'.

In the next chapter, a Finnish jurist, Juha Räikkä, subjects Michael Walzer's concept of a 'nation'[4] to detailed critical analysis with a view to exposing some of the problems of attempting to justify a right to self-determination of nations on grounds that do not extend the same right to many other entities as well. Räikkä concludes that Walzer has usefully drawn attention to the intuition of communal self-determination, but has failed to develop a conception of nationhood that justifies giving it privileged status.

The next two papers address issues of self-determination in decolonisation with particular reference to Africa. Dr Ramose, a South African theologian teaching in Zimbabwe, argues that the supposedly decolonised still suffer the same ills and consequences as they did under colonialism because of the continued dominance of Western social and political philosophies, and indeed theologies, that emphasise individual self-preservation at the expense of justice. Western conceptions of decolonisation and development will remain irrelevant to 'the "Third World's" struggle for life' so long as the powerful reject the immensity and wholeness of Being.

From a radically different, materialist, perspective Professor Issa Shivji of Dar-es-Salaam argues that the right of self-determination, interpreted as a right of peoples rather than of states, expresses both 'the unequal and exploitative relations between African economies and those of the North and the undemocratic character of the African state'. He further argues that the so-called 'right to development' is a spurious concept that diverts attention from the realities of problems of the people of the 'Third World'.

The next chapter by David Gosling, an English philosopher, also addresses the problems of radical inequality between nations in the post-colonial era from yet another perspective. Adopting the standpoint of members of richer nations, especially of former colonial powers, he asks: 'Whose problem is it?' and 'Who has the duty to ameliorate and, if possible, to end the suffering of the poor?' After examining the views of five moral philosophers on the obligations of the developed countries and their citizens to the peoples of the under-developed world, he finds at least a partial answer in the principle of compensatory justice.

Chapters Seven and Eight consider concepts of self-determination in Public International Law. Professor Anna Michalska of Poznan University examines the methodological and conceptual difficulties surrounding these notions as legal concepts and suggests some ways forward for reconceptualising this area in a way which can deal adequately with issues of both external and internal self-determination within the framework of international law.

In Chapter Eight, Dr Bhalla of the University of Nairobi advances a different view. Adopting the approach of an analytical jurist, he argues that the right of self-determination in international law should be confined to the liberation of colonial territories, a much narrower interpretation.

The remaining chapters are geographically more specific and deal mainly, but not exclusively, with internal self-determination. Four of them can be read as case-studies of local nationalism that challenge traditional ideas of statehood and sovereignty in different ways.

Ian Macduff of the University of Wellington examines Maori rights in New Zealand. The sesquicentennial year of the Treaty of Waitangi is being 'celebrated' in 1990. This chapter presents a timely juristic analysis of the con-cept of 'partnership' within the framework of that extraordinary document.

Efrén Rivera-Ramos of the University of Puerto Rico explores a number of general issues raised in other papers in the specific context of Puerto Rico, viewed as a modern colonial welfare state which challenges orthodox conceptions of 'decolonisation' and 'internal self-determination'.

In 'Nationalism and Self-determination: the Basque Case', Joxerramon Bengoetxea argues for a particular version of nationalism in philosophical terms and applies it to the debate on Basque nationalism. He argues for a conception of 'sub-state nationalism' which is justified by self-determination as a democratic principle of personal autonomy extended to a collective level. He builds on MacCormick's institutional theory of law and expresses sympathy with his version of self-determination, but challenges the idea that nationalism is necessarily linked to the idea of the sovereign state. Rather he argues that 'self-determination is the right each nation (and other social entities) has to determine or pronounce itself on the status it wishes to have as a nation'. Applying his general thesis to the complexities of the Basque country, he argues for a moderate and flexible approach to the attainment of Basque nationhood within the framework of the Spanish Constitution, provided that is interpreted as institutionalised practical discourse rather than as a rigid document.

In the final chapter Huw Thomas, an avowed Welsh Nationalist, goes one step further in challenging received notions of state sovereignty. He explores the scope for the recognition of 'sub-state nationalism' within the international framework of the European Community. With the problems of Wales, Scotland, the Isle of Man and the Basques in mind, he analyses the suggestive precedent of Greenland which relatively painlessly acquired OCT (Overseas Countries and Territories) status within the European Community without seceding from Denmark.

A central message of this volume is that there are many hitherto muted or unheard voices that require attention when issues of self-determination are debated. As was pointed out at the Congress this is an important theme of an 'outsider's jurisprudence' that is emerging in the United States and elsewhere. The connection was made by Professor Mari Matsuda of Hawaii who has elsewhere eloquently expressed the idea that there are many kinds of oppressed or disadvantaged people and groups whose experiences of law demand to be heard and whose views challenge entrenched ways of legal and political discourse, praxis and organisation.[5]

This book, then is presented as a cosmopolitan symposium in the English language, conducted with relative detachment and academic decorum, but making no claims to being systematic or comprehensive. It follows three other collections on the same subject which were all published in 1988: *Self-determination in the Commonwealth*, edited by W J Allan McCartney; *Tribal Peoples and Development Issues: A Global Overview*, edited by John H Bodley; and *The Rights of Peoples* edited by James Crawford.[6] All four works were prepared independently and, in three cases, were published before the momentous events of 1989. The timing can hardly be a coincidence, but few, if any, of the contributors could have anticipated the political immediacy of the issues they addressed. It is to be hoped that all four works will be read as part of a continuing series of scholarly exchanges which, taken together, will be seen as making a substantial and constructive contribution to one of the great debates of the age.

NOTES

1   See especially Huw Thomas, ch 12 below.
2   E.g. W J Allan MacCartney, ed, *Self-determination in the Commonwealth* (Aberdeen, 1988).
3   See, however, H Beran in MacCartney, op. cit., ch 2.

4   M Walzer, Spheres of Justice (New York, 1983).
5   Mari Matsuda, 'Looking to the bottom: critical legal studies and reparations', *Harvard Civil Rights—Civil Liberties Law Rev*, 22, p 323 (1987); 'Public response to racist speech: considering the victim's story', *Michigan Law Rev*, 87, p 2320 (1989).
6   MacCartney, op. cit., n 2; this was a selection of papers from the 1986 Edinburgh Colloquium on 'Self-expression and Self-determination in the Commonwealth Context'. John H Bodley, ed, *Tribal Peoples and Development Issues: A Global Overview* (Mayfield Publishing Co, Mountain View, California, 1988) is an anthology which grew out of a graduate seminar on 'Tribal Peoples and Development' at Washington State University in 1985. It usefully relates issues of autonomy and self-determination to the broader literature on development. See also J Brosted ed *Native Power* (1985) and Noel Dyck, ed, *Indigenous Peoples and Nation-states* (Newfoundland, 1985). James Crawford, ed, *The Rights of Peoples* (Oxford, 1988) is a valuable collection of essays, mainly written from the perspectives of legal theory and international law. For a recent, different perspective on the history of ideas about nationhood, see Ann Dummett and Andrew Nicol, *Subjects, Citizens and Aliens* (London, 1990).

CHAPTER 1

The Myth of the Right of Collective Self-determination

Richard T De George

How can we make sense of the frequently asserted right of collective self-determination? Making sense of it is a problem because the right and the claims made in its name are varied and are frequently ambiguous in several ways. The solution I propose is that the right of collective self-determination is best understood as a contemporary myth (in the Lévi-Straussian sense of the term[1]). An analysis that approaches this right as a myth captures its meanings and functions better than such alternatives as considering it a human right, or analysing it as an ideology. Calling the right a myth in the Lévi-Straussian sense does not deny its importance or undermine its possible validity. Rather myths both reveal and hide parts of reality, and serve to make sense of and validate certain actions. They typically form part of a whole, and come in several variations. All of these features are satisfied by the right of collective self-determination.

Meaning and Status

The meaning of the right of collective self-determination is ambiguous. There are various stories that can be and are told about it. In one sense it refers to a claim on the part of any group of people to determine their collective actions. In this sense the right of collective self-determination is a right claimed against a state or against other groups for the given group to carry out its chosen activities free from outside interference. This right, as other rights, is limited only by the right of other groups similarly so to act. The right of collective self-determination in this sense, for instance, is used to defend the formation and activities of voluntary associations, such as labour unions, religious groups,

1

corporations, or other organisations that people are free to join and free to leave.

A second common meaning of the right of collective self-determination—and the one that will be our major concern in this paper—refers to the right of people to choose the form of government under which they will or do live. This meaning is ambiguous in several respects. The first is in the extension of the collective in question. The right extends ambiguously to all individuals, or to all people taken as a whole, or to all or to certain groups or subgroups within a given state. If it is meant to be a collective right that each individual exercises together with other individuals, or that all individuals taken as a whole exercise, then any state established without the consent of every individual would violate the right of the dissenters. Such an interpretation is so strong that according to it no state of any size would be formed, or if formed no state could be justified. If the right is meant to extend to all groups, then minority groups would have the right to establish a state, despite the majority's preference; if it extends only to certain groups, it is unclear why those are privileged. If the special group is 'a people', it is unclear whether that means a tribe, an ethnic group, a cultural group, or something else. It is not clear that there is anything one can call 'the American people', if homogeneity, blood relationships, or cultural history are the determining factors; and the notion of 'the German people' has an historical ring that may cause some to be wary of using the notion of 'a people' as bearers of any rights. If the right refers to the state as such, the relation of the state to its members is unclear.

Another aspect of its ambiguity involves specifying what self-determination means and how it is to be ascertained. Sometimes the right of collective self-determination is used with respect to and forms part of consent theories. Sometimes it is used with and forms part of legitimation theories. At other times it is used with and forms part of revolutionary theories. And at still other times it is used with and forms part of democratic theories. Each of these variants is part of the myth, and all together form the myth-system to which it belongs.

A current dominant sense of the right seems to be in relation to anti-colonial movements and to revolutionary movements against dictatorships. It is a purported right of a people of a given state to determine for themselves how they will be governed when they are in conditions that they and others consider to be violations of that right.

The myth reveals a widespread liberal belief in the autonomy of persons and in the right of peoples to be free of foreign domination and of tyrannous rule. But the myth hides the fact that the right—without any justification being given—is simply not thought appropriate for many groups, or for many minorities within established states.

The American, French, and Russian Revolutions are all instructive in this regard. They can each be seen as in some way using the right of collective self-determination to justify the revolutions that took place in those countries. Yet the justifications for each are very different from one another.

The American Revolution was an anti-colonial revolution. The American

Declaration of Independence states the belief that people should have the right to govern themselves and to be free of tyranny. In effect, the Declaration is a statement of the right of collective self-determination. Clearly it did not affirm that in order to be effective every individual in the territory in question had to agree with it; the Revolution was fought, and those who wished to remain British subjects had no choice but to accept the victorious majority's position or to leave for Britain or Canada. Most significant for our purposes, however, is what happened some eighty-five years later. When the Southern States wished to secede from the Union, they plausibly were expressing their right of collective self-determination. Although the United States was founded on that right, the right to secede did not extend to any group within the established state, nor to any parts of that state. The American Civil War was fought by the North to prevent the Southern States from separating themselves and forming an independent nation.

That war and that result were not anomalies. In fact they represent the dominant interpretation of the right of collective self-determination, at least as practised by contemporary states.

The French Revolution was not an anti-colonial revolution but a revolution by the French to free themselves from the French monarchy. It was fought on the slogan of freedom, equality, and fraternity. Again one can make out the implicit claim of self-determination by a people to overthrow a tyrannous regime and to establish a democracy. We know that soon after overthrowing the monarch, the French were ruled by the Emperor Napoleon and that French armies had no compunction about conquering and subjugating neighbouring states. How such actions squared with the claim of self-determination on the part of all was not raised, at least not by the French.

The Russian Revolution, fought in the name of the workers, was followed by the establishment of a new state, the Soviet Union, a union of many republics. In 1940 Latvia, Lithuania, and Estonia were brought into the Union following a pact between Stalin and Hitler. How such incorporation squares with self-determination remains at best a disputed issue. At the present time, national liberation movements in the Baltic States as well as in other republics such as Soviet Georgia, are generally thought to be comparable to the attempts at secession by the American Southern Confederate States. Once a nation is formed, the right of collective self-determination seems to recede for any minority or group within the state. The consent of the majority of the state as a whole seems to be sufficient to satisfy the collective right of self-determination.

Paradoxically, some of the very states that developed democracy, formed democratic governments, and nurtured the notion of the right of collective self-determination for themselves became colonial powers. One result is that the right has come to mean the right of the majority within a given territory, and, until relatively recently, it was a right of developed nations and not of less developed ones.

Finally, how the territory in question was formed or is defined is in many cases arbitrary. Many of the African states were formed not on the basis of homogeneous peoples but by agreements among colonial powers, or by conquest without respect to the indigenous population. If we interpret the right of collective self-determination to apply not to groups within a nation state but only to the majority of those who happen to be in the political state as defined, we see how anomalous the right of collective self-determination is.

Clearly, the right is not a human right nor a straightforward collective right. The status of myth seems best to capture its reality. As we shall see later, its function is also mythic.

Derivation

The doctrine of the right of collective self-determination is at best a derived right. It is derived from and modelled on the right of individual self-determination. This right is fundamentally a moral right. It comes in its clearest formulation from what it means to be a moral being in the Kantian sense of the term. The right is a statement of the third formulation of Kant's categorical imperative. Moral autonomy is the right of an individual to be subservient to no one, to be subject to the moral law as it derives from reason and not from the fiat of any individual or authority. Autonomy in this sense is equivalent to self-determination because one is morally free. But in the Kantian sense one is only free when one is governed by law and when one acts as the moral law commands. It is this feature that makes autonomy possible in society. If autonomy were simply the right to act as one pleased, society would be impossible.

The collective right of self-determination is derived from the individual right of self-determination insofar as it is simply the individual right exercised by individuals in a joint effort or collectively.

The right collectively to act with others in forming voluntary groups, organisations, unions, churches, etc, corresponds to the first meaning we distinguished. The right of the resulting organisation is not clearly a moral right because the organisation is not clearly a moral entity. Nonetheless, the organisation has the right to do whatever the individuals collectively have the right to do. The right is a derived right, even if its moral status is ambiguous.

The derivation of the collective right of self-determination in its second sense is more problematic, in part because of the ambiguity of that sense. The derivation of the right as applied to 'a people' suffers from the lack of clarity of that term. It certainly requires defence for anyone to claim that the German people have a right to collective self-determination that the American people do not have, even though the former can claim linguistic ties and the latter not. Why and how similar language, or a collective history, or a common culture gives some groups a collective right that other groups do not have is neither self-evident nor clear.

The world is divided into states, and it is not clear what it would mean to say that one has the right either to be free of states or free to set up a state if one is dissatisfied with any of the existing ones. A right that cannot be implemented is vacuous.

How one could derive the collective right of self-determination in the context of the modern state is also not clear. The collective right to organise is derived from individuals collectively exercising their individual rights insofar as their actions do not violate the right of others to similarly exercise the right. Since any state has the exclusive right to the exercise of ultimate force or authority in the territory, it is not compatible with others also so organising in that territory. Hence except in the case of unanimous agreement, no state can legitimately be established on the basis of the right of collective self-determination. Furthermore, even if all the governed consented and originally set up a state using the right of individual self-determination collectively, it would be a mistake to claim that because such a state was initially justified, it continued to be justified if later anyone dissented.

Although this collective right is confused with justification according to the consent of the governed, it would also be a mistake to think that no other justification for a state is possible because of individual autonomy. The individual right of self-determination is compatible with any form of government, not in the sense that every form of government is adequate to the dignity of persons, but in the sense that the individual moral right of self-determination cannot be taken away from anyone, even by slavery.

That people who agree to set up a state should be allowed to do so—a presently impossible demand—does not entail that all legitimate states must be or must have been established in this way. That people should assent to the states in which they live, if those states are to have legitimacy, is not the same as the right of collective self-determination. The right does not specify exactly what legitimacy consists of. Colonies were once governed by mother countries, and there was a presumed acceptance of this state of affairs by most modern states. In some instances, e.g. Canada with respect to Great Britain, this relationship seems to have been acceptable to all the principals concerned. Colonial status by itself does not entail lack of legitimacy or the lack of collective self-determination.

As I noted earlier, however, legitimacy and collective self-determination as presently understood do not require that every citizen or subject of a state acknowledge the right of the government in power to rule. In many countries minorities are denied the right of self-determination by the acceptance of the doctrine of majority rule, perhaps with some guarantee of individual rights. The right of collective self-determination in its second sense is not a moral right and cannot be derived from individual autonomy.

Nor is there any moral or political right of states or nations to self-determination. Nations and states are not moral agents and cannot have moral rights, except in some derivative sense. They exercise sovereignty, which is a political right, recognised in the international arena as much out of self-interest as because of any other reason. Any claimed national right of self-determination either translates into the right of the people collectively to choose their fate and to determine by their established structures how to act, or it means the sovereign right of each state to run its own internal affairs without unsolicited interference from other nations or states.

The mythic aspect of the right is evident in that the specific nature of the right is rarely specified. It is not a right established internally by any system of law, and in international law it is a highly restricted right, limited, for some unspecified reason, only to peoples and only in cases of decolonialisation. Nonetheless, it is sometimes claimed to refer to nations as such, sometimes to majorities in nations, sometimes to peoples, sometimes to other groups. The weight given to the claims made in the name of the collective right of self-determination also varies dramatically, and often depends on one's place in the international balance of power and on the ideological spectrum. Thus claimed wars of liberation may be waged in the name of the collective right of self-determination. But the justice of such wars, and the question of which group really represents the people and is acting in its name and on its behalf are frequently disputed. Any claims to self-determination by minorities in established countries are typically ignored by other established powers, as internal issues to be settled by those within the country. I have already mentioned the Estonians and the Soviet Union; the same is true of the Irish and Great Britain. Nicaragua divides the allegiance of different sides. South Africa is tolerated, even if there is some pressure to end apartheid, which represses the Black majority. Ethiopia's treatment of its minorities is also tolerated, as is Israel's treatment of Arabs on the Left Bank.

Function

The right of collective self-determination thus turns out to be more of a manifesto right than either an enforced or enforceable legal, political, or moral right. It is a term used ambiguously for a variety of political purposes in an attempt to sway public and sometimes world opinion in support of a cause. Sometimes that cause is rebellion; sometimes a call for change; sometimes simply an expression of dissatisfaction; sometimes a claim of justification. Its mythic aspect is congenial to all of these and more.

If the argument so far is persuasive, then it would be inappropriate to evaluate the right of collective self-determination as either a strictly moral claim justifiable in moral terms and on moral grounds, or as a strictly political claim, justifiable in terms of the political structures of nation states. Its status is ambiguous; it resonates with morality, and has political uses. The mode of evaluating a myth, however, is different from that of evaluating a moral or a legal-political right.

Myths are evaluated by how well they perform their function, which is to explain and justify some phenomenon to those who hold them. They are no more scientific than moral. Their explanatory and justificatory functions depend on their being accepted and their cohering with a set of other beliefs. In this case the set of beliefs is most often the justifiability of nation states and national boundaries, the legitimacy of national sovereignty, the defensibility of governments, and the belief in democratic majority rule, among other beliefs. To claim that the evaluation of the right of collective self-determination in the mythic mode depends on how well it coheres with these beliefs neither implies that these components and beliefs are themselves mythical nor that they are not. But one of the conclusions to which this mode of interpretation leads us is that the right of collective self-determination cannot be falsified or be evaluated independently of the whole of which it forms a part.

The right of collective self-determination clearly has a function in the rhetoric and politics of the contemporary world. Analysis can tell us, as it should, that the claimed right is not a moral right, not a human right, not a political right. Mythic analysis can help us to understand it and can provide the justification of which it is most susceptible. The justification of the right is found in its usefulness. When it is no longer useful, it will eventually no longer be used. Such an analysis neither undermines the right nor negates it. Rather it places the right in perspective and keeps those who understand its place from being misled into believing claims sometimes associated with it that are false or unfounded.

If one could mount a thorough-going moral defence of the collective right of self-determination, it would challenge the political status quo in many presently established countries. The myth of collective self-determination hides and allows many who use it to ignore the logic of this challenge, while providing legitimation within limits recognised by traditional nation states. As with many collective rights, its status depends on the recognition of the collective in question—which is most frequently a political and legal determination, rather than a moral one. Its effectiveness as a manifesto right is a function of the conditions under which it is asserted. One can attempt to clarify the meaning of the right to collective self-determination in particular circumstances. But any attempt to restrict it to certain senses which one attempts to justify is to limit it arbitrarily. And any such attempt will fail to change its many current uses. Understanding its mythic status helps us understand why it resists clarification of its ambiguous meaning and status, and why it is sometimes effective when invoked and sometimes not.

NOTE

1. See Claude Lévi-Strauss, 'The structural study of myth', *Journal of American Folklore,* 78 (Oct–Dec 1955), no 270, pp 428–44 (also available, with other writings, in *The Structuralists from Marx to Lévi-Strauss,* Richard and Fernande De George, eds (Garden City, Anchor Books, 1972).

CHAPTER 2

Is Nationalism Philosophically Credible?

Neil MacCormick

The present argument has four main sections. In the first, I raise some questions about the ambiguity of the idea of a free country, and show how some considerations arising from that have led to a disenchantment with nationalism as a philosophical topic rather than a regrettable historical phenomenon. In the second, I take up the perhaps antithetical point that in relation to decolonisation and *perestroika*, most people seem to take a view rather strongly in favour of national self-determination, without really relating this to the first position of reluctance to allow that nationalism has any place in a normative political philosophy. In the third I return to ideas of freedom in the hope of dispelling confusion and perhaps even transcending the contradiction between the first and second sections. Finally, I face directly the question whether nationalism is philosophically credible, and end by commending what I consider to be a moderate and liberal theory of nationalism.

The thesis I commend is one which seeks to avoid the condemnation which in the next chapter Juha Räikkä directs at theories of nations as mystical entities. For there, his attack is upon the theory of Michael Walzer which in effect confines any right of national self-determination to those willing to define themselves as a group by the violent and bloody struggles they are willing to engage in. My own view is no less opposed to the politics of violence than is Räikkä's. But it seems to me possible to construct a non-mystical concept of the nation, and to show how certain rights can plausibly be ascribed to such entities, without thereby committing anyone to a politics of violence. By the same token, I believe one can meet some of the points taken in the preceding chapter by Richard De George, the gravamen of whose case appears to be simply that existing states do not on the whole accede to all or even most claims to self-determination, sometimes having reasons of real persuasive force for the stand they take. This is not wholly convincing of itself, however. If there is a moral right to self-determination, its existence as such is no more negated by the refusal of existing states to honour it than is the existence of human rights as moral rights negated by the refusal of so many states to honour them. On the other hand, the fact that there are sometimes morally respectable reasons which countervail those in favour of self-determination means at most that a right to self-determination cannot be an absolute right in all settings. Nothing in what follows amounts to an absolutist thesis about the rights of nations.

I

We talk often about free human beings, and even today we are all too liable to talk just about free men. In sometimes the same breath, sometimes quite a different one, we talk about free countries. Sometimes we think or speak of a country as being free when it is free from external dominion, sometimes we mean that its internal governance is such as to leave people free to act as they will, often with the implication that they are even free to do undesirable things. "'Mind if I smoke here?'"—"'It's a free country'" is not a dialogue wherein the second speaker registers approval of, far less pleasure at, the prospective exercise by the other of the freedom she or he is conceded to have. Still, a country which is free in this second sense is apt also to be one whose inhabitants are free people, that is people who as individuals are left considerable scope to act according to their own choices and discretions without undue governmental interference, and above all without arbitrary governmental interference. The incompatibility of arbitrary rule with the freedom of humans as individual persons is the ground for our considering the Rule of Law to be one among the absolutely necessary conditions of liberty.

There is clearly a deal of sorting out to be done among senses of freedom, but I hope for the moment that these sketchy remarks sufficiently highlight two distinguishable senses. In that light, we have to ask what if any relations obtain between the two sorts of freedom of free countries I have identified. Can a country be free from external dominion and yet fail to be a free country from the point of view of its citizens' enjoyment of civil liberty? Can individuals have civil liberty even if their country is not self-governing? The answer in both cases appears obviously enough to be 'yes', and accordingly it seems as if civil liberty is not necessary for national independence and national independence not necessary for civil liberty. At best the two concepts seem to be independently variable.

Not merely is this so, but among persons of liberal disposition, exactly those most favourable to freedom as civil liberty, there has been a long-standing suspicion of the notion of national independence, and of politics promoting the values of a nation as a whole as against those that promote the ability of citizens as individuals and in their freely chosen groupings to choose and pursue what they think valuable, even against actual or supposed national preferences. Liberals, that is to say, mistrust nationalism. Nor do they want for examples to exhibit the real grounds for their mistrust. From Hitler to Ceausescu, there has been no shortage of illustrative evils showing how the pursuit of national liberty and national values can lead to denigration, servility, torture and death for those outwith the charmed national circle, and even for many within it. Liberals, needless to say, are not alone in their mistrusting. For most socialists also, the appeal to national values is deeply suspect as at best an ideological device to paper over the cracks of class division and exploitation. Jingoism and xenophobia can be whipped up to mask the realities of division, exploitation and unequal freedom within a country. Some would doubtless see something of an example of this in the startling recovery of political fortunes by the first Thatcher administration consequential upon the war in the Falkland Islands, or Malvinas as I shall also call them in pursuit of a doubtless illusory objectivity. The antics of *soi disant* nationalists such as M. Le Pen on the nastier extreme right of contemporary European politics provide a more unequivocal example of the point.

Thus from the point of view similarly of liberalism and of democratic socialism, it does not appear that there is much to be said for nationalism. This seems to hold good even if such a proponent of conservative liberalism as F A Hayek can argue that in truth socialism itself always amounts to national socialism in the adversative sense, appealing at the deepest level to tribal instinct rather than respecting individual moral agents as such (Hayek, 1944). The fact is that in his eyes socialism is as much and in the same way an enemy of freedom as is nationalism, for at bottom they are the same enemy. From the socialist side of the argument, the response is (in some cases anyway) that the conservative liberal's conception of freedom is an inadequate and impoverished one, precisely in acknowledging a place only for negative freedom, freedom *from* various sorts of public and private interferences and restrictions, while insufficiently attending to positive freedom, freedom *to* participate in the social self-constitution of a community, freedom *to* develop and express one's own personality in the collective, but not necessarily uniform, self-expression of all. Less ambitiously, socialism is at least about freedom *to* in the sense of giving everyone a real chance to do things, by securing everybody a fair, if not perfectly equal, share of commonly available resources in order to make the exercise of even negative liberty similar in worth for all (see, e.g. Crick, 1987).

I have already at best glided over, and at worst begged, more than a few questions even in these opening remarks. But I hope I have done enough to remind you of the quite familiar, not to say hackneyed, questions of freedom which arise the moment one pauses to ponder the credibility of nationalism from a philosophical point of view. It is pretty obvious, and obvious why it is obvious, that the overwhelming consensus of contemporary philosophers towards nationalism is one of hostile dismissiveness. Nationalism is seen as at best a phenomenon to be explained in historical or psychological terms, an aberration of romantic idealism, not a serious topic for normative political philosophy. A brilliant example of this historical-explanatory approach, coupled with the standard consensual critique of nationalism, can be found in Kenneth Minogue's *Nationalism* (1967).

II

Before I proceed to deal with any of the questions I have raised—or begged—so far, I wish in what may be a suitably Hegelian style to introduce some considerations contradictory to the points just made. The contradictions arise out of the way in which people of liberal or otherwise progressive opinion respond towards popular self-determination in the context of decolonisation. The abandonment by the West European imperial states of their colonial possessions overseas, and the nation-state building efforts of the governments of newly independent ex-colonies have on the whole been welcomed, even where nation-building in the odd slices of territory left behind after nineteenth-century European carve-ups has led to authoritarian government, one-party rule, and substantial restrictions in freedom as civil liberty in countries lately come to the freedom of independence from external control. Even where this has happened, there is a common opinion, which I certainly share, that the ending of colonial rule was on the whole and in itself good.

Perhaps even more popular among us western intellectuals have been the movements toward national liberation and greater internal democratisation among the countries of Eastern Europe and, recently, in some internal republics of the USSR. To recall the emotions awakened by and judgements perpended about the Hungarian rising of 1956, or the Prague Spring, or the time of Solidarity in Poland (now happily returned), or to contemplate opinion now about the Baltic republics or Georgia or Armenia or Afghanistan is to see how equivocal opinions as well as terms can be in this area of discussion. In these cases, it seems to be a common conviction that if only countries could become more free in the sense of enjoying enhanced external independence, they could also become more free in the other sense, with their citizens enjoying greater and more secure civil liberty. Even that may be to over-intellectualise the issue. Maybe it is just that, since people so obviously want some new deal from the Soviet state, democratic imperatives require applause for every step taken towards their getting it, and most particularly such steps as themselves involve some form of democratic self-expression.

I was lucky enough to have the opportunity of visiting Poland for the first time myself in October 1988, and the experience of doing so certainly aroused in me pretty much the last-mentioned opinion. Everywhere I had then a sense of a gap between the state and the society, a sense of aspiration unfulfilled through the inability of the state to respond to views of the vast majority of citizens. Everywhere also one had a powerful sense of the Polishness of Poland, and yet of a frustration that this was locked into an inefficient and unpopular system of government. So to say, there was here a nation whose state was serving it ill. (If one were to speak of the Church, that might be a different matter). So any tendency towards a greater democratisation of government, a greater re-inclusion of the nation in the state, would surely be welcome, and that on simply democratic grounds.

Such an example as this, and the others mentioned, do however seem to set up an antithesis to the thesis with which I started. Contemporary moral and political philosophy has on the whole regarded nationalism as a significant but regrettable political phenomenon rather than a political position with a case to make at the level of normative philosophising. (There are, of course, quite a few exceptions, and I am here conscious of indebtedness at least to the late John Plamenatz, to Yael Tamir whose doctoral thesis I had the pleasure to examine in Oxford last year, to Harry Beran (1987), who has explored issues of self-determination and of secession in a powerful series of articles, and to Tim O'Hagan, some of whose ideas on individualism and pluralism I wish to apply or perhaps misapply here.) Yet in the face of the general indifference or hostility to the idea of nationalism, there has been a generally approving response to colonial liberation and national liberation in certain settings, where principles of self-determination of an essentially nationalist sort seem to have been at stake. There appear to be contradictions or at least confusions as to the sorts of free countries it is desirable to have.

In this state of things there is surely a task for philosophy, a challenge to which philosophically-minded persons ought to rise. Can we after all make any sense of nationalism? Can we in any way resolve my questions of freedom by reconciling in any way the two senses of a free country, the country which is free because its citizens have liberty, and the country which is free because it has independence itself? To pursue this task will call for a certain clarification of confused ideas (I do not deny that their confusion owes as much to what I have written so far as to anything in the *Zeitgeist*). So I shall attempt some clarification in the next section, before moving in the fourth and final section to my conclusions.

III

Here, I shall start with a clarification and critique of one civil libertarian conception of a free country. Clearly, there is a great deal to be said for a polity which secures to its citizens the traditional civil and political rights which are broadly constitutive of what Isaiah Berlin taught us to call 'negative liberty', the liberty which consists in *not* being required or forced to do or abstain from things one would not freely choose to do or abstain from (Berlin, 1969, ch 3). The pursuit of happiness requires life and liberty. Mutual respect and self-respect in a moral community require each to have regard to the liberty of others and all ideally to endorse an equal liberty for themselves and everyone else. To this, John Rawls has recently added the useful qualification that unequal liberties can be justified where they strengthen the overall scheme of liberty (Rawls, 1972, p 302). Perhaps parliamentary or judicial privilege give MPs and judges freedoms of speech that the rest of us do not have; but it seems easy to see that the whole scheme of liberty is advanced rather than undermined by such special entitlements. In any event, the flourishing of human good in each and every bearer of humanity seems to be furthered by a regime of civil liberty, on one conception of human good. That is to say, for those who regard autonomy as being of the essence of human and moral value, it is only where conditions of liberty admit of each person's autonomous pursuit of the good as they see it that the good life can be truly realised.

The appeal to autonomy as a human and moral good is not, however, the only possible way to argue the case for liberal civil liberty, and some may even find it a dangerous mode of argument since it itself depends on a so-called perfectionist ground, namely the idea or ideal of autonomy as a constitutive part of human good (See Raz, 1987). Some wish their theory of liberty to be yet more neutral than that as between visions of the good, arguing that the special strength and attractiveness of liberalism lies in its refusal to privilege either any philosophical conception or any individual vision or any state-defined imposition of models for the good life (see Nino, 1989). The natural line for this kind of theoretical approach to take is that of assuming liberty not so much to be conferred on, as to be retained by, the citizen. This suggests that liberty inheres in us in some way anterior to and independently of our social existence, the only question being how far we may lose it or should give it up. Social contract models of legitimation arise almost inevitably in this setting, whether as historical models or, more credibly, as hypothetical or imaginary contracts like that proposed by John Rawls. Hobbes's question, how much of their natural liberty individuals must transfer to the state, is and remains in some form the basic question from this point of view. The question is not what or how much liberty states should give their citizens; rather, it is how much liberty persons should forego in favour of the needs of government, however these needs are conceived. The continuing theme of one strand of liberal thought is that the needs of government must always fall short of the framing and imposition of any one conception of the good life.

This, however, seems to rest on a deeply implausible vision of human society. For it makes absurdly atomistic assumptions about the character of human beings. It is an untenable kind of 'methodological individualism'. It imagines that there could be individuals anterior to any form of organised society who could intelligibly come together and agree to constitute one. Nor is it obvious why the fiction of a merely hypothetical contract can get one round the difficulty. It is one thing to make a hypothesis about what could have happened, but did not; another thing altogether to try and work through an imagining of something which could not conceivably happen.

The truth about human individuals (and it seems to me perhaps Hegel's greatest contribution to philosophy was that he in effect discovered this truth) is that they—we—are social products, not independent atoms capable of constituting society through a voluntary coming together. We are as much constituted by our society as it is by us. The biological facts of birth and early nourishment and the socio-psychological facts of our education and socialisation are essential to constituting us as persons. We are the persons we come to be in the social settings and contexts in which we come to be those persons. At the ground floor of our very sense of our own identity is a personal name. You have completely forgotten who you are if you have forgotten your name. Yet names are in the main given not chosen, and they are given or chosen within a language and an elaborate coding of what counts as a name, and this is significant even for names like 'Malcolm X' which are chosen to make points critical of established naming practices; that is, it is within a web of social practices that we get to be individuals.

Atomistic or methodologically individualistic assumptions cannot but be false. All individuals as they really are fall into the class of 'contextual individuals', if I borrow a term from Yael Tamir's doctoral thesis 'Nationalism within the Bounds of Liberalism'. We have a sense of self because of the way we have learned to be ourselves in the contexts in which we have so learned.

This does not commit me to some kind of mechanistic social determinism. There seems no reason why people cannot come to be autonomous selves within certain kinds of social contexts, and we all have the evidence at least of introspection and also of acquaintance with others to tell us that it is so. It is individuals that we have become in our context, individuals capable of showing autonomy in action. We may value certain sorts of social organisation exactly because and to the extent that they both make possible individuality, individualism and autonomy, and because they create protected spheres of legal liberty within which the exercise of individual autonomy is protected. I take it that Hegel's representation of the constitutional state as the concretisation of reason was intended to make just this point.

So far as it was, we ought to accept his point even if not exactly his way of putting it. In any event, we can now see that the absurdity of methodological individualism in no way entails the rejection of some form of normative individualism (a point I take from Tim O'Hagan, 1990). I may disbelieve that individuals can be conceived as pre-social or extra social atoms whose unions come to be constitutive of societies, and at the same time quite consistently believe that we ought to favour forms of social organisation within which human beings can be constituted as and can flourish as autonomous individuals. For reasons I at least hinted at above, I do in fact commend both this disbelief and this belief. Autonomy is indeed a fundamental human good, and thus it is a great social value to uphold societies which facilitate it. So when we talk about free countries in the sense of countries enjoying secured civil liberty, we should not think of them as though they just contingently happen to be peopled by free humans; each is partly conditional on the existence of the other.

What then about free countries in the other sense? At least I think it will now be becoming clearer that I have to move towards revising my earlier suggestion that the two senses of 'a free country' are quite independent of each other. The first move is to take up the thesis that some form of democratic self-determination has to be considered both justifiable and valuable on rather the same grounds as the simple negative liberties in the list of civil liberties. Some form of collective self-constitution, some kind of active participation in shaping and sustaining the institutions of social or communal government whose aim is to advance liberty and autonomy, seems to be a necessary part of the whole ensemble of conditions in which the autonomy of the contextual individual could be genuinely constituted and upheld. If autonomous individuals require the context of some sort of freedom-enabling society, then the collective autonomy of the society itself seems a part of the necessary context.

No doubt certain sorts of enlightened despotism and certain sorts of enlightened colonial government can create the possibility of civil liberty and economic or professional freedom of trade; these in themselves are valuable as helping to develop autonomy by creating conditions for its full development. But so long as the state stands apart from and above civil society, there is only a partial autonomy of individuals. This stress on the activist and participative character of full autonomy, thus of the need for a collective as well as an individualistic component of autonomy, is a point justly taken by democratic and socialistic critics of mere negative liberty. It is a part of the just reply to Hayek's earlier-mentioned critique of socialism. For democratic institutions depend on the ability of all to take part as the equals of every other, and this requires a whole range of basic conditions in the way of freedom from acute need, satisfactory education and so forth, as well as setting limits, however vague, upon the extremes of economic inequality which are tolerable. Autonomous liberty in a free country requires schemes of redistribution, welfare provision and educational support which would be absolutely excluded by conservative liberalism of the sort which denies the state any role other than that of the night watchman. Very few people nowadays support that view anyway, and much of our political argumentation seems to me to be more about the *how much* than the *whether* of redistribution, welfare, and education. In that sense, it remains true, malgré Mrs Thatcher, Mr Tebbit, Lord Joseph and all, that we are still all socialists now, as Sir William Harcourt remarked all those years ago.

So self-determination is after all a vital part of any acceptable conception of liberty as autonomy, self-determination in a dual sense, meaning that there has to be scope both for individual self-determination inside a political community and for the collective self-determination of the community without external domination.

This should not be thought a particularly novel finding or conclusion. After all, the International Covenant on Civil and Political Rights and the International Covenant on Economic, Social and Cultural Rights both open with the stipulation that:

> All peoples have the right of self-determination. By virtue of that right they freely determine their political status and freely pursue their economic, social and cultural development.

So the theses I have argued so far might perhaps be taken to constitute justifying reasons in favour of an already authoritative doctrine of international law.

IV

All these considerations bring me well towards answering my basic question, whether nationalism can be a philosophically credible doctrine, properly belonging within a normative political philosophy. For the doctrine that 'peoples' have the right to self-determination is itself central to liberal nationalism. And yet this very doctrine itself has been found problematic because of the difficulties of applying it *in concreto*. Woodrow Wilson's famous attempts to apply the doctrine through the Versailles settlement, and all the problems of sorting out people from people, and minorities within minorities within minorities have led many to the same position as Hugh Seton-Watson, that of rejecting the basic idea as not merely impracticable but essentially chimerical, postulating the existence of metaphysical objects such as 'nations' or 'peoples' where no such identifiable entities really exist (Seton-Watson, 1964).

How should we then deal with this challenge? My strategy is to take it up in two stages. The first is to deny the claim that nations are chimerical objects; but the second is to acknowledge the practical problem created by the interweaving and overlapping of nations and national identities, deriving from that the need for a moderate form of nationalism, shorn of some of the more absolutist claims which in my opinion have been the source of the acutest problems about nationalism.

Stage 1 In the earlier discussion, I pointed out that all individuals are 'contextual individuals'. Our sense of identity arises from our experience of belonging within significant communities such as families, schools, workplace communities, religious groups, political associations, sports clubs—and also nations, conceived as cultural communities endowed with political relevance. A nation is constituted by a sense in its members of important (even if internally diverse) cultural community with each other based in a shared past, a 'heritage' of common ways and traditions, including at least some of a family of items such as language, literature, legend and mythology, music, educational usages, legal tradition, religious tradition, all of which cumulatively are regarded as bearing on the legitimacy of government, at least in the sense that governmental decisions which denigrate or belittle any of the focal elements in a given cultural tradition are viewed as abusive of power. Nations exist wherever there are substantial numbers of individuals who share in some degree a common consciousness of this kind.

Observe that I do not say that the nation is made up of the sum of such individuals, for that would be to go back down the rejected road of atomism. The individuals in question necessarily have it as a part of their sense of identity that they are of this culture and heritage, so the nation is as much an essential factor constitutive of their being who they are, as their being so is constitutive of its being what it is. It is rather like the fact that you can no more have shareholders without a company whose shares they hold than you can have a company without shareholders to hold its shares. This does not make either companies or nations mystical or chimerical entities. They are institutional facts, points of imputation, respectively of legal and of moral imputation, essential to the way in which we make sense of economic and of cultural and political life. So the conclusion to this stage of the argument is that nations are quite real and quite identifiable as some among the types of community constitutive of people such as humans now are. They do not exist because of deliberate once-for-all choices or decisions, although the choices and decisions of many contribute to how they are and change and develop or grow or atrophy or wither away. Nor is there anything in this account to guarantee them any special primacy in our consciousness or any sort of natural or necessary exclusiveness or special geographical spheres one as against another. They can and do overlap and intertwine with each other and with other significant political and non-political groups, communities and organisations of all sorts.

Stage 2 The second stage of this part of the argument must now proceed to try and set up some moral or political principles relevant to the state of affairs described in the first stage. If there really are nations with an existence such as I impute to them, what difference does that make? What ought to be done about them, what if any rights do they have, and why?

The answer begins by taking up the basic moral imperative of respect for persons. If, as I claim, a sense of nationality is for many people constitutive in part of their sense of identity and even of selfhood, then respect for this aspect of their selfhood is as incumbent as respect for any other, up to a certain point. The key point is, of course, that at which one national self-expression or self-assertion becomes destructive of another. The Irish joke and the lust for *Lebensraum* are at bottom objectionable on the same ground, albeit with mighty differences of degree. Within the limits set by equal respect and equal allowance of self-respect, respect for persons must include respect for national identities.

But national identities carry political aspirations. The relation between the existence of a nation and the perceived conditions of political legitimacy was noted a moment ago. So respect for nationality does require some acknowledgement of political demands grounded in the needs of national communities for political conditions hospitable to their continuance and free development. Further, the whole idea of the desirability of creating the conditions for autonomous self-determination both of individuals—contextual individuals—and of the groups and collectivities constitutive of them leads back to the claim of self-determination as quite properly a claim on behalf of each nation on similar terms to any and every other.

I insist on this as a universal principle, and couple this universalism with the earlier noted imperative of equal allowance for equal respect among national identities, just like other identities. A part of the odium philosophicum attaching to nationalism (and richly earned by a good few nationalists in political arenas from South Africa to Iraqi Kurdistan and elsewhere) lies precisely in its failure to universalise and treat essentially like claims in like manner. But this in itself can no more discredit the legitimate claims of reasonable nationalism than the rampant selfishness and non-universalism of some individualistic persons discredits of itself universalistic doctrines of political individualism.

A further point of insistence concerns the non-exclusiveness and non-absoluteness of national claims. Since the French Revolution, there was until a few years ago an insistence both on the exclusiveness and on the absoluteness of national rights. Nation states were sovereign states, and sovereignty had to be absolute. There was a parallel doctrine of unity. For every state, but one nation, whatever violence this might do to the facts of history or the consciousness and self-respect of minorities. Historians have tended to treat these theses as paradigmatic for nationalism, and thus to treat nations and nationalism as features exclusively of the post-revolutionary world. I have elsewhere argued that this is an inept model for a theory of nationalism, one which for example makes unintelligible such aspects, say, of Scots history as the response of the community of the realm of Scotland to Edward of England's claim to overlordship in 1286, or the Declaration of Arbroath in 1320, or Barbour's Bruce, or the Covenant of 1638 and much else (MacCormick, 1982). Rather, the virulent doctrine of the sovereign and absolute nation state which arose after the revolution, important though it may have been in the rise of modernity, is but one conception of a concept with a longer past and, I hope, still a future.

That future need not be one that replicates the errors of the past. There are signs in the European Community that we are slowly learning how to transcend the sovereign state without dissolving the nation. In such a setting, the ancient nationalities of Europe can perhaps again come into their own, in conditions of mutual security, mutual respect and a whole variety of interlocking levels of non-sovereign government. Among the friends and colleagues I have made in the course of a fortunately far travelled professional life I can count Basques, Castilians and Catalunyans, Walloons and Flemings, South Tyrolers, Bavarians and Italians and Austrians and Hungarians and Czechs, Scots and Irish and Welsh and of course a great many English, Poles, Ukrainians, Azeris and Russians, Greeks and Turks and Armenians, Finns, Aalanders, Icelanders, Swedes, Norwegians and Danes and of course a great many others. It fills me with a sense of the richness of human experience and culture that there are so many variants on the common human theme and indeed so rewardingly many ways of being European. I hope we can contrive a politics that secures a survivable economy and ecology for us all, enables us to keep peace among ourselves and yet allows for the mutually respectful flourishing of many nationalities.

In that sense, I believe my chief question should be answered in the affirmative. Nationalism can be a philosophically credible doctrine and ought to be embraced in its philosophically credible form. Some of you will know that in my private capacity I regard this as tending in a certain direction so far as concerns our electoral politics of the present. But I shall not trespass out of my role or on to your courtesy by doing any more than to allude to that point.

It occurred to me as I composed all this, that the Grand Old Duke of York made his name by marching his troops to the top of the hill and marching them down again, but I seem to have used the opposite procedure. I started by marching down the hill and casting all kinds of doubt on the case I was to defend. I hope I have succeeded at the end in marching at least a respectable distance back up the hill of my readers' good humoured scepticism.

(Note: this paper was first presented, in a slightly different version, as the Malcolm Knox Memorial Lecture in St Andrews University on 4 May 1989)

BIBLIOGRAPHY

Isaiah Berlin, 'Two Concepts of Liberty', ch 3 of I Berlin, *Four Essays on Liberty* (Oxford University Press, Oxford, 1969)

Bernard Crick, *Socialism* (Milton Keynes, Open University Press, 1987)

F A von Hayek, *The Road to Serfdom* (London, G Routledge and Sons, 1944)

Neil MacCormick, 'Nation and Nationalism', ch 13 of N MacCormick, *Legal Right and Social Democracy* (Oxford, Oxford University Press, 1982)

Kenneth Minogue, *Nationalism* (London, Batsford, 1967)

Carlos S Nino, 'Moral discourse and liberal rights', ch 7 of *Enlightenment Rights and Revolution,* N MacCormick and Z Bankowski, eds (Aberdeen, Aberdeen University Press, 1989)

Tim O'Hagan, 'An unsolved dilemma of liberalism', forthcoming in *Recht und Moral,* Heike Jung, ed, 1990

John Plamenatz *Consent, Freedom and Political Obligation* 2nd edn (London, Oxford University Press, 1968)

John Rawls, *A Theory of Justice* (Cambridge, Mass, Harvard University Press, 1972)

Joseph Raz, *The Morality of Freedom* (Oxford, Oxford University Press, 1987)

Hugh Seton-Watson, *Nationalism and Communism* (New York, Praeger, 1964)

Yael Tamir-Raffaeli, 'Nationalism within the Bounds of Liberalism', (Oxford, Oxford University D Phil Thesis, 1988)

CHAPTER 3

On National Self-determination: Some Problems of Walzer's Definition of Nation

Juha Räikkä

In the history of philosophy and international law there have been many attempts to construct a framework for the morality of intervention in international relations. Often the main queston has been the problem whether there is an obligation to take action to combat moral abuses happening inside the boundaries of another integrated community, nowadays called a nation state. In this essay I pose this question once again. First, Michael Walzer's communitarian theory of the right of nations to self-determination will be reconstructed, and second, a critique will be mapped out by showing that Walzer's definition of 'nation' is highly unclear.

According to Walzer's 'legalist paradigm', every nation state has a moral right to self-determination and, correspondingly, every nation state or its government is under obligation to respect the integrity of other communities' internal affairs (Walzer, 1977; 1985). In Walzer's view, nation states are moral entities in which autonomous processes of social life take place and in which there exists a union of people and government, constituted by mutually accepted historical conventions, communal sentiment, loyalties, and resentments. As Walzer puts it, 'community rests most deeply on a contract, Burkeian in character, among 'the living, the dead, and those who are yet to be born''' (Walzer 1985, p 219). The point is that moral meanings are seen as being grounded in this special kind of contract: communal life and its normative structures require self-enclosed political arenas, and global pluralism is the basis of all morality (ibid., pp 217–37). Although all this may sound somewhat obscure, the intuition behind Walzer's argument is clear and well-known: people cannot be given liberty.

Walzer thinks that individual rights are both analogous to nation states' rights and the basis for these. He writes that 'when we describe individual rights, we are assigning to individuals a certain authority to shape their own lives, and we are denying that officials, even well-meaning officials, are authorized to interfere'. A claim of analogy is made when he goes on to say that 'the description of communal rights makes a similar assertation and a similar denial', for 'in the individual case, we fix a certain area for personal choice; in the communal case, we fix a certain area for political choice', a choice which is of course collective in its nature although not necessarily a 'democratic' one. Hence Walzer does not think that the right of self-determination is grounded on the usual consent-argument. Walzer says that individual rights are also a ground of communal rights. According to him, 'rights are only enforceable within political communities where they have been collectively recognized, and the process by which they come to be recognized, and the process by which they come to be recognized is a political process which requires a political arena'. Further, Walzer writes that 'against foreigners, individuals have a right to a state of their own' and 'against state officials, they have a right to political and civil liberty', but 'without the first of these rights the second is meaningless: as individuals need a home, so rights require a location' (ibid.). Therefore, Walzer sees communal rights as a necessary condition of the morally acceptable enforcement of individual rights.

Improbable as it seems, however, Walzer allows that external states may unilaterally suspend the ban against intervention in three specific cases. First, when one foreign power intervenes in support of one side in a civil war, other powers may rightfully intervene in support of the unaided party. Second, humanitarian intervention in the affairs of another community is allowed in cases of massacre or enslavement, for these make 'talk of community or self-determination cynical and irrelevant'. And finally, a point of especial interest, intervention is justified when what is at issue is national liberation or secession: for the principle of self-determination is maximised when new nations are helped to achieve their own freedom (Walzer 1977, p 90). Hence the right to self-determination is in fact unconditional.

It is important for Walzer to be able to distinguish between civil war and national liberation, for only in the latter case is intervention legitimate. Practically speaking, however, making this distinction is not a very easy task. In any case, Walzer suggests that one can be sure that a struggling group in fact represents a distinct community (and not just a rebelling minority) if it has 'rallied its own people and made some headway in the "arduous struggle" for freedom' and if it appeals to the principle of self-determination. In his view there is 'the need for political or military struggle sustained over time', for 'evidence must be provided that a community actually exists whose members are committed to independence and ready and able to determine the conditions of their own existence' (ibid., p 93). Consequently, Walzer is driven to call fighting a morally relevant property: communities which do not fight are not entitled to self-determination, for, actually, they are not genuine communities at all.[1]

For the sake of argument, let us now presume that a presupposition of

Walzer's argument is correct: that a theory can indeed be formulated which, first, makes true respect for communal life possible and, second, avoids the problems of ethical relativism; that there is a plausible theory which (universally) denies interventions between special social entities while it justifies independent norm-formation inside them; that there are indeed social entities which have a right to form their own moral structures and even structures which are not consistent with the universal or impartial moral codes. Clearly, this is the main thesis of Walzer's argument: in his theory these entities are called nations. And here Walzer meets one of the most persistent lines of theoretical criticism of the principle of self-determination: the definition of this mystical entity.

In Walzer's view the significant criteria by which we can identify the relevant entities are its struggle for existence and its appeal to the principle of self-determination. Only if an entity fights does it deserve a right to autonomous existence. But why exactly is it a morally relevant feature that an entity struggles? Surely it is an implausible viewpoint that war and political antagonism enjoy crucial moral value.

First, one cannot say that the fighting criterion is necessary to demonstrate when a community really exists: the consequence of this would be that nations which do not fight would lose their right. Moreover, in this case we would have a merely contingent principle of self-determination, for we would have to respect only those historical communities which have been bellicose. Second, it cannot be claimed that a nation's fighting is identical with its being a community. Such a claim would not only use language in confused manner but would also invent a wave of interventions: obviously, if every group called a 'nation' in some weak sense 'fights' and if fighting justifies external support of a fighting party, then we can forget the principles of non-intervention and self-determination. It is clear that this is not what Walzer intends to say. Therefore, there are two conclusions to draw. For one thing, Walzer does not seem to talk about 'nations' in a conventional way. Of course he hopes that he does, but the radical consequences, a wave of interventions, does not make it possible.[2] And for another, he does not give us a morally relevant definition of an entity entitled to self-determination, for fighting is not a property which could entitle a group to self-determination.

Clearly, Walzer's failure is a traditional one: he fails to give a morally adequate description of the 'nation'. On the one hand, fighting and an appeal to the principle of self-determination are not adequate criteria morally to entitle an entity to self-determination. On the other hand, if we find a more sophisticated version of 'fighting' as an acceptable criterion for entities entitled to self-determination, it cannot easily be a property which distinguishes the nation from other autonomous entities: families, cultures and even particular professions, for instance; for, obviously, these too are committed to autonomy in their norm-formation and mutual life, and these too 'fight' in some complex sense to achieve their rights. (On the analogy between nations and families see Elfstrom, 1983.)

A theory which avoids these problems is a challenging project. First, one must answer the question as to what transforms an 'ordinary' social entity into the kind of community entitled to unconditional self-determination. The unconditionality is an especially problematic condition, although—contrary to widely held belief— it surely is crucial to any argument about entitlement to communal rights. It is crucial, since if we say that a relevant social entity is entitled to self-determination only when it has this or that quality, then our argument for self-determination is only pseudo-argument: for in this case we are imposing from outside the community the way in which it is entitled to 'determine' itself. (An entity is entitled to determine itself only how it is determined from the outside to determine itself.) This has nothing to do with true self-determination, of course. And the problematic nature of this necessary unconditionality of self-determination is also clear. Counter-intuitively, Mafia groups or Nazi nations would then be clearly entitled to self-determination. For if a peaceful nation is entitled to self-determination because of its internal relations, or if a normal family is entitled to autonomy because of its internal integrity, then morally unacceptable entities must also be entitled to self-determination, provided that they have the relevant internal relations, or whatever it is which is the criterion for an autonomous entity.

The second problem is how to distinguish the nation from other 'communal' entities such as cultures, families and so on. It is not enough to describe what it is which makes an entity eligible for self-determination; for, to reiterate, surely we will find the same sort of morally relevant properties in entities which are not called nations as in entities which are called nations. But to talk about the right of national self-determination and not about social entities' right to self-determination in general, there must be something special in 'being a nation'.

There are two ways to try to capture this special quality: one is to give some internal attribute of a nation, and the other is to argue for some external criterion. However, both of these methods are problematic. There seem to be no credible internal and morally relevant demarcation criteria by which we can distinguish a nation from other social entities: neither language nor internal altruism is such a criterion, nor is territoriality, authority or isolation from other entities, for instance. Attempts to find a demarcation criterion are well known and so are their failures (see French and Gutman, 1974). The problem of external criteria is also easy to see. In a word, the use of external criteria to answer the question why it is just nations (and not other integrated social entities) which are entitled to self-determination, is against the 'spirit' of the principle of self-determination. For example, if we think that the right of self-determination must be given to nations and not to families or highly homogeneous cultures because it is reasonable from a utilitarian point of view, then we are once again presenting a pseudo-argument for self-determination. For if we allow a nation autonomy only on utilitarian grounds, then we can forget a true principle of self-determination: once again we are imposing from outside the community the acceptable ways of 'self-determination'. (For example, we are saying that 'now your community is big enough but not too big for integrity and autonomy'.) It is of course possible that it indeed is reasonable from a utilitarian point of view to give the right of self-determination only to nations; but this is not what is of interest here.

From the foregoing, it will be clear that Walzer does not pay sufficient attention to the central problems of the right of nations to self-determination. In conclusion, then, we can say that if one tries to assign a right of self-determination to nations in a 'true form' and not only in a 'pseudo-form, then the whole paradox of communal morality must be solved first, a paradox which says that if we want to assign a right of self-determination to nations we are committed to allowing it for very many other entities too, and this, unsurprisingly, leads to contradiction in practice. In his attempt to solve this paradox Michael Walzer has not succeeded especially well. Nevertheless, he acknowledges the intuition of communal self-determination, an intuition which many others have failed to notice, and the problem Walzer encounters can be attributed to any argument which acknowledges this—very important—intuition.

NOTES

1 In his *Spheres of Justice* (New York, 1983) Walzer again presents an argument to which the notion of national community is crucial, but one cannot found any clear definition of it.
2 Walzer, too, thinks that there is a danger of allowing too many interventions.

BIBLIOGRAPHY

Gerald Elfstrom, 'On dilemmas of intervention', *Ethics,* 93 (1983)
Stanley French and Andres Gutman, 'The principle of national self-determination', in *Philosophy, Morality, and International Affairs*, Virginia Held *et al.*, eds (New York, 1974)
Michael Walzer, *Just and Unjust Wars* (New York, 1977)
Michael Walzer, 'The moral standing of states: a response to four critics', in *International Ethics,* Charles Beitz *et al.*, eds (Princeton, 1985)

CHAPTER 4

Self-determination in Decolonisation

M B Ramose

Introduction

The foundation of decolonisation is the recognition and indeed the acceptance of the principle that the consequences of colonial conquest need to be reversed! This recognition includes the correlative principle that the process of reversal must be upon a just basis and that justice should be a manifest consequence in the new order brought about by decolonisation. Historically, colonial conquest consisted of the following general characteristics:

1   the fact of the military defeat of the conquered by the colonials;
2   land disseisin or expropriation;
3   imposition of colonial rule by way of:
    (a) destabilising the indigenous socio-economic systems in order to adapt and adjust them to the order desired by the colonial conquerors,
    (b) modification or outright rejection of the indigenous culture wherever and whenever it conflicted with the culture of the colonial conquerors. This was designed to ensure the overall dominance of the colonial conquerors over the indigenous ways of life;
4   systematic and continual subjugation of the conquered people or indigenous societies in order to ensure the preservation of all that has been mentioned in 1,2, and 3 above. Subjugation revolves around the principle that the relationship between the conqueror and the conquered will be in the character of dominance-subservience.

In the light of the foregoing the question that arises is the following: in what way and to what extent has decolonisation been a veritable reversal of the consequences following upon the military defeat of the conquered indigenous people? Apart from the fact of military defeat of the conquered indigenous peoples, have all the general characteristics of colonial conquest, already mentioned, been really removed through decolonisation? The fact of military defeat of the conquered indigenous peoples is set apart for the simple reason that it is historically unrepeatable. It does not therefore follow that the conquered indigenous people are precluded from pursuing the military option in their quest to remove the general characteristics of conquest. Our reflections with regard to the questions posed will apply, with due modifications, to the so called 'Third World' and more specifically to Africa in general. It goes without saying that even in this latter case specificities in terms of time and place call for modification of the generality of our discourse. However, since it is our intention to bring to bear a characteristically philosophical response to the questions posed, we will remain at the level of generality—speculative thought—fully recognising that such speculation will be meaningless without due regard for specific concretions. Yet it goes without saying that speculative thought is always based upon concrete reality.

Our philosophical reflections then will hopefully illumine the following thesis:

> Colonisation and decolonisation are based upon naturalistic deontology or self-preservation. Although the face of colonisation has changed under the appellation of self-determination and decolonisation, the underlying naturalistic deontology remains unaltered. This latter consists of two basic interactive tendencies, namely, the constructive and the destructive. These tendencies continue to shape human history. With particular reference to Africa the destructive tendency of self-preservation manifestly regulates and dominates the behaviour of the former colonialists. On this basis the African experience of self-determination through decolonisation is that international relations proceed from a complex structure which continues to deprive the African people of authentic self-realisation. Accordingly, a relevant social and political philosophy for Africa, nay, for the so called 'Third World', must proceed from the reality, the experience of the 'Third World's struggle for life. The former colonialists should rid themselves of rigidity, formalism, conceptualism and absolutism in order to be able to participate constructively in the reading of the 'Third World's' experience of the struggle for life. Without this, self-determination and decolonisation will remain irrelevant to the crucial issue of the 'Third World's' struggle for life.

The Philosophy of Decolonisation

Ontology

The fact of being-in-the-world has mainly been understood as expressive of the separation between the human entity (consciousness, the self) and the world at large (cosmos). No doubt another way of understanding the fact of being-in-the-world is that all entities in their multiplicity and diversity are expressive of the oneness or unity of the world or cosmos. On this view separation is no more than a specific manifestation of the oneness of being. The ontology of colonisation—colonial conquest—is based upon the first view. According to this view the cosmos exists for the sake of the human being. In this sense the human being is the centre of the cosmos. Consequently, the human being as a specific individual entity is entitled to use all that there is in the world to preserve its own life. So it is that the central meaning of being human is to recognise the gratuity of life (being thrown into existence for no specific reason) and from there to take the decision to choose life, that is, to preserve one's own life. Thus non-life or death is regarded as something that ought not to be preferred. The will to live then becomes the reason that justifies the gratuity of life. The reason for the gratuity of life is to live. This justification means that being-human-in-the-world is to be confronted with a fundamental choice, namely, the choice between life and non-life or death.[2] The praxis of the will to live means that the world(being) must respond to the needs of the individual human by being the same as the individual needs demand. Thus the sameness of being becomes both the regulative principle and the guarantee in practice for the preservation of individual life. The will to live is a command to the world to remain the same. In terms of colonisation this ontological framework means that the colonials perceive the indigenous peoples as a threat to the life of the colonials. On the ground of this perception of the other as an agent of death, the other was then to be eliminated, reduced to non-life. Therefore, 'Before the *ego cogito* there is an *ego conquiro*; 'I conquer' is the practical foundation of the 'I think'.[3]

The Other as an Invitation to Life

The conception of the human being as the centre of the world together with the ontology of the will to live discussed above, have led to colonisation and its ensuing consequences. The elimination of the other through actual death or the reduction of the other to non-life through subjugation affirms the colonial conqueror as the centre of the world and is a practical guarantee of his will to live. Contrary to the ontology upon which the praxis of the colonial conqueror continues to unfold, the apparition of the other is primarily a beckoning, an invitation to life. The other—the conquered indigenous peoples—shares with the colonial conqueror the will to live but not the conception that the self is the centre of the cosmos. The decentring of the self from the cosmos allows for the invitation of the other to life. The opposition between these two conceptions of the will to live means that the colonial conqueror has arbitrarily and selfishly chosen and imposed death upon the conquered people. Decolonisation is a belated though not entirely voluntary recognition of the fact that this arbitrary and selfish imposition of death upon the conquered people is both unjust and an outright contradiction of the pre-eminent meaning of the other as an invitation to life. Although decolonisation has come to this recognition, it is clear that in the sphere of international politics as well as international relations the former colonial powers do not understand the meaning of the apparition of the other as an invitation to life to be the abandonment of the conception that the human being is the centre of the world. Consequently, the decolonised continue to suffer the same ills and consequences, and sometimes even more, than those that they have experienced under the yoke of colonialism.

Self-Determination In Decolonisation

The fact that the conquered people continue to suffer the same ills and consequences—and sometimes even more—as those that they have experienced under the burden of colonialism means that decolonisation has not ushered in self-determination. If this latter term means authentic, independent and free self-expression as well as the pursuit of self-realisation with due regard for the interests of the other on the basis of justice, then this has not yet become the experience of the decolonised.[4] On the contrary, the former colonials have understood decolonisation to mean:

(i) systematic and limited physical withdrawal by themselves from the erstwhile colonised territory;

(ii) adherence to the conception of the individual self as the centre of the world. In consequence of this the decolonised people were:

    (a) to continue to be subjugated despite the granting of political independence;

    (b) to continue to be denied economic independence which is an indispensable element of political independence;

    (c) to be encouraged and even manipulated into aspiring for admission—especially—to Western 'civilisation', and, following upon such admission to remain faithful servants of Western 'civilisation'. This was clearly designed to ensure the dominance of the culture of the colonial conquerors over that of the conquered peoples. In this way the latter would remain the junior partners in a philosophical discourse as well as a corresponding praxis within the framework of Western 'civilisation'. This was designed to keep the progeny of the conquered peoples as the perpetual servants of Western 'civilisation'. The ideology of the sameness of being, which, as we have already suggested, is part and parcel of colonialism held, therefore, that decolonisation would mean the deliberate and systematic inhibition of the self-determination of the conquered peoples. Through philosophical mimesis translatable into appropriate praxis the progeny of the conquered peoples were to be made to lead a life of unauthentic existence and be purposely obstructed in their quest for self-realisation. So it is that self-determination as an experience of the progeny of the conquered peoples in the supposedly new order brought about by decolonisation means that, from the point of view of the posterity of the colonial conquerors, self-determination must remain still-born even in decolonisation. The still-birth of self-determination in decolonisation means the institutionalisation of the condition of dependency to which the progeny of the conquered people continue to be subjected since the military defeat of their ancestors by the colonial conquerors. Thus present-day international relations can be described, with particular reference to the so called 'Third World', as the ongoing experience of self-determination in decolonisation.

Development in Servitude

The ontological conception of the apparition of the other as an invitation to life as well as a demand to decentre the self from the cosmos constitutes the foundation for authentic development. The quest to ensure individual and collective survival and continually to improve the quality of human life is the essence of development. Development then has got two interrelated aspects to it. First, it is an affirmation of 'I am' in the context of 'we are' and second, it is the quest to perpetuate this condition through the continual improvement of human life in order to sustain it for as long as possible. Development as the avoidance and postponement of death represents the general human reluctance to return to our unknown origin once we have experienced life as we know it. It is beyond question, therefore, that human life is at the centre of development.

When the system of states expanded beyond the confines of Western Europe in the emergent global international system, the relations between the West European states in particular and the new member states of the international community were no longer based upon the erstwhile principles of mutual respect and fair play.[5] Instead, verticality replaced horizontality with regard to relations between the West European states and the new member states of the international community. Verticality pointed to both the assumed superiority and the corresponding dominance of the West European states in the conduct of international affairs. Despite the changed situation in international politics, especially in the aftermath of decolonisation, both the superiority complex and the persistent dominance of Western states remain more than apparent. In the sphere of international politics a sharp division is made between national individuality—the state as the individual writ large—and international community. This fragmentation on the basis of verticality underlines the division between *us* and *them*. Accordingly, what we have here is the apotheosis of the 'I am' which seeks the exclusive satisfaction of the needs of the individual self. Justice is rendered irrelevant in this context and, indeed development as well, because the survival of the other and the continual improvement of the quality of the other's life are subordinated to what is regarded as the prior claim of 'I am' to the same. As a result the life of the other becomes conditional upon the 'I am' first ensuring his survival and improving the quality of his life. Thus it is not profoundly recognised here that both the 'I am' and the other have an equal claim to survival as well as to the improvement of the quality of their life. On this reasoning, reciprocity in the sense of fair and mutually beneficial dealings is excluded. This then captures the essence of the Western conception and model of development which is dominant in the structure, organisation and conduct of international affairs. In decolonised Africa and the so-called 'Third World', development as a substitute for colonisation is in reality an insurance for underdevelopment. The Western model for development is yet another instance of the arbitrary and selfish imposition of the death sentence upon vast innocent multitudes of people in Africa and the so-called 'Third World'. As such it is not a model of development *for the life of human beings.* In the light of this it is clear that the development that the dominant West continues to impose upon the so-called 'Third World' is, in reality, development for servitude.

Justice in Development

The 'Third World' experience of a still-born self-determination in decolonisation is a reality that demands transformation on the basis of justice. The misery and poverty that ineluctably lead to the death of multitudes in the 'Third World' are the consequence of a model of development designed to deprive the poor of life. Yet the poor as a collective alterity is simultaneously an invitation to life and a cry for justice. The poor are an invitation to life because they are not a threat to the life of the other. Instead of being a threat to the life of the other, the poor are a challenge to the other to live and construct social relations on the principle of the forgetfulness of the self.[6] Life, according to this principle, is a recognition that the poor are dialectically poor in the double sense of their being kept systematically poor by the rich and powerful and also because of their opposition to the rich and powerful. Life according to the principle of the forgetfulness of the self means, therefore, the will to give up one's life in order to give life. In the era of decolonisation the reality of the North–South relations shows that the Northerners either eschew or are unwilling to live according to the principle of the obliviousness of the self. This is precisely what prevents the realisation of justice in the North–South relations. Yet, the alterity of the poor is a cry for justice; justice that recognises the imperative of restoration and restitution to the dialectically poor. The basis of authentic development then is to give life to the poor but along with and together with the poor. Giving life then will be according to the poor but for the sake of other human beings, especially the rich and the powerful, since their participation in this process will mean a willingness to live according to the principle of obliviousness of the self. This is the essence of justice in development.

Life Without a Centre

Life according to the principle of the forgetfulness of the self means voluntary self-immersion into Being. It means the willingness to be absorbed into Being. Such a willingness is impossible unless the individual human being recognises that he is infinitely insignificant and even almost invisible in the face of the immensity and wholeness of Being. Accordingly, openness to being requires a profound sense of humility as the foundation of the willingness to be in the service of Being by giving life to the other.

   Self-preservation then means, in the first instance, a fundamental option to give life in recognition of the fact that ultimately only Being is the giver of life. Yet, up until now the world has been dominated by social and political philosophies which are opposed to the principle that only Being is the giver of life. These social and political philosophies are based upon a fundamentally wrong premise, namely that naturalistic deontology or self-preservation belongs in the first instance to the single individual human being. Consequently, the human being is said to be bound by nature to seek and secure the preservation of its individuality, that is, the 'I' that the human individual is supposed to be. This type of reasoning is isolative. It is fragmentative in that it proceeds by breaking Down being into separate, discrete and isolated entities and then assumes that the myriad divisions it has constructed reflect the true character of Being.[7] In practice this fragmentative thinking has led to divisions of humanity—sometimes deadly divisions—into noble and commoner, superior and inferior race as well as theist and atheist to name but a few. It is well known that this type of fragmentative thinking, which is a clear manifestation of the destructive aspect of self-preservation, continues to plunge humanity into suffering, conflict and death. In our day the threat of nuclear omnicide hangs over humanity because of the illusion of self-preservation. The reverse perspective, namely, to give life according to the principle of the forgetfulness of the self as a service to the self-preservation of Being, the ultimate giver of life, is a challenge to the dominant social and political philosophies including all the religions in our day.

NOTES

1   B Davidson, *Discovering Africa's Past* (Longman Group Limited, London, 1978), pp 185–209.

2   J Sobrino, *Spirituality of Liberation: Toward Political Holiness* (Orbis Books, Maryknoll, New York, 1985, 1988), p 111.

3   E Dussel, *Philosophy of Liberation,* A E Marinez and C Morkovsky, trans (Orbis Books, Maryknoll, New York 1985), p 3.

4   C A Dior, *Black Africa: The Economic and Cultural Bases for a Federated State,* H C Samuelson, trans (Lawrence Hill and Company, Westport, Connecticut, 1978), p 34.

5   G Stern, 'Morality and international order', in *The Bases of International Order* (Oxford University Press, London, 1973), pp 140–1.

6   J Sobrino, op. cit., pp 32–3; *The True Church And The Poor,* M O'Connell trans (Orbis Books, Maryknoll, New York, 1984, p 178.

7   D Bohm, *Wholeness and the Implicate Order* (Routledge and Kegan Paul, London 1980), pp2–3.

CHAPTER 5

The Right of Peoples to Self-determination: an African Perspective

Issa G Shivji

Introduction

The argument of this chapter is that the right to self-determination is a central right in the contemporary African situation. It captures some of the fundamental tensions in the socio-economic and political set-ups of Africa. It expresses within it the unequal and exploitative relations between the African economies and those of the North as well as the authoritarian and undemocratic character of the African state.

Precisely for these reasons the right to self-determination, we submit, is a hotly contested terrain. On the one hand we have the practices of the African states (including those of the Eastern 'socialist' countries) which attempt to restrict the right to self-determination to colonial or colonial-type situations. On the other hand, we have a series of 'civil wars' raging on the continent which seem to take the 'right to self-determination' way beyond a typical colonial situation to the internal aspects of national and nationality-oppression within the juridically sovereign states. It is this contest that we seek to highlight in this chapter. The chapter makes a critique of the existing state practice and proposes a re-conceptualisation of the 'right to self-determination' from the standpoint of the vast majority of the African people.

The chapter also compares the 'right to self-determination' with the 'right to development' and argues that the latter fails to express the interests of the people of Africa. Rather it is a *statist* proposition expressing, at best, the interests of the ruling classes.

The Constituent Elements of the Right to Self-determination

A Limitations of the Right to Self-determination in the Soviet and African State Practice and the Consequences Thereof

The 'right to self-determination' is eminently a democratic right or principle. It first arose during the bourgeois democratic revolutions in eighteenth- and ninetheenth-century Europe. Its comprehensive theorisation is to be found in Lenin's writings, where it was elaborated as a 'Right of Nations to Self-determination'. The Soviet state was the first to put it into practice when in the 'Declaration of Rights of the Working and Exploited People' it proclaimed complete independence of Finland, evacuation of troops from Persia and freedom of self-determination for Armenia.[2] In the League of Nations practice it was not yet recognised as a principle of international law.[3] It was for the first time included in the United Nations Charter at the insistence of the Soviet Union, albeit in a truncated form.[4] Significantly it does not appear in the Universal Declaration of Human Rights and did not find a clearer formulation until 1966 in the International Covenants.[5]

The principle of self-determination, or as it has now been formulated, 'right of people to self-determination', is now generally recognised as a *right* in international law.[6] What is contentious is of course what it implies, includes and excludes. We briefly look at that debate.

In Lenin's thesis on the 'Right of Nations to Self-determination', it is very clear that he was referring to the right of *oppressed* nations to independence and formation of their own separate states. Hence there the right includes the right to secede.[7] In the *Decree on Peace* which was written by Lenin, he gave a definition of annexation which also serves very well as a definition of self-determination, for annexation is nothing but a 'violation of the self-determination of a nation'.[8] Lenin characterised annexation as

> any incorporation of a small or weak nation into a large or powerful state without the precisely, clearly and voluntarily expressed consent and wish of that nation, irrespective of the time when such forcible incorporation took place, irrespective also of the degree of development or backwardness of the nation forcibly annexed to the given state, or forcibly retained within its borders, and irrespective, finally, of whether this nation is in Europe or in distant overseas countries.[9]

Since the Second World War, and during the era of decolonisation, the Soviet practice has consistently applied only one aspect of Lenin's thesis, i.e. formation of sovereign states by the formerly *colonised* people, but it has otherwise resolutely upheld the principle of territorial integrity, state sovereignty and non-intervention. In Lenin, it is clear, that the principle applied not only to colonial nations 'in distant overseas countries' but also to nations in independent states such as in Europe. Secondly, the Soviet practice has been that the principle is implemented once a colonised country gains independence, while for Lenin it was a *continuing* principle and could be invoked at any time by an *oppressed* nation even in a sovereign state.[10]

The Soviet practice is akin to the UN, the OAU and the Afro-Asian *state* practice. In its own relations with African states, the USSR has applied that position even in opposition to a struggle for national self-determination as in Eritrea.[11] Cassese puts it succinctly:

> According to socialist countries, self-determination, considered as the right to non-intervention, means the right that foreign States shall not interfere in the life of the community *against the will of the government*. It does not include the right that a foreign state shall not interfere in the life of the community *against the interests of the population* but at the request or at any rate with the tacit approval of the government.[12]

What has been stated by Cassese was best illustrated in the case of Idi Amin's Uganda where the Soviet Union supplied that fascist dictator with arms to slaughter the population.[13]

Restriction of the right to self-determination to colonial and colonial-like situations (South Africa) in the state practice of the Soviet Union and African countries and the absolutising of the principle of territorial integrity is based on a two-fold rationale. On the one hand there is the fear that the recognition of this right would lead to dismemberment of states and encouragement of secessionist movements and on the other it would provide a fertile ground to foreign powers to support such movements, thereby weakening the sovereignty of African states. Of course, underlying both these 'reasons' is the very nature of the African states which have failed to apply both consistent anti-imperialism and democracy. Recognition of the right to secede does not automatically mean that every nation or people have a *duty* to secede; indeed the fathers of this right believed that the very *recognition* of the right to secede and the democratic treatment of all nations and nationalities within a particular state led to a situation of voluntary *union* of nations rather than secession. For, to emphasise once again, the right belongs to an *oppressed* nation and if a nation is not oppressed, that is to say, if it is treated democratically and accorded equality, both the reason and rationale for secession disappear. The problem in Africa has been precisely that the existing states have not treated nations and nationalities under them democratically; hence their fear that the recognition of this 'right' will lead to secession. As a matter of fact, oppression of nations and nationalities in Africa has led to devastating civil wars and gross violations of the rights of the whole masses of people.[14]

A very good illustration in this regard is the case of Sudan. The central problems of the Sudan and the causes underlying the present war have been well-summed up by Akol as:

> the dominance of one nationality over the others, the sectarian and religious bigotry that has dominated the Sudanese political scene since independence, and the unequal development in the country.[15]

In other words, Akol has identified precisely those factors—national oppression, undemocratic, authoritarian state system, and imperialist domination—which are supposed to be countered by the principle and concept of self-determination. The history of the Sudan itself illustrates these tensions and the fact that their relative resolution is intricately tied up with these factors.

The only time the Sudan had 'peace', so far as the question of Southern Sudan is concerned, was after the signing of the Addis Ababa agreement in 1972.[16] The agreement provided for fairly comprehensive self-government for Southern Sudan. And during the first period of the operation of the agreement some intention was shown to redress extreme underdevelopment in the South.[17] But the irony of the agreement was that while Southern Sudan was granted certain democratic rights, the central government continued to be run on the basis of Nimeiry's authoritarian state and party structures. It is doubtful if even the original signing of the agreement was based on a principled stand or simply an expediency for Nimeiry to survive. With the benefit of hindsight, it is not far-fetched to say that it was expediency.[18] Over the next ten years Nimeiry gradually made inroads into the agreement and finally abrogated it in June 1983 and, among other things, imposed Shari'ah law contrary to the 1973 Constitution which had recognised Islam, Christianity, and traditional religions although 'none of them was permitted to compromise, through constitutional and legal means, the political and civil rights of any citizens.[19] Nimeiry's scrapping of the agreement almost immediately broke the 'peace' giving rise to the Sudan People's Liberation Movement and the Sudan People's Liberation Army (SPLM/SPLA) under John Garang.

It is significant that the SPLM's programme basically sets out its goal as to build a New Sudan based on New Democracy embracing essentially all the important elements of the 'right of people to self-determination'.[20] A leading member of the organisation puts it thus:

> To bring about such a New Sudan, the edifice of the old Sudan must be destroyed in its entirety. . . . The formation of the New Sudan involves two processes which must go on concurrently because of the nature of Sudan's weary historical epoch; and to be meaningful revolutions, they must consummate in the democracy that brings peace and prosperity to the masses of our people. The two processes are: Nation-formation and National Liberation. Nation-formation is to fuse the many nationalities in the Sudan into a nation. . . .
>
> National liberation, the second process, is necessarily to liberate the Sudan from external dependency and internal exploitation.[21]

But it is not only the Sudanese state, supported by Western imperialism, which has failed to implement the 'right to self-determination': even the so-called 'socialist' state of Mengistu supported by the so-called 'developed socialist' state, the Soviet Union, has resorted to military suppression of the struggle of nations and nationalities for self-determination in Ethiopia. To be sure, even during Lenin's time, the Soviet state had begun to deviate from its principled stand on the question of self-determination.[22] But to his credit, Lenin in his last days severely criticised the practice of Great-Russian chauvinism and warned

of the dangers of trampling on nationality rights.[23] That critique and warning
are as valid today:

> It would be unpardonable opportunism if, on the eve of the *debut* of the East, just
> as it is awakening, we undermined our prestige with its peoples, even if only by the
> slightest crudity or injustice towards our own non-Russian nationalities. The need
> to rally against the imperialists of the West, who are defending the capitalist world,
> is one thing. There can be no doubt about that and it would be superfluous for me
> to speak about my unconditional approval of it. It is another thing when we
> ourselves lapse, even if only in trifles, into imperialist attitudes towards oppressed
> nationalities, thus undermining all our principled sincerity, all our principled
> defence of the struggle against imperialism.[24]

The preceding discussion helps us to sum up one plank of the principle of
political self-determination. Principally it involves the right to *independence* of
the colonised or non-self-governing countries and the establishment of their
own separate states. Cassese refers to this as the 'external' aspect of the
principle. But it also involves, as a principal element, the right of oppressed
nations, within otherwise sovereign states, to self-determination: this ranges
from some form of autonomy up to and including secession i.e. formation of
a separate state. (This is the 'internal' aspect.) The bed-rock of this principle,
as of all democratic principles, is the *standard of equality* of all nations and
peoples.[25] Other elements, which are often an expression of this principle, are
derivative. These are, for example, the principle of state sovereignty, territorial
integrity and non-intervention. Such practices as voluntary federations and
unions of nations and countries are also practices which express the principle
of self-determination—the converse of secession. it is submitted that the
existing state practice in Africa (including the Soviet and East European state
practice) has isolated only one element in the principle, the element of anti-
colonialism, and *absolutised* it. It has also raised the derivative element, state
sovereignty and territorial integrity as well as non-intervention, to the level of
the main principle and often made it the *overriding* element.[26] As should
become clear in the course of this discussion, this practice has therefore robbed
the right of self-determination of its fundamental defining characteristic—
anti-imperialism. This is so because national oppression, which in Africa is
often an expression of unequal and uneven national (regional) development,
is derived from colonial history and perpetuated by independent states in
alliance with imperialism whose local manifestation is the neo-colonial
political economy.

Within the conception of national oppression and the concomitant rights
are included the cultural, social and religious rights of nationalities, minorities
and national groups.[27] This is recognised by the International Covenants,
where it is clearly stipulated that the right of peoples to self-determination
includes their right to 'freely pursue their economic, social, and cultural
development'.[28] Both practically and politically the full recognition and
realisation of this right is extremely crucial to the democratisation process in
Africa. Colonial heritage where the African people, more than any other

colonised people, literally suffered cultural annihilation and oppression has not only survived but even found newer manifestation in post-independence Africa. One of the common colonialist policies was to raise a particular nationality to the status of a favoured group in terms of education and other 'privileges' thus leaving behind not only uneven economic development but also uneven cultural and social development. The practice of African states in this regard too has been anything but democratic as many examples from Algeria to Zimbabwe testify. The principle of non-discrimination and equality, central to the right to self-determination, is thrown overboard as some cultures, languages or religions are accorded superior, while others, inferior status within the same state boundaries, leading to friction and even wars. The results have been awesome as nationalities and minorities find their culture, traditions and languages despised and attempts made to eradicate them. This question in its own right calls for debate and discussion of practical political approaches within the larger question of democracy and anti-imperialism.

The second plank of the 'internal' aspect of political self-determination refers to the freedom of the 'people' to choose the form of their governance and government. This is where the Western doctrine and particularly propaganda relate the principle of self-determination to fundamental freedoms and human rights. But in practice Western powers themselves fall far short of implementing the anti-authoritarian thrust of this aspect of the principle. The first instrument according to Cassese, which fully stipulates this plank in the 'internal' aspect of the principle is the Helsinki Accords where it is provided that

> By virtue of the principle of equal rights and self-determination of peoples, all peoples always have the right, in full freedom, to determine when and as they wish, their internal and external political status, without external interference, and to pursue as they wish their political, economic, social and cultural development.

Cassese has interpreted this to mean that all peoples always have a right to choose a new social or political regime free from oppression of an authoritarian government.[29] Although somewhat weakly formulated, the African Charter could be interpreted in a similar fashion when it provides in Article 20(1):

> All peoples shall have the right to existence. They shall have the unquestionable and inalienable right to self-determination. They shall freely determine their political status and shall pursue their economic and social development according to the policy they have freely chosen.

While these formulations are capable of *democratic* interpretations, it does not mean that conceptions of democracy from the standpoint of the state, as opposed to that of the 'people', are necessarily the same. Indeed often they are not, for even authoritarian, compradorial states may and do go through the motions of periodic elections and setting up of representative institutions. But at this stage, what I am trying to establish is simply that the 'right to self-determination' has within it this broad democratic conceptualisation recognising fully that there are underlying tensions expressing contradictory class perspectives.

The other aspect of the 'right to self-determination' is *economic self-determination*. Historically, the genesis of this aspect lies again in the Bolshevik Revolution of 1917. Hitherto what had reigned and exercised hegemony both in international law and practice was the right to private property. It was the Soviet state which for the first time in any significant way breached this hegemony by nationalising private property. In 1917 this was only a breach. Students of international law are familiar with the resultant contradiction in international law since then about the legitimacy or otherwise of the right to nationalise without compensation. This need not delay us further. With the march of socialist revolutions and the upsurge of national liberation movements in the Third World, the hegemony of the right to private property was gradually but definitely eroded. While the Universal Declaration of Human Rights in 1948 still paid homage to this right, the 1966 Covenants do not include the right to private property.[30] The UN Resolution on *Permanent Sovereignty over Natural Resouces*, 1962[31] is a further manifestation of the continuing fall in the fortunes of the sanctity of private property. However, while these developments have no doubt made serious ideological incursions into the right of private property, in practice these have been at the level of phenomenon rather than in essence. Let us explain.

Anyone familar with Marxist and Leninist paradigms knows that the concept of private property refers to and embraces essentially the relations of exploitation between classes. Further that it is not simply confined to *legal* ownership of the means of production. Juridical ownership is only one form that private property, understood as a relation of exploitation, takes under capitalism. Over a period of time, the Soviet state theory and ideology have fundamentally departed from this conceptual framework. What is counterpoised to private property is *state property* not *social property*. In other words, the concept of private property is reduced to and collapsed with legal ownership of the means of production. It is in this restricted and distorted form that the concept of private property/state property has found its way in much of the debate so far as the right to or freedom of private property is concerned.

On a more specific level, the African state practice has interpreted the principle of economic self-determination almost exclusively in terms of their 'trade union' demands for the so-called New International Economic Order and against some of the grossly inequitable practices of the multi-national corporations, other economic institutions (e.g. World Bank, IMF etc) and the world capitalist market. These demands, which are made under the rubric of economic self-determination (the term often used is economic independence), *a fortiori* are seen as the rights of *states* rather than 'people'. This conception too results in a truncated form of anti-imperialism rather than a comprehensive conceptualisation where imperialism is seen as manifesting itself in dominant/exploitative relations of production and exploitation on the economic level while socially and politically maintained by compradorial alliances which find concrete expression in authoritarian, undemocratic states.

The African state practice discussed above has found expression in the African Charter on Human and Peoples' Rights. Read together with the OAU Charter and the OAU Resolution of 1964, the Charter reproduces all the limitations of the African state practice in the area of the right to self-determination as we show briefly in the next section.

B   *Right to Self-determination in the African Charter*

The African Charter confines the right to political self-determination ('external') to colonial, non-self-governing countries. There is therefore no right of oppressed nations within the sovereign states to secede. Territorial integrity is upheld at all costs:

> In effect, then, Article 20(1) gives sovereign states the right to self-determination, while Article 29 seems to deny this right to communities within sovereign states.[32]

Nor does the Charter take acount of the rights of nationalities and minorities to freely pursue their culture, languages, traditions, etc. The Charter is satisfied with an individualistic, and even then a very weak, formulation in article 17(2) where it says 'Every individual may freely take part in the cultural life of his community'. This on a continent which is literally strewn with so-called 'ethnic' conflicts and where some grievous violations of cultural etc, rights have taken place.[33] Yet, it may be emphasised again, these omissions are consistent with the practices of the states in Africa.

On 'internal self-determination' the authors of the African Charter seem to be satisfied with a hesitant and ambiguous formulation (and probably the spirit too).

> Every citizen shall have the right to participate freely in the government of his country, either directly or through freely chosen representatives in accordance with the provisions of the law.

At best this provides for a *representative* government which need not necessarily be a *democratic* one. And to add salt to the wound, the clawback clause could enable any African government which has put the relevant law on the statute book and goes through the motions of electing representatives—as most of them do—to claim that they fulfil the requirements of this provision.[34]

It is important to underscore that the African Charter raises the secondary elements in the principle of self-determination i.e. non-intervention and territorial integrity to the level of principal elements. It is not without irony that the OAU debate on Tanzania's invasion of Uganda *on all sides* was conducted on the level of the 'principle' of non-intervention and territorial integrity rather than that of self-determination. Thus President Nyerere justified his action in terms of self-defence and the territorial integrity of his country since Amin had first invaded Tanzania.[35] Clearly, this was a very weak argument once the Tanzanian troops went beyond repulsing the invading Amin troops and actually moved into Uganda up to the capital Kampala to 'liberate' it. The principle of self-determination implies the right of the oppressed people to liberate *themselves* and not a foreign army doing it for them.

Those who attacked Nyerere though never based their argument on the principle of self-determination either.[36] They actually defended Amin by arguing on the level of territorial integrity and non-intervention. This debate, and the ideological paradigms within which it was conducted, is a profound illustration of the truncated form in which African states have appropriated the principle of self-determination and emasculated it of its anti-imperialist and democratic content.

Economic self-determination in the African Charter very closely follows the UN and UNCTAD-type tradition. It does not go further than the UN Resolution on Permanent Sovereignty over Natural Resources and backtracks even from that position by making the right (1) exercisable by *states* and (2) subjecting it 'to the obligation of promoting international economic co-operation based on mutual respect, equitable exchange and the principles of international law', (art 21).[37] Laudable as these may sound, 'mutuality' and 'co-operation' in the typical African situation, where the economies are invariably dominated and exploited by foreign finance capital and multi-nationals, can, in practice, only mean an endorsement of the existing unequal, inequitable and exploitative imperialist relationships.

The weakness of the provisions of the African Charter stand out in sharp relief when contrasted with the Algiers Declaration,[38] for example.

The 'fathers' of the Algiers Declaration leave no doubt as to their awareness of the *colonial* roots, including the plunder and spoliation that went with it, of the present underdevelopment in the Third World. Besides providing for the people's 'exclusive right over its natural wealth and resources' (art 8), the Declaration has some powerful provisions on the right to indemnity and restitution. The people have a right 'to recover them [i.e. natural wealth and resources][39] if they have been despoiled, as well as any unjustly paid indemnities'. Under the section entitled 'Guarantees and Sanction', three articles provide further elucidation of the concept of unjust enrichment, historical and contemporary. These provisions deserve quotation *in extenso*:

Article 24
   Any enrichment to the detriment of the people in violation of the provisions of this Declaration shall give rise to the restitution of profits thus obtained. The same shall be applied to all excessive profits on investments of foreign origin.

Article 25
   Any unequal treaties, agreements or contracts concluded in disregard of the fundamental rights shall have no effect.

Article 26
   External financial charges which become excessive and unbearable for the people shall cease to be due.

The neo-colonial character of the African Charter is even more starkly revealed in the resurrection of unbridled respect for private property. We have seen that this is a backward step compared to the UN Conventions. Even the European Convention does not contain it and it was included more or less as an afterthought in the First Protocol.[40] Even moderate African commentators have found it difficult to swallow it. Rembe suggests that one of the 'push-factors' for the inclusion of this right might have been to attract foreign aid and investments.[41] Indeed, what else! Rembe has further observed that this provision flies in the face of African states' oft-repeated obeisance to sovereignty over natural resources and the declarations of quite a few of them to socialism. It blatantly negates the concepts of property in African traditions and values which are supposed to have been the guiding light of the Charter. Rembe rightly points out the contradiction between the right to private property and the provisions on sovereignty over natural resources or eminent domain. Unlike Rembe, who seems to entertain some hope that a 'balance must be made between property ownership and eminent domain',[42] I do not see any such balance in the Charter or in the minds of the framers. Rather, taking into account the principles of international law to which the right to sovereignty over natural resources has been subordinated, it is clear that the right to private property has clearly come out on top. Who would be prepared to argue that that was not the *intention* of the 'founding fathers'?

C   *Re-conceptualising the Right to Self-determination*

Our preceding discussion and the critique we have made of the existing state practice may now be summed-up in a reconceptualisation and reformulation of the right to self-determination. The constituent elements of the 'right of people to self-determination', it is submitted are:

Principal elements: (a) equality of all peoples and nations;
(b) right of colonised people to independence and formation of their own sovereign states;
(c) right of oppressed nations to self-determination including the right to secede;
(d) right of all peoples, nations, nationalities, national groups and minorities to freely pursue and develop their culture, traditions, religion and language;
(e) freedom of all peoples from alien subjugation, domination and exploitation;
(f) right of all peoples to determine democratically their own socio-economic and political system of governance and government;

Secondary or derivative elements:
(a) right of all peoples to seek assistance from other peoples in its struggle for self-determination;
(b) principle of *state* sovereignty, territorial integrity and non-intervention by one state in the internal affairs of another *state*.[43]

In short, what is being proposed here is a broadening and deepening of the concept of the right to self-determination embodying the principal contradiction between imperialism and its compradorial allies *vis-à-vis* the people on the one hand, and oppressor *vis-à-vis* oppressed nations, on the other. This conceptualisation, ideologically and legally, captures the most important elements of the anti-imperialist democratic struggles within the framework of a New Democratic Revolution as at the same time showing historical continuity with democracy in general and revolutionary tradition in particular. During its revolutionary days the Chinese Communist Party summed up the main trends in the Third World as:

> Countries want Independence;
> Nations want Liberation and
> People want Revolution.

The reconceptualisation of the 'right to self-determination' attempts to capture these trends on an ideological/legal plane within the framework of human rights discourse.

Finally, it should be clear from the thrust of our discussion of the right that the right to self-determination is a *collective* right. It is a continuing right, 'a right that keeps its validity even after a people has chosen a certain form of government or a certain international status'.[44] The right-holders in the right to self-determination are dominated/exploited people and oppressed nations, nationalities, national groups and minorities identifiable specifically in each concrete situation. The duty-bearers are states, oppressor nations and nationalities and imperialist countries.

It is further submitted that conceptualised as it is here, the 'right to self-determination' is superior to and has advantages over the so-called 'right to development'. This is discussed next.

Right to Self-determination and Right to Development compared

The 'right to development' is considered a specifically African contribution to the international human rights discourse. Keba M'Baye, a Senegalese jurist, is credited with having first propounded this right in 1972[45] and later getting it formally recognised in resolution 4(XXXIII) of the UN Commission on Human Rights in 1977 when he presided over its thirty-third session.[46] Since then there have been a couple of conferences on the 'right to development' and a score of writings by Africanists on the same theme, sometimes purporting to expand and elaborate on M'Baye's proposal and at other times criticising it. It has also found a formal recognition in the preamble of the African Charter of Human and Peoples' Rights. And finally the UN General Assembly has adopted a *Declaration on the Right to Development* by its resolution 41/128 of 4 December 1986.[47]

Although the 'right to development' has been enthusiastically adopted by African states and vigorously propagated by African human rights writers, it is the argument of this author that this 'right' suffers from serious legal and political draw-backs compared to the 'right to self-determination'.

The genesis of the right to self-determination lies in the struggles of the people from the days of bourgeois revolutions in eighteenth- and nineteenth-century Europe to the post-war national liberation struggles of the people of the Third World. It thus has a historical legitimacy which the right to development does not. The right to development finds its roots in the contemporary demands of the Third World states for better terms in the international market, greater aid and assistance and generally in what has come to be known as the demand for the new international economic order. At best these are statist 'trade union' demands which seek a little more comfortable accommodation for the Third World ruling classes within the existing order. At worst, they amount to no more than a new way of asserting a 'right' to charity.

On the level of international law, as the right to self-determination has developed over more than half a century, it has come to be recognised by international law and has found place in UN treaties (the 1966 Covenants) as well as in a considerable number of other international treaties among states of both the North and the South.[48] To be sure, the conceptualisation and the content of this right, as we have seen, remains contentious, as indeed it should, given the underlying contradictions of the world imperialist system. That it captures some of these important contradictions is its strength rather than weakness. The right to development, on the other hand, is an assertion of a 'new' right. It does not therefore have the legitimacy of international legality. True, its development has been fast from the original conception to the Declaration by the General Assembly. It has been enthusiastically taken over by liberals of the West, supported by Soviet-oriented theorists and almost unanimously advocated by African international lawyers. Even if it eventually finds a place in an international covenant, the question remains: Does it serve the interests of the *people* of Africa?

Conceptually the right to development has very weak foundations. Development itself has either been expanded to include everything (and therefore nothing!) as in the UN Declaration,[49] or more often narrowed to economic development in its economistic, and increasingly, even econometric sense. Either way it blunts, if not eliminates, the ideological and political sting and sharpness which are central to the concept of self-determination.

Under the right of self-determination, the right-holders are *a collective*, whether people, nations, nationalities or national groups. Besides the fact that each one of these concepts has strong theoretical foundations, they are practically and politically of immediate relevance to Africa in its struggle against imperialism and authoritarianism. Secondly, these concepts are not tied to existing state structures and systems but rather have an independent dynamism of their own with a capacity to comprehend and guide change. In a word, they express class struggle rather than a statist *status quo*. The concept of the right to development, on the contrary, is both static as well as statist. The right here generally belongs to 'states' as is clearly expressed in the Declaration. The Preamble 'recognises' that 'the creation of conditions favourable to the development of peoples and individuals is the primary responsibility of their States'. 'States have the *right and duty* to formulate appropriate national development policies', (art, 2(3)) [emphasis supplied]; states have a duty to co-operate with each other in ensuring development (art 3(3)) and in formulating international development policies (art 4(1)); even popular participation is supposed to be encouraged by states (art 8(2)) and 'States should fulfil their rights and duties in such a manner as to promote a new international economic order based on sovereign equality, interdependence, mutual interest and co-operation among all States, as well as to encourage the observance and realization of human rights' (art 3(3)). The 'state' here has been presented out from a fairytale as the embodiment of all virtues and interests of the people which, needless to say, flies in the face of historical evidence and is certainly nowhere close to the real-life authoritarian states of Africa used ruthlessly by imperialism and compradorial ruling classes in the exploitation and oppression of the African people and nations.

Finally, underlying the right to development is a conception which sees development/democracy as a gift/charity *from above* rather than the result of struggles *from below*. On the international plane, it is based on an illusory model of *co-operation and solidarity* (à la M'Baye). This is like crying for the moon, for how can there be solidarity between rider and horse?

Under the right to development the human person is seen as a 'participant and beneficiary' (art 2(1)) of development. Development, therefore, is someone else's (the state's?!) project. Under self-determination people are themselves the creators of and the struggling force for development and democracy which are *reclaimed and asserted* as *their* project. People are neither pitiable victims of the state's excesses nor recipients of it's handouts. In the latter conceptualisation the state takes its rightful place as a historical and social category both as a participant in and an embodiment of class struggles.

The right to development fits in neatly in the ideology of developmentalism which has been the hallmark of African states since independence in rationalising the depoliticisation and demobilisation of the African masses. It has managed to occupy many conferences and discussions. Given its spurious nature, in our opinion it has played a diversionary role in shifting attention from the reality of the Third World and its struggling people.

Conclusion

In this chapter we have tried to show that the 'right of peoples to self-determination' (together with the right to organise[50]) is a central right in the present African conjuncture. It continues to capture and express some of the major tensions obtaining in the continent since independence. However, there is no single African perspective on this right. Rather there are at least two major African perspectives: a statist perspective expressing the interests of the African state and the ruling classes and a people's perspective expressing the interests of the large majority.

It is our argument that the 'right of peoples to self-determination' unlike, for instance, the so-called 'right to development', is capable of expressing both these perspectives. Hence the content and the formulation of the 'right to self-determination' constitute a contested terrain just as democracy, which is the soil from which it has grown, continues to sustain some of the major debates and struggles in Africa today between the forces of change and those of the *status quo*.

NOTES

1   This chapter is based on the author's book *The Concept of Human Rights in Africa* (Dakar, Codesria 1989).

2   See V I Lenin, *Selected Works* (Moscow, Progress Publishers 1977), vol 2, p 475.

3   Akram H Chowdhury, 'The question of self-determination of indigenous populations under international law: the case of Chittagong Hill tracts', mimeo. Codesria Documents, pp 7 *et seq.*

4   Antonio Cassese, 'Political self-determination—old Concepts and new developments', in *UN Law/Fundamental Rights: Two Topics in International Law*, Antonio Cassese, ed (The Netherlands, Sijthoff & Noordhoff, 1979), p 138.

5   It was included in the *UN Declaration on the Granting of Independence to Colonial Countries* adopted on 14 December 1960 when significantly the USA, Great Britain, France, Belgium, Portugal, South Africa, Australia, Dominican Republic and Spain abstained. Ibid, p 141.

6   Ian Brownlie, *Principles of Public International Law* (Oxford, Clarendon Press, 1979) 3rd edn, p 593.

7   See *Selected Works*, vol 1 op. cit., pp 598-9.

8   Lenin, 'The discussion on self-determination summed up', in *On the National Question and Proletarian Internationalism* (Moscow, Novosty Press, 1970) p 100.

9   Quoted in *International Law: A Textbook*, G I Tunkin, ed (Moscow, Progress Publishers, 1966), pp 46-9.

10   Cassese has argued that the formulation of this principle in the Helsinki Accords goes further than the traditional UN and Soviet position on self-determination. The Soviet Union itself had suggested the 'traditional' formulation. But the fact that it finally agreed to the broader formulation shows the Soviet Union's pragmatic rather than principled position on this issue and even discriminatory approaches depending on whether it is dealing with weaker Afro-Asian countries or fellow super-powers in Europe. Cassese, op. cit., pp 148–53. For the text of the Helsinki Accords see Ian Brownlie, *Basic Documents in Human Rights* (Oxford University Press, 1981), 2nd edn, p 320.

11   See B Habte Selassie, *Conflict and Intervention in the Horn* (New York, Monthly Review Press, 1980).

12 Op. cit., p 140.
13 See Mahmood Mamdani, *Imperialism and Fascism in Uganda* (London, Heinemann, 1983).
14 Witness the refugee situation in Africa. With one-tenth of the world's population, Africa is estimated to have almost half the world's refugees. And the majority of these refugees have run away from political oppression and problems of civil wars in their countries. See Edward Kannyo, 'Banjul Charter', in *Human Rights and Development in Africa*, Claude E Welch Jr and Ronald I Meltzer, eds, Albany, State University of New York, 1984), p 131, p 137. See also Zdenek Cervenka, 'The effects of militarisation of Africa on human rights', *Africa To-day*, vol 34, pp 69–84 (1987).
15 Lam Akol, 'The present war and its solution', in Francis Mading Deng and Prosser Gifford, eds, *The Search for Peace and Unity in the Sudan* (Washington, The Wilson Center Press, 1987), pp 15–23 at p 15.
16 Mohammed Beshir Hamid, 'Devolution and the problems of national integration in the Sudan'. *Ethnic Studies Report* II, no 2, July 1984, p 61. See also SPLM/SPLA publication *Sudan To-day* (London, 1985).
17 B Yongo-Bure, 'Prospects for socio-economic development of the South', in Deng and Prosser, eds, op. cit., pp 36–50 at p 48.
18 Elias Nyamlell Wakoson, 'The dilemmas of south-north conflict', in Deng and Prosser, eds, op. cit., pp 90–106 at p 92 and Mansour Khalid, 'External factors in the Sudanese Conflict', in ibid., pp 109–26 at p 113.
19 Bona Malwal, 'The roots of current contention', in ibid., pp 7–14 at p 14.
20 See Akol, op. cit., p 16 *et seq*.
21 Ibid., p 20.
22 See Lenin, 'The Question of nationalities or "Autonomisation"', in Lenin, *On the National Question*, op. cit., pp 141 *et seq*.
23 With 'perestroika' there has been a resurgence of the 'national question' in the Soviet Union which may not be unconnected with the Great-Russian chauvinism of the Stalin and post-Stalin eras.
24 Lenin, op. cit., p 168.
25 On the concept of equality in International Law see the Dissenting Opinion of Judge Tanaka in the 'South West Africa Cases (Second Phase), 1966' reproduced in Brownlie, *Human Rights*, op. cit., pp 441–70.
26 See for instance the OAU Charter and Cassese, op. cit.
27 The use of these concepts is not without problems. In the bourgeois 'international law' jurisprudence, as a matter of fact, these concepts are used most confusedly where often state, country, nation, people etc, are used interchangeably. In the Marxist literature, on the other hand, these terms have a definite conceptual content. The use of these terms in this work is in the latter tradition. However, it must be pointed out that 'minority' is not part of the Marxist conceptual framework and does pose some theoretical problems. For an example of total confusion on these concepts in the bourgeois literature, see Yoram Dinstein, 'Collective human rights of peoples and minorities', in *International Comparative and Law Quarterly*, 25, pp 102–20 (1976) where the meaning of the terms 'nation' and 'people' is reversed. This confusion, however, may not be totally innocent; it is probably meant to justify the claims of zionists to a separate state.
28 Vernon Van Dyke, 'The cultural rights of peoples', *Universal Human Rights*, 2, no 2, pp 1–21 (April–June, 1980).
29 Op. cit., p 152.

30   Interestingly, even the European Convention seems to give it an inferior status by including it in the First Protocol, more or less as an afterthought.

31   Resolution 1803 (XVII).

32   Ibid., p 6.

33   Steven Neff, *Human Rights in Botswana, Lesotho and Swaziland: Implications of Adherence to International Human Rights Treaties* (Lesotho, Institute of Southern African Studies, 1986), p 9.

34   See Neff, ibid.

35   Kannyo, 'Banjul Charter', op. cit., p 146.

36   The hegemony of the statist interpretation of the principle of self-determination is further evidenced by the fact that even among intellectual and progressive circles in East Africa the debate on the so-called 'liberation' of Uganda was never conducted within the Leninist paradigms of self-determination.

37   This would in effect mean recognition of the traditional rule of international law which forbids nationalisation of property without adequate, fair and prompt compensation.

38   Universal Declaration on the Rights of Peoples adopted by National Liberation Movements, trade unions and other NGOs in Algeria in July, 1976. For text see Issa G Shivji, *The Concept of Human Rights in Africa*, op. cit., appendix.

39   To be sure, the Charter has one obscure provision which says 'In case of spoliation the dispossessed people shall have the right to the *lawful* recovery of its property as well as to an adequate compensation.' The use of the term 'lawful' is worrisome; it probably means in accordance with the provisions of international law, in which case the apparent, progressive content of the article is nullified.

40   Nasila Rembe, *Africa and the International Law of the Sea* (Sijthoff and Noordhoff, 1980). p 117.

41   Ibid., p 220, fn 31. The printing of footnotes in this book is badly done as the order of the footnotes to chapters three and four is reversed.

42   Ibid., p 117.

43   Notice that here the concept of 'people' is primary and state is seen as subordinate, rather than the other way round as in the existing literature.

44   Cassese, op. cit., p 150.

45   Keba M'Baye, 'Emergence of the "right to development" as a human right in the context of a new international economic order', paper presented to the UNESCO Meeting of Experts on Human Rights, Human Needs and the Establishment of a New International Economic Order, Paris, UNESCO, 19–23 June 1978, Doc SS-78/CONF 630/8.

46   Jack Donnelly, 'The "right to development": how not to link rights and development', in Welch and Meltzer, eds, op. cit., p 261.

47   The text is reprinted in the International Commission of Jurists, *The Review*, no 38: 53–6 (June 1987).

48   The Helsinki Accords and the OAU Charter, for example.

49   The Preamble states:

> . . . [T]hat development is a comprehensive economic, social, cultural and political process, which aims at the constant improvement of the well-being of the entire population and of all individuals on the basis of their active, free and meaningful participation in development and in the fair distribution of benefits resulting therefrom, . . .

50   For a discussion of the 'right to organise' see Shivji, *The Concept of Human Rights in Africa* op. cit.

CHAPTER 6

Obligations of Affluent Nations to the Poor in the Situation of 'Radical Inequality'

David Gosling

Introduction

The contrast between the affluent nations of the world and the desperate poverty of the majority of people in other nations remains as stark today as ever, despite much material progress and continued wealth-creation in wealthy states. Although even the richest countries have their own poor and their own injustices, the global problem of 'radical inequality' (Nagel, 1977, p 55) constitutes one of the most important moral problems of our time and one which is currently becoming still more severe.[1] But whose problem is it? And who has the duty to ameliorate, and, if possible, to end the suffering of the poor?

The recent popularity in the West of fund-raising events[2] for aid charities has shown that many citizens in affluent nations have concern for the plight of the poor in Africa and elsewhere, but in no way does it indicate an acceptance of any *obligation* to alleviate global poverty, but rather, it affirms the right of individuals in wealthy societies to contribute or not, as a matter of preference, to ameliorative efforts. Since 'appeals' are normally made only in response to specific circumstances such as a drought, flood or war which are perceived to be beyond the control of either donors or victims, no responsibility is accepted for the *status quo* of radical inequality which persists outside the circumstances of specific disasters. While the giving of 'aid' remains within the category of *charity*, not only is responsibility *denied*, but the assumed superiority of the rich nations is affirmed both symbolically and in real economic terms. Arguments which have been advanced by moral philosophers have challenged this voluntarist framework and have attempted to make the relief of famine the responsibility of all who are in a position to give assistance, but all such arguments run into some considerable difficulties.

In this paper I attempt to show that, in addition to the universal obligation which falls on all who have it within their power to contribute towards the alleviation of poverty, the continuity between present problems of global distributive justice and the effects of historically shared communities of interdependence give rise to special obligations imposed on many wealthy nations to those countries who are especially vulnerable to their economic and political policies. The argument gives some support to claims based on a principle of compensation,[3] but it is also necessary to examine the reasons for the limited application of this principle. By reasserting the grounds of obligation, we can go beyond the voluntarist assumptions of the charity movement and establish a basis for the alleviation of the circumstances of global inequality which nevertheless recognises rights of self-determination.

From Third Estate to Third World

Two hundred years ago the Third Estate in France demanded recognition of the 'Rights of Man'. Today, in economically advanced Western countries, many of these rights are largely established and recognised in law—and in some cases the demands of the French Revolution have been far exceeded. But it needed revolutionary activity and the creation of new structures of political authority to establish the political framework within which Rousseauian rhetoric could be translated into realist politics. Today the global Third Estate, or Third World as it is sometimes controversially called, not only has no effective court of appeal where it can pursue its claims, but it has no prospect of establishing the kind of world authority that could have jurisdiction over just claims.[4]

The rights of peoples detailed in the Declaration of Human Rights made by the United Nations remain empty, pious hopes, unenforceable and far removed from the prospect of becoming political reality. Article 25 of the Universal Declaration of Human Rights states that 'Everyone has the right to a standard of living adequate for the health and well-being of himself and of his family, including food, clothing, housing and medical care and necessary social services'.[5] Despite this declaration it is estimated that 30 per cent of the developing world is threatened by food deficiencies, and even on a conservative estimate at least 100 million adults and children face chronic food shortages in Africa alone.[6]

Herein lies the problem—the enormous gulf between the language of 'human rights'[7] and the failure to provide the means to fulfil the duties those rights entail. Within the sphere of international relations there is no political mechanism to enable 'moral' options to become political reality and no institutions through which majorities can vote for a change in the world economic/political order or enforce such changes. Judging by results, the UN, the World Bank, and other such international institutions are clearly not in a position to implement policies which could translate declarations of rights into political reality.

Ethical Idealism and Economic Realism Contrasted

In response to this situation we appear to be faced with two polarised alternative sources of analysis—the *idealist*, which seeks to give a prescriptive account of how relations between states, and between individuals within states, should be conducted from consideration of ethical principles alone, and the *realist* which is premised on the assumption that the operation of market forces and the *realpolitik* of international relations are human activities to which moral judgements have no application. Economic and political realists suggest that the moving forces of international relations are not primarily the result of individual decision and are therefore to be thought of as morally neutral. In so far as individual politicians and commercial entrepreneurs do act as personal agents they do so at the bidding of the 'interests' they serve and are driven by forces they do not control. According to this view, we can no more pass moral judgement on market and political forces than we can on, say, the force of gravity. On this view any enduring economic situation, whether contemporary or historical, is simply the result of an intersection of the components of a situation (commercial, demographic, technological, geographic and so on) in which agents must react rationally to optimise their own interests. The justice of the outcomes is judged by reference only to 'entitlements' established by ownership, production and exchange.[8]

On this view, European traders who were able to drive bargains with cash-crop growers in Africa which were much to the advantage of the Europeans, were able to do so because of their advantages in technology, transport, access to markets, responses to demands and so on which gave the crops the 'value' in the market which they had. Merchants could not be blamed for setting the price they could get, nor were they responsible for that price. They were entitled to take profits as rewards for the risks they undertook, and in any case benefits did accrue to local economies by stimulating trade, production, and the development of infrastructures. Moral judgements about distributive justice simply do not come into it.

Similarly the scramble for Africa should be understood as a response by the European powers to the perceived need to protect their international political standing and to expand into new markets which they believed would solve the 'problem of over-production'. From the agents' point of view this was a rational policy made necessary by their perception of political and economic realities.

Within the moral discourse of contemporary liberalism both the actions of European traders and the carving up of the political map of Africa may be judged unethical. The European traders may be said to have offended against deontological principles which should regulate trading relations and were therefore guilty of exploitation, causing undue and unreasonable hardship to the peasant farmers, making coercive contracts rather than the bargains between equally autonomous peoples demanded by the principle of fairness. Similarly the colonial powers use of force to expropriate territory may be judged to be morally unjustifiable on the grounds that they had no right to the territory, which they used illegitimately to foster their own ends without any proper compensation to the dispossessed indigenous peoples.[9]

The discourse of realism, however, proclaims the irrelevance of the vocabulary of moral *judgement* and operates within the terms of national interest, market forces, institutions, and power. Moral considerations may only be given some recognition as a motivational factor in international economic and political relations. For example, the anti-slavery motivation may have been a partial explanation of British policies of penetration into Africa in the nineteenth century, but, on a realist analysis, British governments' decisions to lend their support to the opening of the African interior should be judged by criteria of commercial and national interests alone.[10] Within the terms of economic realism, moral concerns which have affected trade policies, such as the provision of minimal institutions for the promotion of education and health, have to be regarded merely as a cost to be born, to be set *against* the economic gains to be made, rather than regarded as a gain in their own right. Economically they are debits, not credits!

Ethical idealism

If the discourse of economic realism excludes the vocabulary of moral judgement, it is equally true that the discourse of moral philosophy rarely concerns itself with economic or historical realities.[11] It is in this sense that ethical debates about obligations to the world's poor are 'idealist,' working with terms such as justice, rights, obligation, benevolence, personal responsibility and issuing in claims on our charity, or in declarations of moral duty, which seem remote from the actual practices of either politicians or ordinary citizens.

Let me illustrate this point by reference to five accounts in moral philosophy which have advanced arguments for establishing that developed countries and their citizens have obligations to the peoples of the under-developed world. These are; 1   Singer (1973, 1983); 2   Beitz (1979); 3   Harris (1980); 4   Shue (1980, 1984) and 5   O'Neill (1977, 1986). I shall only give an outline characterisation of each of these accounts before discussing what I take to be some general problems faced by them all.

1   Singer's utilitarianism demands that welfare should be maximised on a strictly impartial basis. He, therefore, argues that,

> If it is in our power to prevent something bad from happening, without thereby sacrificing anything of comparable moral importance, we ought, morally, to do it.[12]

The application of this principle demands that we should always devote our resources to the person whose welfare can be most significantly improved, irrespective of their distance from, or their relationship to, the agent. Since the money I might spend on another item of clothing when I already have an adequate wardrobe would clearly benefit the hungry of the poorest nations far more than the benefit I receive from an additional item of clothing, I am under an obligation to spend the money on the poor. Singer claims that our 'traditional moral categories', which distinguish between duty and charity, must be rejected, since it is the improvement of another's welfare which should determine the allocation of resources, not any preconceived notion of duty to specific individuals or groups close to home. In response to the criticism that such a morality makes impossible demands on our capacity for impartiality Singer does, in his later work, recognise the need to 'make use of existing tendencies in human nature' (Singer, 1983, p 155), but this is on the grounds that harnessing the inclinations of many to follow a less rigid standard of impartiality will be more likely to achieve the utilitarian goal of maximisation of the welfare of all than by insisting on an ethic which only the impartially rational could follow

2   Beitz (1979) argues that 'realists' are wrong to attempt to take international relations out of the arena of morality and proposes an extension of a Rawlsian conception of justice on a global scale. This would involve denying that

> citizens of wealthy nations have general rights to retain their domestic products, which override their obligations to advance the welfare of less-advantaged persons elsewhere. (Beitz, 1979, p 172)

The effect of Beitz's programme would be to create 'global redistributive obligations' which would take aid out of the category of charity and into the category of duty. The formulation of all policies should on this view, in line with Rawls's 'difference principle', aim to make improvements for the world's worst-off groups. He rejects the assumption that states have entitlements to their own resources because parties meeting in the original position would not accept the arbitrary inequalities between states which would result, but, rather, he thinks they would demand an allocation which would only allow inequalities to the extent that they benefit the most disadvantaged groups.

3   Harris (1980) argues that there is no difference in principle between the positive duty not to harm anyone by performing avoidable and harmful actions and the 'negative responsibility' not to harm anyone by failing to perform actions which could be performed and which, if performed, would prevent harm happening to them. (Harris, 1980, p 60). Failure to prevent a harm which we could have prevented, on this view, makes us causally responsible for that harm. Harris accepts that if we ought to prevent literally

all the harm we can this imposes a 'saintly' duty on us which we are unlikely to be able to meet, but thinks that this does not in any way diminish the strength of what we *ought* to do (Harris, 1980, p 153).

4   Shue (1980) argues that if we recognise any liberty or welfare rights we must also acknowledge that they all presume 'basic' subsistence rights without which nothing else is possible. Non-interference cannot be justified when it leads to the inability of another to survive. Basic rights to life itself place obligations on others for positive action involving threefold correlative duties, namely:

I   To avoid depriving
II   To protect from deprivation
     1   By enforcing duty (I) and
     2   By designing institutions that avoid the creation of strong incentives to violate duty (I).
III To aid the deprived
     1   Who are one's special responsibility
     2   Who are the victims of social failures in the performance of duties (I), (II-1), (II-2), and
     3   Who are the victims of natural disasters. (Shue, 1980, p 60).

Shue argues that the duty to fulfil people's basic rights by building effective institutions which will enable them to enjoy those rights falls on all. Once we know of the harm we are causing by our failure to create such institutions (or by the recognition that we should have known of that harm) then we must take responsibility for having failed to take due care (Shue, 1984, p 91–2).

5   Finally, O'Neill's (1977) analysis focuses on the obligation not to kill, arguing that, where there are sufficient resources available on 'lifeboat earth', any distribution which leads to a death is a killing. Since people have a right not to be killed, any distribution of resources, for example by foreign investment and commodity pricing policies, which lead to deaths, amounts to unjustified killing (O'Neill, 1977, p 157). More recently O'Neill has advanced an argument using the Kantian principle of the overriding duty to protect human autonomy to show that material justice demands that we should organise both production and distribution 'to meet needs, including material needs, which destroy capacities or power to act autonomously' (O'Neill, 1986, p 149). If accepted this proposal would require a revision of the accepted categories of inter-national economics and would impose a *universal* obligation to refrain from action based on maxims of coercion or deception.'[13]

One characteristic which is common to all these arguments is a refusal to regard distance as morally relevant.[14] Moral responsibility requires fulfilment of only two conditions, knowledge and capacity, that is a person incurs moral responsibility if (a) she has knowledge of a wrong—(or more stringently should have had knowledge of a wrong) and (b) has some capacity, even if limited, to act in a way that it is believed will ameliorate or prevent that wrong. A proviso may be added to deal with priority problems, namely that moral responsibility is not incurred if it entails the sacrifice of anything of comparable moral significance. Distance is only relevant because it makes our knowledge of situations (and what we can do about them) more indirect than if we had personal acquaintance with them, but although media coverage of famines and Third World problems is patchy and inconsistent, it has effectively removed the possibility of our remaining ignorant of many of the events which call for moral concern.[15]

Each of these theories requires a willingness to 'expand the circle' of our moral obligations to include all humankind. Singer's principle is explicitly based on the utilitarian principle of impartial beneficence, but each of the other 'ideal' theories I have referred to also requires a setting aside of particularist loyalties. In Beitz, the redistribution of resources according to a Rawlsian difference principle requires us to maximise the position of the 'globally least advantaged representative' (Beitz, 1979, p 152); in Harris we must accept responsibility for *all* the wrongs that we could have prevented or ameliorated, no matter how remote those wrongs might be;[16] in Shue the duty to 'aid' those whose rights have been infringed is imposed on all who can assist without themselves losing their basic rights,[17] and finally, in O'Neill we are asked to regard the attainment of the Kantian ideal of autonomy as an object of our moral relations with *all* those affected by our actions, no matter how remote they may be.

But diluting our responsibilities across the 'global community' can be self-defeating; by stretching our obligations beyond our moral motivations we run into the familiar problem of seemingly limitless moral obligation.[18] If we perceive our obligations as limitless then any action may appear as futile as any other, resulting in a sense of moral arbitrariness. The demands of a universal morality, it has been argued, lead to the counter-intuitive conclusion that all other values, all other commitments and projects, become submerged under the flood of impossible moral ends.[19] It is not necessary for the purposes of this paper to determine the rights and wrongs of the issue about the limits of obligation. I am inclined to think that moral obligations cannot be arbitrarily limited by psychological considerations of 'overload' although the extent to which we meet our moral obligations is so limited. But *in practice* we are deterred by a fear of becoming morally overloaded and this fact is a relevant consideration in allocating moral responsibility.

Membership and perceived relationships

I want to focus on one particular objection which has been brought against the widening of the circle of moral responsibility, which may point to a fruitful way forward. It has often been argued that if membership of a state, or region, town or family means anything it must imply that I have some duties to members of my own community that I do not owe to those who are strangers.[20] To ignore this point is to see the world as a single community without any differentiation of rights and duties, of loyalties and affiliations, commitments and responsibilities. Such an undifferentiated view of the world would ultimately lead, as Walzer has suggested, to a 'world state whose redistributive processes would tend over time to annul the historical particularity of the national clubs and families.' (Walzer, 1983, p 48) . Where we draw the boundaries of our 'community' will vary in relation to different interests, which entails that the notion of a 'global community' has meaning within some, but not all contexts (Vincent, 1986, p 99). Determining these boundaries is a difficult and contentious matter, but universalist moralities which ignore the significance of such boundaries altogether fail to appreciate the significance of commitments and practices which give meaning to human lives.[21] Furthermore, such boundaries are also necessary to protect the autonomy of associations, families, neighbourhoods, regions and states, and are necessarily required by any claim to self-determination. This is not to deny the significance of relationships of interdependence, nor that duties may cross boundaries, but it is a reminder that any solution to the problem of duties of the affluent nations to the underdeveloped must recognise the loyalties of the peoples within the affluent nations, and, more importantly, must recognise the integrity of the poor nations and not merely recreate in a new form the policies of economic dominance and cultural assimilation that characterised colonialism.

This general point has implications for the manner in which we approach the problem of radical inequality. Firstly, in order to achieve some degree of redistribution it is essential to explore the nature of, and our perceptions of, the relationships between sets of people between whom the redistribution is proposed. For, as Miller has suggested,

> Our ideas of distributive justice are powerfully affected by our perception of the relationships generally prevailing in the set of people within which the distribution will occur. (Miller, 1989, p 58)

Since neither the nature of the relationship nor our perceptions of it are fixed, there is considerable scope for altering those perceptions. The current fashion for fund-raising for charities tends to perpetuate the perception of the Third World as a huge begging bowl—absorbing what seem to be enormous amounts of money (though they are only 'enormous' by the standard of 'gifts', not by the standard of government expenditure). When this image is linked to media portrayals of African governments as corrupt, spendthrift and militaristic, the stability of this source of aid becomes viciously unstable. If long-term redistribution of wealth is to become part of political policy within affluent nations a clearer understanding of the relationship between the rich and the poor and the extent to which we are interdependent needs to enter into public debate and opinion.

The arguments against the particularist alternative are in a sense the converse of the objections to universalist ethics, namely that appeals to community are always liable to result in selfishness, partiality and chauvinism. But it would be wrong to think that community-based ties preclude all forms of redistribution, or that duties to members of our community should always take priority over general duties to the world at large (Goodin, 1985, p 157). What must be retained from universalism is the thought that it is wrong to close our minds to the wider consequences of the decisions we take within our own political communities and wrong to deny responsibility for the harms which can be causally linked to those decisions. These causal networks are more far-reaching than many suspect and one way forward towards the affluent meeting their obligations to the Third World is to map out the links where causal responsibility can be identified. [22]

Attempt to base claims on historical injustices

Establishing the basis for obligations deriving from past relationships requires recognition of three features of the current situation of radical inequality. 1   The 'common life' between rich and poor which colonisation created and which neo-colonisalism perpetuates; 2   the identification of past wrongs and 3   the contemporary impact of this shared history on the practices and relationships which characterise neo-colonialism.

1   Colonisation and Neo-colonialism—the creation of a 'common life'

The importance of the 'Empires' to colonial powers such as Britain, France, Spain, Portugal, and to a lesser extent Belgium and Holland, is a matter of some dispute among historians. On some views of Britain's industrialisation the slave trade, the 'plunder' of India and later the trade with the colonies were crucial to making Britain a world military and economic power (Fryer, 1988). Others have disputed the degree of importance that should be given to this element in Britain's history. [23] However, what cannot be denied is that in their different ways the colonial powers incorporated their colonial conquests into their political communities. Whereas Portuguese territories were declared to be 'an integral part of the Portuguese State' [24] and French acquisitions became part of 'Metropolitan France', the British doctrine of the 'Dual Mandate' maintained a more decentralised political administration, but which never-theless attempted to impose on the colonies British values, culture and institutions. From when Queen Victoria was declared Empress of India in 1876, to Harold Macmillan's 'winds of change' in the 1960s the British sense of identity was closely bound up with its Imperial self-image.

Although the peoples drawn into the Empire were not given the full rights of citizenship and membership was discriminantly distributed, they were encouraged to think of Britain as the motherland protecting their interests and pursuing 'liberty and self-development' (Fetter, 1979, p 96). The impact on the colonies of the imperial culture was, and continues to be, enormous—on the boundaries of states, on education and legal systems, language, religion, political and administrative systems, economic and political ties and so on. Since the 1960s politicians have often found it convenient to distance themselves from the common world that colonialism created, although in Britain the 'Commonwealth' is still occasionally paraded as a matter of national pride. But, international capitalism has created a commonality of culture through the processes of neo-colonialism which is either ignored or taken for granted by western states. Also nations such as the United States have a considerable interest in this global system of economic interdependence although never having been an imperial power. The 'Coca-Cola' empire[25] is a reality, and one which creates a 'common life' between rich and poor nations although of a different kind to historically based colonial affiliations.

2 Past Wrongs and their Contemporary impact

Despite the rhetoric of colonialism which emphasised the 'white man's burden' unselfishly bringing civilisation to benighted areas of the globe, the period of colonialism was often characterised by exploitation, violence, denial of rights, expropriation, and the repatriation of profits. Colonialism systematically distorted African economies to the detriment of indigenous people and to the advantage of externally-orientated European interests.[26] In the judgement of one historian of Central and Southern Africa,

> Colonialism systematically undermined pre-existing agricultural and trading systems in order to coerce Africans into providing the low-cost labour needed to produce cheap raw materials for export to the factories of Europe.[27]

This is not to say that colonialism was evil in every respect. The balance sheet must take into account some beneficial effects, and recognise the work of altruistic and idealistic individuals in the colonial service who devoted their lives to their perception of the good of Africa, but the evidence that the colonial governments and their trading companies simply used territorial acquisitions to advance their own interests with little concern or consideration for the indigenous peoples is overwhelming. These injustices are not simply an historical matter; the structure and problems of Africa today largely derive from their recent colonial past. The continuing prosperity of the West and the racial minority in South Africa is in part dependent on the perpetuation of colonial relationships. Neo-colonialism, by which I understand the dominance of Third World economies by the economic interests of Western capitalism, has in many cases exacerbated the distortion of African economies, preventing any substantial improvement in rural poverty.[28] Multinational companies continue to exploit and dominate the economies of the Third World[29] and the system of international financing has 'tended to impose unnecessary and unacceptable political burdens on the poorest' (Brandt, 1980, p 216).

The inherited colonial economies of Africa cannot be changed to eliminate famine without understanding the origin of contemporary social and economic structures, since a good case can be made for saying that the 'colonial legacy' is among the root causes of many of the continuing political and economic problems that face underdeveloped countries today.[30] We may cite from the history of colonialism, for example, forced labour (a century or more after slavery was abolished), land annexation, punitive taxation, arbitrary justice and imprisonment, and monopolistic trading. From the more recent practices of neo-colonialism we may cite examples of the export of profits, subsistence level wages, unsafe practices (such as the dumping of toxic wastes), distortion of economies away from the production of food for the home market, over-dependence on imports from the manufacturing nations which push up national debts and create further dependence on foreign loans and capital.

Passing judgement on the past

One response to this kind of analysis has been to suggest that the victims of past wrongs should be able to demand some form of rectification of the problems inherited from the colonial period, and furthermore that the cost of this process of rectification should be borne by those states who are the continuing beneficiaries of those past wrongs and who are also guilty of collusion with the contemporary wrongs of neo-colonialism and the global economic system. The attractions of this approach are that: 1 it does not depend on an appeal to charity, since the obligation is imposed on the wealthy states as a strict duty; 2 nor does it require infinite obligation, since the obligation is owed to specified groups by virtue of an established relationship; 3 it may be pursued according to principles that an adherent of the entitlement view of justice could accept and therefore may provide a common standard of judgement between idealist and realist analyses; and 4 by focusing on restructuring economic relationships, it may have more prospect of success than piecemeal aid projects funded from charitable sources. By claiming that the poor nations are owed rectification, the right of the wealthy states to distribute their wealth according to their own self-interested inclinations is challenged. It makes the wealthy indebted to the poor, instead of the poor indebted to the wealthy.

We must be careful here to distinguish between a number of different demands for rectification which can be made; between retribution, restitution and compensation (O'Neill, 1986, p 74). The demand for *retribution* as punishment for past wrongs runs into two insuperable problems, firstly the difficulties in determining how to apportion blame to agents whose actions were consistent with the moral rhetoric of their own time and, secondly, the injustice of punishing a present generation for the wrongs committed by those in the past. The basis for retrospective judgement is not only unclear, its implications are equally uncertain—for if it is a judgement on the past alone, then the contemporary generation cannot bear the guilt for past wrongs, nor be liable for compensation resulting from them. Any punitive element in a scheme of compensation can therefore only apply to the wrongs of contemporaries. But the first problem we encounter with any attempt to determine where contemporary wrongs are being committed is the refusal of the political and economic realist to recognise the legitimacy of concepts of blame and guilt in the context of international relations. If the actions of the multinationals are no more than those of rational agents operating within market forces there can be no agreement about what is a wrong and therefore on what appropriate punishment should be imposed. A further issue here is whether present generations are under any moral obligation to deny themselves the benefits accruing from the advantageous trading position occupied by the wealthy states today, which is at least in part a consequence of past wrongs. As Dr Ramose argues elsewhere in this volume, neo-colonialism has perpetuated the 'assumed superiority and the corresponding dominance of the Western European states in the conduct of international affairs.' (Ramose, 1991, p 29). But once again the realist will argue that the present generation in affluent nations cannot be held responsible for the historical inequalities from which it derives its power to promote its own legitimate interests.

If the demand is understood in terms of restitution rather than retribution, a different set of problems arise. Whereas it is appropriate for a householder whose property has suffered damage to demand that her property be restored to its original state, we may safely assume that no nation will demand that it be restored to the levels of wealth of the period before which the alleged systematic wrongs of capitalism occurred. Rather the principle to be applied is that restitution requires 'the restoration of a good or level of well-being to that which someone would have enjoyed if they had not been adversely affected by another's wrong acts' (Sher, 1981, p 6). The application of this principle would, however, require that we should be able to reconstruct what Africa would have been like if it had never been colonised and then compare it to today's actual situation. In doing so we would have to make a number of counterfactual assumptions about how and to what extent indigenous peoples would have employed Western technology on their own terms to maximise their own benefits. Using the most favourable set of assumptions it might be argued that Third World countries could have been much better off than they actually are if much of their wealth had not been syphoned off to support the interests of the colonial power.

But in practice it is impossible to calculate what the course of African history might have been since such counterfactual speculation is full of so many uncertainties. We cannot be sure that things would necessarily have gone better if the indigenous people had not been colonised (Kitching, 1982, p 154; O'Neill, 1986, p 110). Also problematic would be judgements about what would have been a fair return for resources extracted under conditions other than colonialism (Goodin, 1985, p 159). Furthermore, the transferability of entitlements to compensation diminishes over time because the longer it is since the original wrong, the less the contemporary situation may be assumed to be causally dependent on the original wrong and the more difficult it becomes to determine responsibility (Sher, 1981, p 13). It is therefore impossible to calculate what 'reparations' may be due to the ex-colonies from colonial and neo-colonial powers.

Does the demand for compensation for past wrongs, rather than retribution or restitution, offer a more constructive way forward? As O'Neill has argued, compensation may be due whether or not 'the harm suffered constitutes an injury inflicted by identifiable agents', it is independent of any judgement of guilt and is in the form of a good which substitutes for, rather than restores, the original good (O'Neill, 1986, p 85). However, arguments must be provided which show why particular agents should bear the burden of compensatory measures to aid states whose citizens have had their opportunities reduced by the legacies of colonialism. The causal links between the harms caused by historical colonialism and the continuing advantages enjoyed by the contemporaries of wealthy states must do the job of placing responsibility on those who, collectively, enjoy those advantages. Furthermore, it may be argued that colonisation created a *de facto* acceptance of responsibility by the claim to have authority over the territories. A substantial and far-reaching 'common life' was established and celebrated by the colonial powers which cannot now be denied or conveniently forgotten.

The role of counterfactual reasoning is not eliminated from two aspects of the compensation argument, since (a) at least on a consequentialist view, establishing that harms occurred requires the judgement that different and more favourable consequences would have followed if different decisions had been taken by agents in the past, and (b) any attempt to calculate the compensation due must make estimates of what might have been the situation of the ex-colonies if they had not suffered the damages attributable to colonialism and its legacies. But the need for these excursions into other historically possible worlds can be restricted. I do not have to establish that I would not have been cheated if I'd played cards with B in order to establish that I was cheated by A. It is enough to show that the ex-colonies had their interests systematically undermined by the colonial powers to show that real harm was inflicted. The evidence in favour of this view is strong, as I have argued in the last section. On the historical nature of the wrongs, we must remember that they were not once and for all events but, as we have seen, are intimately connected with continuing structures of economic and political control, both internally in the newly independent countries and in the terms of international trade. The discriminatory actions of the colonial period created inequalities that continue to affect entitlements. We are not dealing with ancient wrongs alone, but the perpetuation of past wrongs in the contemporary world.

Making such judgements and justifying them is not a quasi-judicial process. Consider a parallel case, a legally legitimate but regressive tax system that is now judged to have created major injustices by the standards of social justice now favoured by that society. Because agents operating within that framework did not do 'wrong' by legal standards, there cannot be any question of retribution, nor can what is necessary for restitution be clearly calculated or demanded. But the inequalities created by such taxation may be taken to justify a programme which gives the balance of benefits to the groups which had previously suffered from the unjust system. The reformist taxation policy would not need to make reparations for past wrongs in the sense of determinate payments of compensation but it would need to put into effect certain principles:

1. Non-perpetuation: the new system must not perpetuate the wrongs committed by the previous system.
2. Equalisation of opportunities: the opportunities gainedby the privileged in the old system must be granted to those previously denied them.
3. Affirmative action: certain special terms may be granted to the previously under-privileged in order to achieve 'non-perpetuation' and 'equalisation of opportunities'.[31]

Such proposals are familiar within the literature of positive discrimination, for example in the context of preferential hiring, and have been subject to much debate. An objection that has often been brought against such compensatory programmes is that they are an inefficient means of achieving rectificatory transfers because they cannot guarantee to distribute benefits to those who most deserve them (i.e. those who have suffered most discrimination) nor impose their greatest burdens on those who can best afford to bear them. In the case of economic measures to assist the poorest nations, it might be said that positive discrimination will tend disprorortionately to favour entitlement holders within the recipient nations, and only at a cost of creating further injustice against the poor of the affluent nations. But if the justification for the policy of discrimination in favour of the poor is in terms of an improvement in their overall welfare rather than in terms of 'corrective justice', then this criticism loses much of its significance. The measures of 'positive discrimin-ation' are justified by the contribution they can make to rectifying the situation of radical inequality.

Implications for the Obligations of Affluent Nations

How useful would such compensatory principles be if they were applied to relations between wealthy and poor states? How confident can we be that they would contribute towards a solution to the problem of radical inequality? It seems likely that compensatory justice, the recognition by wealthy nations of the extent to which obligations to the poor depend on acceptance of responsibility for past and contemporary injustice, can only constitute a partial fulfilment of duties to aid those who suffer malnutrition. For those in a position to give aid 'ideal' moral duties still apply and beneficence will still be needed. Let us see why this is so.

First we must consider limitations on the application of compensatory justice. An important objection to the approach we have been considering is that it perpetuates old patterns of dependency by seeing the problem as a reflection of historical connections and continues to bind the development of the poor nations to the economic power of their erstwhile masters. By concentrating on the perspective of the poor as victims, which the demand for compensation necessarily does, the fundamental power relationships are neither sundered nor weakened. Indeed it might be suggested that compensation would operate to the advantage of the major economic powers, since having wiped the slate clean as it were, they could then continue to exercise their dominance with a clear conscience. Such an outcome would clearly make little impact on the problem of radical inequality.

Whilst it is difficult to imagine any solution that will completely eradicate the differentials of economic and political power, this utterly pessimistic view of the outcome of a solution based on principles of compensatory justice is not justified. To show this it is necessary to elaborate on the three features of the proposal: (a) assumptions about the possibility of self-determination within this framework, (b) the forward-looking nature of the proposal, (c) the possibility of fair contracts between unequal powers.

If we accept de George's argument in this volume (de George, above, ch. 1) that the right to self-determination is at best a 'manifesto right' and not a substantive one, we cannot assume that any realignment of economic policies would necessarily be premised on recognising this right. However, in this respect, the right to self-determination of states is not in a different position to even the most basic of individual rights to subsistence. But under an agreement which sought to compensate for the harms of the past, the ex-colonial powers would be under an obligation to recognise states as self-determining, since a failure to do so would perpetuate past wrongs, not compensate for them. Any new strategies for economic growth could not be controlled by the interests of the affluent nations, since it is a basic principle of rectification of past wrongs that the agent responsible for the wrong should not determine the victim's future. Imposed solutions from institutions working within the economic network of the developed world, e.g. the World Bank, have rarely given sufficient credibility to 'evaluator relative solutions'. That is, the recognition that the evaluation of what is to count as a 'solution' is relative to the values and aspirations of the agents affected by it. The history of imposed solutions premised on a monolithic conception of what counts as development on a Western model has not been good (particularly in Africa) and any way forward which is to respect the autonomy of nations must allow for local solutions which are compatible with separate and distinct cultural and social traditions.

A significant problem with the assumption of the possibility of self-determination is whether the governments of the ex-colonies are in a position to be the representatives of the poor. According to some views, post-colonial authorities have tended to perpetuate colonial power in a different guise, continuing policies which give little power to the poor and effect little redistribution of wealth. If, as Sen (1981) has argued, it has been people's lack of entitlements that has led to their starvation, not the lack of available food, unless there are internal changes to the patterns of entitlement little progress will be made towards eliminating poverty. If self-determination is restricted to its 'external' aspect, (Shivji, 1991, p 37), as a feature of states rather than of peoples, it cannot necessarily operate in the interests of the poor, but even if, on this view, it is the internal policies of the autonomous Third World countries which are crucially important in achieving internal redistribution of wealth, the globally powerful nations have a responsibility (a) not to resist governments which attempt to make the necessary reforms of entitlements and (b) to support investment policies which can contribute to the redistribution of wealth within these poorest states. The internal aspect of self-determination cannot be realised when the controllers of capital use their economic strength to maintain state systems which serve their interests rather than the peoples'. This means that powerful nations must refrain from interfering, either militarily or by manipulating economic pressures, when independent nations adopt policies which protect the interests of the poor.

The second point is that when the proposal for compensation is couched in terms of the principles by which future policies should be pursued, rather than in terms of a 'lump-sum' redistribution, the ties that bind countries to their past allegiances can be loosened rather than perpetuated. Regulatory principles which give a greater degree of equality of benefits from a relationship create the possibility of freedom for the previously subservient partner. Assuming that some relationship will continue to be desirable between the states, since to be isolated from possible trading partners would be even more regressive than the present situation, then what is important is to regulate the conditions under which that trading should take place over a considerable period of time in the future.

Of course, the economic superiority of the developed world cannot be simply set aside, which raises the third issue, whether a negotiated basis for compensation is possible between such unequal powers. The application of the principles outlined above to North/South relations would depend on an acceptance of the proposition that there have been past wrongs, which continue to have unjustified and deleterious effects today. To hope for such an admission may seem to reintroduce 'idealist' considerations which are as unrealistic as the arguments criticised earlier. This would be so if there were *no* ethical restraints on the pursuit of realist economics and politics. But this is not so. International Law exists to constrain states and corporations within some ethical frames, and within domestic capitalist economies there is a host of legislation which is designed to set ethical standards for business practice— including for example, legislation on 'fair trading', health and safety at work, consumer protection, prohibitions on 'insider dealing', restrictions on monopolistic mergers, environmental protection measures and so on. Extra-economic pressures can be employed when there is the political will, for example when governments have used economic boycotts for political purposes.

Economic systems must be judged by their results. It is a mistake to think of economic systems as if they were natural. Market forces are *not* like physical forces, for, unlike say gravity, they are largely constructed, not discovered, they are responsive to legislation, and they reflect moral choices. The resistance to such changes comes not from the impossibility of altering trading relationships, but from the self-interest of the affluent who fear the loss of economic superiority. There are two sorts of answers to this resistance; one appeals to long term reciprocal benefits, and the second appeals to standards, already in operation domestically but not applied internationally. However, one must be sceptical as to whether 'reciprocal benefits' can be achieved without perpetuating the hegemony of the neo-colonial powers, and whether progress is possible towards acceptance of the need to apply ethical standards in international relations will depend on achieving some dialogue between ethically based claims by the poor and the realist assumptions of the rich nations.

On one view this possibility depends crucially on establishing common standards of justification independent of what is particular to the contending parties. MacIntyre has argued that, where there is no resort to such standards, human relationships are perforce relationships of will and power unmediated by rationality. The appeal to impersonal standards of judgement opens the prospect for 'unmasking and dethroning arbitrary exercises of power, tyrannical power within communities and imperialist power between communities' (MacIntyre, 1988, pp 396–7). The gulf between the positions of the poor and the rich make implausible the supposition that common agreement is possible. If, as seems probable, it is an inescapable feature of the dialogue that all appeals to justification will operate within forms of discourse which reflect or are determined by institutionalised distributions of power, then the dialogue itself (and the definition of the terms of the dialogue) will necessarily be part of a strategy to achieve the resolution of conflict through struggle. Finding common ground will not depend on an appeal to impersonal standards but on whether political pressures may be applied to bring about some redefinitions of the negotiating positions of both sides.

The terms within which the dialogue between rich and poor is pursued are not fixed, but reflect shifts in political priorities. Whilst full agreement on judgements about the past may continue to be impossible, a change of public opinion based on a fuller awareness of colonial and neo-colonial practices is not out of the question. Just as we have seen, in recent years a successful campaign to shift public opinion in favour of control over industrialists who pollute the environment, in much the same way the dimensions of the public debate over the Third World are open to change. One of the distancing factors in this matter is lack of knowledge, not so much of the existence of famines, which are given considerable media attention, but of long-term hunger and its causes in the imbalances in the global economic system. If awareness of the network of causal links which tie every consumer and shareholder in affluent countries to conditions in the Third World were to be significantly increased, a change in the perception of the 'South' from merely the recipients of aid to that of interdependent economic partners to whom obligations are owed may become possible. Such a change of perceptions following a political campaign to raise public consciousness could succeed in having a more radical effect by altering the terms under which the dialogue between the poor and the rich is pursued than the present tactics of charities which are aimed at individuals' generosity and good will. [32]

The terms of the dialogue at present continue to be dominated by the definitions imposed by the neo-colonial powers through agencies such as the

World Bank, and in these circumstances the demand for rectification of past wrongs is likely to be understood on conditions which will not match the principles I have outlined as required. Since the recognition of self-determination is also limited by the self-interest of the dominant economic powers, this gives us further grounds for thinking that appeals to idealist standards will continue to be necessary.

But there are two other reasons why at best compensatory justice would only constitute a partial fulfilment of our duties to aid those who suffer malnutrition, firstly because not all of the causes of inequality can be traced to past wrongs. Where natural disasters such as droughts contribute to famine 'ideal' moral duties still apply and beneficence is still needed. It would be quite wrong to suggest that other factors such as climatic difficulties, demography, and the lack of natural resources have not played their part in creating hunger, but the capacity of the ex-colonial nations to respond adequately to these natural disasters and endemic problems has been hampered by both colonialism and its neo-colonial legacy. But overwhelming natural disasters always place an obligation to assist on those who are in a position to do so.

Secondly, whilst the argument places the burden of compensation on those nations primarily responsible for the colonial system, other affluent, but non-colonial nations may be in a position to offer substantial aid. Nevertheless, all of the wealthy nations have to some extent been participants in, and able to make use of, the neo-colonial economic system which places some responsibility on them to compensate those nations who have been the victims of this system.

Where people are vulnerable to the problems created by the situation of radical inequality, all those who recognise the enormous need of the hungry must respond with concern and practical help. But because of the power of governments, corporations and international banking to bring about shifts in policies of production, trade and ownership, action at this level can have the most substantial impact. The demand to alter the terms of the dialogue between rich and poor, from domination by the assumptions of realism to some consideration of ethical principles, can occur if public opinion in the affluent nations were to recognise the need to alter the basis of their economic relationships with the poorest nations.

The obligation to assist the poorest nations of the world is greatest where those who are at least in part responsible for the past injustices are also those who are in the best position to help the countries most vulnerable to their policies. This is, I suggest, the situation of most ex-colonial and present neo-colonial powers, but only when the public is made aware of its complicity in perpetuating injustice can opinion become a force for long-term change.

NOTES

1   See the most recent evidence provided by The World Bank in *Sub-Saharan Africa, from Crisis to Sustainable Growth* (1989).
2   The best known of these was Live Aid associated with the leadership of Bob Geldof in 1985. Since then, in the UK, for example there has been Band Aid, Comic Relief, 'I Ran the World', Action Aid.
3   For example, in the Universal Declaration on the Rights of Peoples adopted in Algiers, July 1976 (see Shivji, p 41 of this volume).
4   See Hoffman, 1981, Ch 3. This is not to say that some local improvements cannot be justifiably attempted by revolutionary action (see Honderich (1980), but the kind of world authority proposed by Russell or more recently Verghese (1976) is clearly beyond the scope of any imaginable revolution, apart from its being open to some substantial objections.
5   Adopted by the General Assembly of the United Nations in 1948. This right was further elaborated and affirmed in the 1966 Covenant on Economic, Social and Cultural Rights.
6   Cole (1976), George (1976), Brandt (1980), Alston (1984), World Bank (1989).
7   Although the right to adequate food has been endorsed by the United Nations, it is instructive to note that both the USA and the UK have opposed the inclusion of economic rights on the grounds that they are inappropriate for judicial enforcement and that they go beyond rights recognised in their own legislation. See Alston (1979), (1984). For a challenge to this view see Fried van Hoof in Alston and Tomasevski (1984).
8   For example, Nozick (1974). For a survey of 'realism' in international relations see McKinlay and R Little, *Closed Problems and The World Order* (London, Francis Pitta, 1986).
9   For the classic statement of this kind of judgement, see Rodney (1972) or more recently Fryer (1988).
10   See discussions in for example, Hynes (1979) and Austen (1987).
11   For an argument that economists and ethical philosophers would both benefit from contact with each other, see Sen (1987).
12   Singer in Aiken and La Follette (1977) p 24. A slightly amended statement of the principle states that 'if it is in our power to prevent something bad from happening, without thereby sacrificing anything else morally significant, we ought, morally, to do it.' (p 27). The significance of the different formulations is discussed by Arthur (1977).
13   O'Neill does not think that the demands of beneficence are unlimited, but she does argue that 'amid unjust institutions there is no limit to the needs to which the imperfect obligations of beneficence may have to turn to ensure that capacities to act are developed and maintained.' O'Neill (1986) p 152.
14   For discussions of the relevance of 'distance' in moral argument, see for example Becker (1975), Glover (1977), Honderich (1980), Singer (1983), Goodin (1985), O'Neill (1986).
15   See Singer (1973) 'From the moral point of view, the development of the world into a "global village" has made an important, though still unrecognised, difference to our moral situation.' In Aiken and La Follette (1977), p 25.
16   'If there is something we genuinely *can* do to prevent death and starvation, then if we are not to be responsible for those deaths we must prevent them . . . What possible difference could remoteness make?' (Harris (1980) p 144).

17 'One is required to sacrifice, as necessary, anything but one's basic rights in order to honor the basic rights of others.' Shue (1980), p 116.

18 For discussion of this point see, for example, Sidgwick (1907), Urmson (1958), Williams (1973), Harris (1980), Fishkin (1982), Kagan (1984).

19 'We would then each be morally *required* to give up our entire way of life and devote ourselves full time to the amelioration of world poverty, disease, and over-population.' Fishkin (1982), p 75. See also Williams (1973).

20 For a review of the literature on this point, see Goodin (1985).

21 A useful discussion of this approach is to be found in Beiner (1983).

22 Here I follow the suggestion made by James (1982), but I am also mindful of the objections raised by Goodin (1985) p 125ff and pp 159–61; O'Neill (1986) p 110.

23 For example Austen (1987) p 109 argues that the value of the slave trade to Britain may have been exaggerated. His conclusion, in relation specifically to Africa, is that 'on the aggregrate, the colonial venture remained of questionable value' (p 117).

24 The Constitution of Portugal (1951) Articles 133–6, quoted in Fetter (1979).

25 Of course Coca Cola is only one such brand name—many multinational companies operate under a variety fo brand names in virtually every country in the world.

26 The most forceful accusations along these lines are Williams (1944) and Rodney (1972), but see also Palmer and Parsons (1977); Crowder (1968, 1987), Fryer (1988).

27 A Seidman, in Palmer and Parsons (1977).

28 'It is clearly shown that in many instances underdevelopment was not merely a matter of increasing economic distortion, dependency and subordination for the masses of the people; it was also a matter of absolute impoverishment against previous standards of living. Wealth was being extracted and in many cases is still being extracted from the rural areas by force, fraud and fiat.' Palmer and Parsons (1977).

29 See Bergsten, Horst and Moran (1978) and Austen (1987), who argues that 'foreign investments (are) not guided by any realistic concern for the continent's own needs' (p 217).

30 Crowder (1987) discusses the following relevant factors (1) colonial violence, (2) arbitrary judicial processes, (3) poverty resulting from colonial policies, (4) deprivation of political experience prior to independence, (5) inherited state structures, (6) colonial political exploitation of internal divisions.

31 For discussions of the application of parallel forms of equalisation of opportunities through 'positive discrimination' see J J Thompson (1974), Sher (1975), T Nagel (1979), L W Sumner (1987), J Edwards (1987).

32 On the need for a political approach to the problem see Nagel (1977) p 56, Beitz (1979) e.g. p 173–4, Brandt (1980), Goodin (1985) p 104, and O'Neill (1986) p 162.

BIBLIOGRAPHY

W Aiken and H La Follette, eds, *World Hunger and Moral Obligation* (Englewood Cliffs, Prentice Hall, 1977)

P Alston, *Making and Breaking Human Rights* (Anti-Slavery Society, London, 1979)

P Alston, 'International law and the human right to food', in Alston and Tomasevski (1984)

P Alston and K Tomasevski, eds *The Right to Food* (Dordrecht, Nijhoff, 1984)

J Arthur, *Rights and the Duty to Bring Aid* (Aiken and La Follette, 1977)

R A Austen, *African Economic History: Internal Development and External Dependency* (James Curry, 1987)

L Becker, 'The neglect of virtue', *Ethics*, 85, 2 (Jan 1975)

R Beiner, *Political Judgement* (Methuen, 1983)

C Beitz, *Political Theory and International Relations* (Princeton, 1979)

C F Bergsten, T O Horst and T H Moran, *American Multinationals and American Interests* (Washington DC, Brookings Institution, 1978)

W Brandt, *North-South: A Programme for Survival* (Pan, 1980)

P Brown and H Shue, eds, 'Food policy: the responsibility of the United States' in *Life and Death Choices* (New York, Free Press, 1977)

J Cole, *The Poor of the Earth* (Macmillan, 1976)

M Crowder, *West Africa Under Colonial Rule* (Hutchinson, 1968)

M Crowder, 'Whose dream was it anyway? twenty five years of African independence', *African Affairs*, 86, 342 (1987), pp 7–24

R T De George, 'The Myth of the Right of Collective Self-determination,' Chapter One, *supra*.

J Edwards, *Positive Discrimination, Social Justice and Social Policy* (London, Tavistock, 1987)

B Fetter, ed, *Colonial Rule in Africa: Readings from Primary Sources* (Univ of Wisconsin Press, 1979)

J S Fishkin, *The Limits of Obligation* (Yale Univ Press, 1982).

P Fryer, *Black People in the British Empire: An Introduction* (Pluto, 1988)

S George *How the Other Half Dies: The Real Reasons for World Hunger* (Penguin, 1976)

A Gewirth, 'Starvation and human rights', in A Gewirth *Human Rights* (Univ of Chicago Press, 1982)

J Glover, *Causing Death and Saving Lives* (Penguin, 1977)

R Goodin, *Protecting the Vulnerable: A Reanalysis of Our Social Responsibilities* (Univ of Chicago Press, 1985)

G Hardin, *The Limits of Altruism* (Bloomington, Univ of Indiana Press, 1977)

J Harris, *Violence and Responsibility* (London, Routledge, 1980), p 144

S Hoffman, *Duties Beyond Borders* (Syracuse Univ Press, 1981)

T Honderich, *Violence for Equality* (London, Penguin, 1980)

W G Hynes, *The Economics of Empire* (Longman, 1979)

J Iliffe, *The African Poor, a History* (Cambridge, 1988)

S James, 'The duty to relieve suffering', *Ethics* 93, Oct 1982)

S Kagan, 'Does consequentialism demand too much? Recent work on the limits of obligation, *PPA*, 13, 3 (1984), pp 239–54

G Kitching, *Development and Underdevelopment in Historical Perspective* (Methuen, 1982)

D Lake, 'Power and the Third World: toward a realist political economy of north south relations', *International Studies Quart*, 31 (June 1987), pp 217–34

G R Lucas and T Ogletree, eds *Lifeboat Ethics: The Moral Dilemmas of World Hunger* (New York, Harper and Row, 1976)

A MacIntyre, *Whose Justice, Which Rationality* (London, Duckworth, 1988)

J Mackie, *Ethics: Inventing Right and Wrong* (Pelican, 1977)

D T Meyers, 'Human rights in pre-affluent societies', *Phil Quart*, 31, 123 (April 1981)

D Miller, 'In what sense must socialism be communitarian?', *Social Philosophy and Policy*, 6, 2 (1989)

T Nagel, 'Poverty and Food: why charity is not enough', in Brown and Shue (1977)

T Nagel, 'The policy of preference, *Philosophy of Public Affairs*, II, no 4 (Summer 1973). Reprinted in Thomas Nagel, *Mortal Questions* (CUP, 1979)

R Nozick, *Anarchy, State and Utopia* (Blackwell, 1974)

O O'Neill, 'Lifeboat earth', in Aiken and La Follette (1977)

O O'Neill, *Faces of Hunger* (Allen & Unwin, 1986)

R Palmer and N Parsons, eds *The Roots of Rural Poverty in Central and Southern Africa* (Heineman, 1977)

M B Ramose, 'Self-determination in Decolonisation', Chapter Four, *supra*.

W Rodney, *How Europe Underdeveloped Africa* (London, Bogle L'Ouverture, 1972)

A Sen, *Poverty and Famines: An Essay on Entitlement and Deprivation* (Oxford, Clarendon Press, 1981)

A Sen, *On Ethics and Economics* (Blackwell, 1987)

G Sher, 'Justifying reverse discrimination in employment, *PPA*, 4, 2 (Winter 1975)

G Sher, 'Ancient wrongs', *PPA* (1981), pp 3–17.

I G Shivji, 'The Right of Peoples to Self-determination: an African Perspective', Chapter Five, *supra*.

H Shue, *Basic Rights: Subsistence, Affluence and US Foreign Policy* (Princeton, 1980)

H Shue, 'The Interdependence of Duties', in Alston and Tomasevski (1984)

H Sidgwick *The Methods of Ethics* 7th ed (Macmillan, 1907)

P Singer, 'Famine affluence and morality', *PPA* 1 (1973). Reprinted in Aiken and La Follette (1977)

P Singer, *The Expanding Circle* (Oxford, OUP, 1983)

L W Sumner, 'Positive sexism', *Social Philosophy and Policy*, 5, 1 (Autumn, 1987)

J J Thompson, 'Preferential hiring', *Philosophy and Public Affairs*, 4 (1973), p 364

J O Urmson, 'Saints and heroes', in A I Melden, *Essays in Moral Philosophy* (Seattle, Univ Washington Press, 1958)

P Verghese, 'Muddled Metaphors', in Lucas and Ogletree (1976).

R J Vincent, *Human Rights and International Relations* (Cambridge Univ Press, 1986)

M Walzer, 'The moral standing of states', in *Philosophy and Public Affairs*, 9, 3 (Spring 1980)

M Walzer, *Spheres of Justice* (Blackwell, 1983)

B Williams, 'A critique of utilitarianism', in J J C Smart and B Williams, *Utilitarianism, For and Against* (Cambridge Univ Press, 1973)

E Williams, *Capitalism and Slavery* (Chapel Hill, Univ of North Carolina Press, 1944)

World Bank, *Sub-Saharan Africa, from Crisis to Sustainable Growth* (Washington DC, 1989)

CHAPTER 7

Rights of Peoples to Self-determination in International Law

Anna Michalska

Human Rights and Rights of Peoples: Scope and Methodological Assumptions

(a) Human Rights

The notion of human rights expresses various meanings. It can be understood as conveying philosophical or moral propositions, as principles of a political system or as a particular type of legal norms. There are certain ideas and principles concerning human rights rooted in individual or national consciousness which do not always coincide with the 'official' ideology expressed in the norms of internal law. Some claims concerning human rights have a long story behind them, while others are formulated because of the effect of changing socio-economic relations, as the response to threats brought about by progress in civilisation, science and technology.

The notion of human rights has strong emotional overtones. The postulate of human rights protection was advanced at various historical periods and it has been used extensively to justify very different political intents and moves. Human rights were written on the banners of those who fought for the freedom of the individual and the liberation of peoples as well as on those who under the cover of rights committed terrible crimes against mankind. The expression 'human rights' is not only used in various meanings but is also often misused.

Neither international law as a practice nor international law as a discipline has formulated a definition of human rights. Such a definition was probably relevant at the time the first international instruments were prepared. Today such a definition is not indispensable since it has been replaced by the international list of human rights.

The 'list of human rights' as specified internationally is adopted here as a point of departure for the analysis of the promotion and protection of those rights. This paper will therefore deal only with those human rights which are contained in universal and regional treaties, and in general and specific treaties. Only exceptionally has the paper drawn on resolutions and declarations of the General Assembly of the UN. The second part of this paper will discuss human rights which are laid down in constitutions and laws of some States.

The International Bill of Human Rights has been received in a variety of ways. Some writers claim that this international agreement has an ideal character, and international norms are interpreted and applied by the respective states according to the political and ideological concepts adopted by them. Others are of the opinion that international instruments in the field of human rights are the expression of a will to adopt and accept some common and universal values by states of various socio-economic and political systems, ideologies, and traditions in culture, civilisation and religion. This paper shares the latter view. It also claims that international instruments are the expression of a certain compromise, the expression of the universal concept of the basic human rights, the *sine qua non* prerequisite to analyse those instruments.

The formation of a new separate branch of international law can be observed today: international law of human rights, which ought to be interpreted in accordance with the general principles of international law and with the basic principles in the field of human rights which have been formulated in international fora. In consequence, this paper does not include problems of interpretation and application of the treaties in domestic law of individual states. The interpretation of treaties should be based mainly on international materials. These consist of all the international instruments and also minutes of the discussions in various international organs and the stand international organs adopted in the process of controlling the execution of the treaties. These materials can supply us with an interpretation and the information necessary to understand the contents of the specific regulation as well as the intentions pursued by their authors. It would appear to be understood that such an interpretation has to some extent a 'supra-state' character and expresses the position of the international community and not of individual states.

This opinion might as well be considered as illusionary and shelved as wishful thinking *vis-à-vis* possible different interpretations of human rights in respective states. But if we consider that international law of human rights is the expression of the universal concept of human rights, then the meaning of the rights must be established on the grounds of instruments and international materials.

(b) Rights of peoples

For many reasons, the analysis of rights of peoples would appear to be a much more complex and difficult task than the study of human rights. This is primarily because the notion 'people' is ambiguous and used in different contexts. For instance, it can be related to a community which is organised in its own state; to 'people' of a colonial state; to a community which does not have its own state and is not part of any other state. The notion can refer to minorities of various kinds. It is again very easy to identify 'people' with 'nation'. The second difficulty encountered in defining this notion is the very diversity of subjects or social groups which are subserved. The third, and as it appears the main difficulty, lies in the various research perspectives which preclude the construction of one given definition. The meaning of the notion 'people' is subject to whom, for what purpose and under what conditions this notion is used. 'People' could be identified with 'nation' in a homogeneous state. 'People' could also refer in a given state to one part of it; e.g. the 'people' as opposed to the bourgeoisie. People who have their own state would interpret the meaning of that notion differently from people who are striving to create their own state. The interests of peoples in colonial states generally correspond to interests of nations in periods of struggle for their independence. Yet, it appears that individual nations tend to create their own states in the name of self-determination of peoples. One research perspective has to be adopted for peoples organised in a multinational federal state and another for a state in which the federal structure has an administrative nature and not a national one. The question of defining peoples is still not resolved. Should it include ethnic minorities, linguistic minorities, or religious minorities, etc, it has to be accepted that the notion 'people' denotes different meanings. It is also worth mentioning that the notion 'people' conveys different meanings in legal norms in national and international law. And it cannot always be explicitly taken from a legal context.

The notion 'people' has been used in international instruments in many contexts. Yet, at the same time, no definition of that notion is provided by international law. Jouve is right in saying that 'peuple, c'est, en quelque sorte, un mot caméléon'. [1] However, lawyers cannot be released from the obligation of attempting to state the precise meaning or meanings of that notion. In spite of the fact that 'people' is a sociological and not a legal notion, '. . . il entre dans des catégories qui ont une signification juridique'. [2]

It is first and foremost the meaning and the scope of 'rights of peoples' and not the meaning of 'people' itself which is analysed in the doctrine of international law. It is also common practice in both international instruments and doctrine to subsume various 'rights of peoples' in the general category of 'right to self-determination'.

In my opinion that concept does not seem to be well-grounded. The notion of 'self-determination' is vague, lacking precision, used in a variety of ways and often misused altogether. The focus of this study will be on the 'rights of peoples' rather than on the broader issue of 'self-determination'.

The *Dictionary of the Terminology of International Law* states that the 'right of peoples to self-determination' has two basic meanings. One is attributed to a state and is 'l'intention de respecter l'indépendance de celui-ci', while in its other meaning it can be referred 'à une collectivité humaine considérée comme constituant un peuple en raison de ses caractères géographiques, ethniques, religieux, linguistiques, etc., et de ses aspirations politiques'. Self-determination is understood as granting those peoples 'la faculté de choisir son appartenance politique par voie de rattachement plus ou moins étroit à un Etat, de changement de souveraineté ou d'accession à l'indépendance politique'.[3]

The quoted definition proves that two radically different subjects are entitled the 'right of peoples to self-determination'. I cannot accept the concept that a State is vested with the 'right of peoples to self-determination'. A number of international norms can be quoted in which principles of sovereignty and independence in international relations are expressly voiced, therefore since the right of states to independence is proved there is no need here to recall 'the right of peoples to self-determination'. Besides, identifying 'state' with 'people' brings the danger of relaxing the international protection of rights of peoples.

On the other hand the second meeting attributed to the notion 'people' by the *Dictionnaire* deserves careful attention: 'Un peuple en raison de ses caractères . . .'. Still even that denomination cannot constitute a starting point for the analysis of international instruments; criteria which are the basis for differentiating separate types of peoples are examples of such criteria and not exhaustive. The right to self-determination is not precisely stated here.

It seems that the above definition ought to be understood as expressing a doctrinal view—by no means the only one—for it is not explicitly related to the contents of international instruments. Taking account of the year of publication of the said *Dictionaire* (1959), the definition 'people' is based mainly on the international instruments of the inter-war period.

It is significant that no unambiguous definition of the notion 'people' can be found, even in the 'Universal Declaration of the Rights of Peoples', also referred to as the Algiers Declaration. It is used in the Declaration in at least three different ways:

(a) Le peuple est une communauté humaine qui se signale par des différences suffisamment significatives à l'égard des autres peuples.

(b) Le peuple est l'ensemble ou la majorité de la population d'un Etat dont un des droits fondamentaux est de n'être pas soumis au pouvoir d'une minorité.

(c) Le peuple est tantôt un peuple homogène structuré en Etat, tantôt une minorité nationale dont les droits collectifs sont reconnus à l'intérieur de cet Etat.[4]

Consequently different types of peoples are vested with the rights described in the Declaration.

In my opinion no unequivocal definition of the notion 'people' can be generated. One can only attempt to differentiate various types of people who are protected by international instruments. But as a result, one should be aware that different peoples are vested with various series of rights on the basis of international law.

Charpentier, analysing the international instruments, arrives at the conclusion that the expression 'right of people to self-determination' is used in at least four different ways

(a) Le droit des peuples à être consultés sur toutes cessions territoriales.

(b) Le droit des peuples à choisir leur forme de gouvernement.

(c) Le droit des peuples à être protégés contre toute intervention extérieure.

(d) Le droit des peuple à se libérer d'une domination qui les opprime.[5]

The author does not analyse these different interpretations of the right to self-determination. It is the contents of the right to self-determination which are the starting point of Charpentier's deliberations. I would suggest the adoption of another criterion, namely the types of peoples which are vested with the right to self-determination by the international instruments.

Right of Peoples to Self-Determination in International Law

(a) Before 1945

1 The principle of self-determination of peoples gained world-wide importance during the First World War. First, international instruments recognised rights of peoples, reiterating the principle of nationality. In implementing the fourteen points of President Wilson, a number of nations in Central and Eastern Europe gained independence. In the peace treaties, careful attention was given to the protection of ethnic minorities. In the Covenant of the League of Nations no express mention of self-determination was to be found. The principle, however, dominated history between the two World Wars. It is sufficient to mention the case of Bohemia where self-determination was denied to a large ethnic minority.

Between the wars self-determination was understood as a political principle which applied to all 'peoples' without distinction. The term was used in the following instances:

A 'People' living as a minority (or even as a majority) group all in one state, ruled, however, by another 'people'.

'People' living as minority groups in more than one state without their own statehood.

A 'people' living as a minority group in a state but perceiving itself as part of the 'people' of a neighbouring state.

A 'people' or 'nation' forced by external influence to live in separate states.

A 'people' living as a majority (or even as a minority) group within the limits of a territory with a special status under foreign domination.

In all five cases it was required that the respective 'peoples' settle in certain parts of the country where they then formed the majority of the population. The principle of self-determination of peoples relates mainly to ethnic minorities living together within the limits of a given territory inside a pre-existing state or empire.[6]

2 During the Second World War, two major aspects of self-determination were emphasised in the Atlantic Charter. The authors of the Charter:

> . . . desire to see no territorial changes that do not accord with the freely expressed wishes of the peoples concerned.

> . . . respect the right of all peoples to choose the form of government under which they will live and they wish to see sovereign rights and self-government restored to those who have been forcibly deprived of them.

This text is still conceived in the spirit of the pre-war period.

(b) Relevant provisions of the United Nations Charter

The UN Charter speaks of the rights of peoples in several provisions.

1 The Preamble reads as follows: 'We the peoples of the United Nations determined . . . to employ international machinery for the promotion of the economic and social advancement of all peoples . . .'

2 One of the purposes of the United Nations as set out in Article 1, paragraph 2, is: 'To develop friendly relations among nations based on respect for the principle of equal rights and self-determination of peoples . . .'

3 The introductory part of Article 55 which deals with international economic and social co-operation reads as follows: 'With a view to the creation of conditions of stability and well-being which are necessary for peaceful and friendly relations among nations based on respect for the principle of equal rights and self-determination of peoples . . .'

4 In Chapter XI entitled 'Declaration Regarding Non-Self Governing Territories', Article 73 provides that 'Members of the United Nations which have or assume responsibilities for the administration of territories whose peoples have not yet attained a full measure of self-government recognize the principle that the interests of the inhabitants of these territories are paramount . . . and to this end . . . to develop self-government.'

5 In Chapter XII, entitled 'International Trusteeship System', Article 76 provides that: 'The basic objectives of the trusteeship . . . shall be: to promote the political, economic, social and educational advancement of the inhabitants . . . and their progressive development towards self-government or independence as may be appropriate . . .'

The formation of the United Nations Charter in this respect could give rise to various interpretations:

Is the term 'people' used in the Preamble in the same way as in the operative paragraphs? (From the minutes of the San Francisco Conference it could be inferred that the term 'peoples' in the Preamble refers to the international community as legally organised in the United Nations.)

Does the notion 'self-determination' have the same meaning as the notion 'self-government'?

If we assume that the authors of the United Nations Charter deliberately introduced distinctions between 'self-determination' and 'self-government', would the difference be conceptual or would it depend on the subject (different types of 'peoples') to which it applies? Since the notion 'self-government' is used in relation to the Non-Self Governing and Trusteeship Territories could it be inferred that the principle of 'self-determination' is related to peoples in independent states?

The text of the United Nations Charter does not bring a ready answer to the above questions and doubts.

There are two principles expressly formulated in the United Nations Charter: 1 'Equal rights of peoples', and 2 'Self-determination of peoples'. The third principle can also be inferred from Article 55 of the Charter: the relation between equal rights and self-determination of peoples on the one hand and human rights on the other. The international co-operation prescribed in the Charter must be directed toward the realisation of the equal rights of individuals with due regard to the principle of equal rights of peoples. The fundamental rights of individuals appear side by side with the principle of self-determination of peoples.

Interpretations of the United Nations Charter provisions is brought about, to some extent at least, in the consecutive international instruments adopted by the UN and in the practice of that organisation. The basic question, in my opinion, is to find what types of peoples are vested with the right to self-determination by the rule of international norms. An attempt at analysing the contents of that right can be taken up only subsequently.

It is not in my opinion essential—at least for the purposes of this paper—to answer the question as to whether self-determination has a character of principle or right. Self-determination is provided by norms of international law and this is a sufficient argument to say that it is a case of imposing legal obligations on a state. Whether they are rooted in the principle or in the right, is not important. I am using the term 'right to self-determination' but I do not advocate that it has any other meaning than the 'principle of self-determination'.

The international instruments adopted by the United Nations Organisation after 1945 can in my opinion secure the right to self-determination for two kinds of peoples; i.e.:

1 Peoples of colonial and dependent states.

2 Peoples understood as a community in an independent state. However,

special protection is also granted to special social groups identified by the international instruments. Different criteria are used to identify these groups. Therefore, it is not essential to know if these special social groups live in an independent or a colonial state. One must of course be aware that the above types of 'peoples' have some common features and international reality is much too complex to be approached by means of terms that have been defined once and for all.

(c) Self-determination of colonial and dependent peoples

According to the widely adopted, present-day view only peoples under colonial rule have the right to self-determination, which involves accession to independent statehood. The ethnic composition of such a territory is irrelevant. As soon as independent statehood is reached, the territorial integrity of the country is protected against any attempt to destroy national unity, even if a given ethnic group is in this way brought under alien domination. Partsch sees this as a new concept of self-determination,[7] in comparison with the already discussed concept of the inter-war period. This view is based on the practice of the United Nations bodies, and the practice validates it to a large extent.

Right to self-determination of colonial peoples has been recognised—in a way not to allow any further doubts—in the Declaration of the Granting Independence to Colonial Countries and Peoples adopted by the UN General Assembly in the Resolution 1514/XV on 14 December 1960. In the Preamble of the Declaration, the General Assembly referred to 'the need for the creation of conditions of stability . . . based on respect for the principles of equal rights and self-determination of all peoples . . .' The General Assembly solemnly proclaimed 'the necessity of bringing to a speedy and unconditional end colonialism in all its forms and manifestations'. The operative part begins with the declaration that 'the subjugation of peoples to alien subjugation, domination and exploitation constitutes a denial of fundamental rights'. Article 1.

Article 2 of the Declaration states precisely the contents of the right to self-determination; by virtue of that right people freely determine their political status and freely pursue their economic, social and cultural development. At the same time, the above quoted provisions of the Preamble, together with Article 5, unambiguously define the subject of that right: Trust and Non-Self-Governing-Territories or all other territories which have not yet attained independence.

The above Declaration is supplemented by the General Assembly Resolution 1803/XVII of 14 December 1962, 'permanent sovereignty over natural resources'. The first-mentioned of the declarations aims at liquidation of colonialism and other forms of dependence, while the other is directed mostly against neo-colonial practices.

The right to self-determination is expressly related to colonial peoples by numerous international instruments. Interpretation of that kind can be among others inferred from the Resolution VIII of 11 May 1968 adopted by the International Conference on Human Rights entitled: 'The importance of the universal realization of the right of peoples to self-determination and of the speedy granting of independence to colonial countries and peoples for the effective guarantee and observance of human rights'. The conference called upon the General Assembly 'to draw up the specific programme for the granting of independence to territories under colonial rule' and called upon the Security Council 'to resume consideration of the question of decolonization and expedite the granting of independence and self-determination to colonial peoples and countries'.

General Assembly Resolution 637A/VII declared that 'the right of peoples and nations to self-determination is a prerequisite to the full enjoyment of all fundamental human rights', and recommended that UN members 'uphold the principle of self-determination of all peoples and nations' and called for information under Art 73c of the Charter on 'the extent to which the right of peoples and nations to self-determination is exercised by the peoples of Non-Self-Governing Territories, and in particular regarding their political progress'.

Resolution 2621/XXV deserves particular attention as it contains a programme of action for full implementation of the Declaration. That view has also been reflected in the reports of the Human Rights Committee related to a study of reports submitted by the states.[8]

A wider interpretation of the right to self-determination—it could also be argued that it would be a different one—has recently been observed in UN practice. It increases the range of peoples which are vested with that right. The new interpretation has not always been taken into account, it seems, by the doctrine. Numerous international instruments seem to relate more and more to the realisation of the Declaration of the Granting of Independence with the necessity to liquidate racial discrimination and apartheid in colonial and dependent territories. For instance, Resolution 34/42 of 7 December 1977 of the General Assembly expresses its conviction

> that a total eradication of racial discrimination, apartheid and violation of the human rights of the peoples in colonial territories will be achieved most expeditiously by the faithful and complete implementation of the Declaration . . . and by the speediest possible complete elimination of the presence of the racist minority régimes therefrom.

In the same resolution the General Assembly affirmed again

> that continuation of colonialism in all its forms and manifestations, including racism, apartheid, the exploitation by foreign and other interests of economic and human resources . . . is incompatible with the Charter of the United Nations, the Universal Declaration of Human Rights and Declaration of the Granting of Independence.

Numerous resolutions concerning the right to self-determination refer not only to peoples under colonial domination but also to peoples 'under alien domination'. One can quote as a case in point Resolution 2649/XXV which refers to South Africa and to the Palestinian people. Other resolutions refer to the right to self-determination of peoples within the context of 'foreign domination and alien subjugation'. Resolution 2787/XXVI is an example of this, while at the same time it confirms the legality of the Palestinian people's struggle for self-determination. The interpretation of the Resolution on Permanent Sovereignty over National Resources has recently evolved in the same direction. The General Assembly supported 'the efforts of the developing countries and peoples of the territories under colonial and racial domination and foreign occupation in their struggle to regain effective control over their natural resources' (see for example Resolutions 2158/XX, 2386/XXIII, 2625/XXV and 3171/XXVIII).

The right to self-determination in the international instruments quoted above asserts a right for peoples to be granted independence and to create their own state. Not only people under colonial rule are entitled to it but also peoples under alien and racist domination. The General Assembly considered that 'the acquisition and retention of territory in contravention of the right of people of that territory to self-determination is inadmissible and a gross violation of the Charter' (Resolution 2649/XXV).

This wider concept of the right to self-determination is adopted in the provisions of the African Charter on Human and Peoples' Rights. The Preamble states that in order to achieve the total liberation of Africa, the peoples '. . . are undertaking to eliminate colonialism, neo-colonialism, apartheid, zionism, and to dismantle aggressive foreign military bases . . .' It is also noteworthy that the African Charter provides for a right of colonised or oppressed peoples to free themselves from the bonds of domination by resorting to any means recognised by the international community (art 20 point 2). It states as well that 'All peoples shall have the right to the assistance of the states parties to the present Charter in their liberation struggle against foreign domination, be it political, economic, or other' (art 20, point 3). A right to be granted assistance from alien states in the process of realising the right to self-determination is not prescribed in international instruments. Art 1, point 3 of the Covenants affirms that 'State Parties . . . including those having responsibility for the administration of Non-Self-Governing and Trust Territories, shall promote the realisation of the right to self-determination, and shall respect that right.' There is therefore an interesting evolution of the principle of self-determination and the relations of that principle to human rights in the African Charter. The right of peoples to self-determination was confirmed by the provisions listing the principles adopted by the OAU. However, there seems to emerge a dualistic conception: on the one hand, the right of peoples to self-determination and, on the other hand, human rights. This does not proceed from the single fact that the realisation of the right of peoples to self-determination is a prerequisite for the protection of human rights but rather is due to the importance laid on the former.

The concept of the OAU Charter is not only dualistic in its approach but also preferential and selective: Member States are bound by specific provisions to respect the right of peoples to self-determination but no such obligation exists in the case of the respect of human rights. Nevertheless, unlike other international instruments, the African Charter indicates the inseparable link between the right of peoples to self-determination and other human rights, as well as the relationship between human rights and the rights of peoples. This can be observed not only in the very title of the Charter, but also in the Preamble and various specific provisions. For example, the Preamble states that '. . . the reality and respect of peoples' rights should necessarily guarantee human rights'.

The right of colonial and dependent peoples to self-determination is also provided for in other international instruments besides those already discussed. Both International Covenants state the right of peoples to self-determination, although neither one nor the other introduce any new elements. The provision in Art 1 of both Covenants is however important because for the first time this right has been formulated within a universal document concerning human rights i.e. a universal instrument which recognises the legal obligations of the states parties. Placing the right to self-determination at the beginning of both Covenants (and not within the list of the other human rights) is an indication that this right was considered as a prerequisite for the realisation of all other human rights.

Some authors examine the right to self-determination within the context of the principle of territorial integrity of the state and with the right to secession. For example, Charpentier writes that '. . . se pose la question de savoir si la pratique contemporaine de la décolonisation consacre l'application aux peuples colonisés d'un droit à sécession . . .' and further that 'l'impossibilité d'expliquer pourquoi un droit à la sécession est ouvert aux peuples coloniaux et interdit aux autres peuples dominés'.[9] Formulating the question in such forms implies in my opinion some misunderstanding. The principle of territorial integrity refers to relations between states, while the right to self-determination—as understood in this paper—refers to specific peoples. Charpentier maintains that 'c'est l'obligation de décoloniser qu'a consacrée la pratique et non le droit des peuples à disposer de leur sort'. On the one hand, this formulation is consistent with the view that the right to self-determination must also include the right to secession. On the other hand the author seems to ignore a certain evolution in the contents and range of application of the right to self-determination which has already been indicated in this paper, i.e. that colonial peoples are no longer the only subjects of the right to self-determination.

The right of colonial and dependent peoples to self-determination does not imply the right to secession for minority groups living in an independent state. Achieving independence for a territory which is not self-governed cannot be considered as a secession. Dependent territories, from the standpoint of international law, do not constitute an integral part of the territory of the state which is administering them.

The Declaration of the Granting of Independence triggered off a rapid process of decolonisation. The colonial and trusteeship system belongs, in fact, almost to the past. That change in international relations has been reflected in the proceedings of the General Assembly. The resolutions adopted in recent years have concerned mostly the right to self-determination of peoples which have been identified by name (e.g. former Southern Rhodesia, South Africa and Palestine). Nowadays, resolutions concerning the right to self-determination are adopted by the General Assembly on rare occasions. Therefore, one can legitimately wonder whether this right, as defined here, is an obsolete question. The answer is, however, negative because of, among other things, a certain evolution in defining this right, as already indicated. Subjects of this right are not only colonial peoples but also peoples living under foreign domination, in racist systems and under the regime of apartheid. Besides, the right to self-determination is also directed against neo-colonialism. Restricting the right to self-determination solely to colonial territories would now be obsolete because in the context of the few colonial territories left it does not impose any obligations for most of the states parties.

In concluding this section, the following can be stressed:

1   The principle of territorial integrity and inviolability of borders cannot bar the process of decolonisation. But at the same time, this principle sets limits to the right of colonial peoples to self-determination. When a colonial territory is granted independence, then the peoples who would compose this new state cannot claim the right to self-determination for secession purposes.

One cannot ignore the fact that colonial states were often artificially created: they were composed of different national, ethnic and religious groups (which sometimes remained markedly different). Thus it often happened that after peoples had acceded to independence they became embroiled in internal struggles in the name of the 'right to self-determination'. But such a right has already been exercised if an independent state has been created and therefore the peoples cannot refer to it in a struggle for secession. Can such an exercise of the right to self-determination of colonial and dependent peoples fully satisfy peoples?

2   For many years the UN has paid a great deal of attention to the right of colonial and dependent peoples to self-determination. The question arises whether this has not been to the detriment of international protection of the right to self-determination of other subjects. As Cassese has said:

> l'ONU tend à ne protéger, en général, que certaines catégories de peuples: les peuples dépendants, c'est-à-dire les peuples soumis à une domination coloniale ou à l'occupation étrangère et, parmi les peuples souverains, seulement ceux qui vivent sous un régime raciste. Les autres peuples ou minorités au sein d'Etats souverains ne sont pas l'objet de sollicitudes de L'ONU, même s'ils sont opprimés, ou tyrannisés par leurs gouvernements.[10]

But does the UN, an international organisation of a universal character, offer effective legal means to respond to situations other than those mentioned?

3   The right to self-determination of colonial and dependent peoples relates to external self-determination. The international instruments quoted above do not explicitly indicate how one should interpret the right to self-determination of peoples under racist and apartheid regimes. Are the international instruments applicable only in situations when racism and apartheid are imposed by a foreign state, or are the said international instruments equally applicable in the case of racist and apartheid policies determined by a state within its borders?

4   All modern doctrines of human rights offer similar interpretations of the right to external self-determination of colonial and other dependent peoples as formulated in international instruments. Divergencies, if any, related only to details concerning the exercise of that right and not its principle.

(d) Self-determination of peoples living in independent states

In one of his important papers on the right of peoples to self-determination, Cassese attempted to devise a new concept of this right. Namely, he formulates the concept of the right of peoples to 'political' self-determination.[11]

Cassese maintains that a new and more meaningful concept of political self-determination has emerged in international law, particularly within the sphere of a so-called internal self-determination. He considers political self-determination to be more consonant with new demands for freedom at the present time.

Colonial and dependent peoples are the subject of external self-determination, and the exercise of that right, as already stated, relates to liberation from external dependence (from another state). The right to internal self-determination is directed against authoritarian régimes, therefore, not only against external interference but mainly against internal interference. This is a right to struggle against all forms of arbitrary oppression of peoples. It is aimed, Cassese tells us 'against those forms of authoritarianism which have taken root in different areas of the world where colonialism was unknown'. It embraces all peoples and is not restricted to peoples under colonial domination. This concept was brought to the forefront in the International Covenant on Civil and Political Rights and in the Final Act of Helsinki. But above all, in the author's opinion, it was formulated in the Algiers Declaration.

As a matter of fact Cassese analyses only one aspect of the right to self-determination (internal) that is political self-determination. The yardstick against which he measures the implementation of the right to self-determination is the safeguarding of the civil and political rights of the individual.

Reducing the right to internal self-determination only to political self-determination was strongly criticised by Graefrath.[12] His criticism is based on the grounds of the Marxist doctrine of human rights and Graefrath considers that Cassese's views on this subject express a bourgeois doctrine.

The socialist concept presents the right to self-determination as a comprehensive complex of internal and external self-determination. This theory does not restrict the right to self-determination to colonially-oppressed peoples and at the same time does not consider that the exercise of such a right has been exhausted after the creation of an independent state.

Graefrath indicates that the exercise of the right to self-determination in terms of a bourgeois democracy is based on the dissociation of civil and political rights from economic, social and cultural ones, on the abstraction of property relations and on the isolated treatment of the political sphere irrespective of its class content and its functions within the framework of social development.

The basic allegation against Cassese's concept is the following: it is not the sovereignty of the people which determines whether or not a state exercises the right of peoples to self-determination, but the safeguarding of political and civil rights which are considered as characteristic of the system of bourgeois democracy. The socialist concept of the right to self-determination has emphasised the close link between the freedom of the individual and the freedom of society.

The Marxist concept of the right to self-determination is not restricted, as Cassese claimed, to the question of external (national) self-determination. This concept combines in one definition of the right of peoples to self-determination, the social liberation struggles of the oppressed and exploited peoples with the national and colonial liberation struggles. Social liberation struggles are considered by Graefrath solely as liberation of peoples from the capitalist system.[13]

While both authors agree that the right to self-determination has internal aspects and controversies, they disagree as to the content of this right. Cassese refers exclusively to political self-determination, while Graefrath refers exclusively to social determination.

As far as the question of the scope and methods of safeguarding the right to internal self-determination is concerned, a substantial divergence of opinions can be observed between Western and Marxist states. This has been frequently expressed in international fora. It relates to the question of different understandings of democracy and, consequently, of a role prescribed to particular categories of human rights. Therefore, I have purposely presented here two extreme positions in both doctrines in order to clarify the controversial issues under consideration, although some intermediary views have been expressed in the literature.

The concepts of international instruments are the expression of a compromise as to the ways of understanding the right to self-determination. The compromise can be observed both in the contents of general principles and in the list of human rights.

Peoples of a given state are the subject of the right to internal self-determination and this is exercised in relation to state authority. This is a principle of internal democracy: every people should be allowed to decide upon its own institutions. Self-determination in domestic law is safeguarded by the constitutional principle that 'people are the source of authority' or the principle of 'sovereignty of the people'. Those principles are applied through numerous specific provisions and mostly by human rights provisions.

The Universal Declaration of Human Rights does not refer *expressis verbis* to self-determination, but it declares that 'the will of the people shall be the basis of authority of government' (Art 21, point 3). In the light of the preparatory work preceding the Universal Declaration this provision can be understood as: 'Le principe fondamental est que la volonté du peuple est la base de l'autorité des pouvoir publics'.[14]

Article 2 of both Covenants provides: 'All peoples have the right to self-determination. By virtue of that right they freely determine their political status and freely pursue their economic, social and cultural development'. Animated discussions both at the Commission of Human Rights and in the General Assembly's Third Committee preceded the adoption of that specific provision. In opposing the inclusion of that article some delegates contended that the Charter of the United Nations referred to the 'principle of self-determination' not to the 'right to self-determination'. They further argued that as a principle, it had a very strong moral force, but that it was too complex to be translated in legal terms in an instrument which aimed at legal enforcement. They added that the various terms used—'peoples', 'nations', 'right to self-determination'—were not defined; that the principle of self-determination was interpreted in different ways in different places; that the problem of minorities and the right to secession were involved. Finally, they argued that self-determination did not constitute an individual right; it was a collective right and, therefore, inappropriate for inclusion in a Covenant which attempted to lay the ground for individual rights; it had been placed in the Covenants before all individual rights and seemed to imply that individual rights were of a secondary importance as compared to self-determination.

The proponents of the right to self-determination, on the other hand, insisted that this right was essential for the enjoyment of all human rights and should, therefore, appear in the forefront of the Covenants. In many cases individual rights could not be exercised because peoples did not enjoy the right to self-determination. They pointed out that self-determination was proclaimed as a principle in the Charter and that it was clear that any Member State which had accepted that principle was committed to the right which derived from it. Member States were already committed to respect the right to self-determination through Articles 1 and 55 of the United Nations Charter. Similar difficulties arose also with respect to the right of economic self-determination, the right of peoples to dispose freely of their natural wealth and resources because, as some delegations contended, it could be interpreted to justify expropriation without just compensation. The entire article was adopted by 33 votes to 12 and there were 15 abstentions.

Preparatory work on both Covenants proves clearly that the notion of 'self-determination' was used in various ways and in numerous contexts. The minutes of the discussions at the Commission of Human Rights and the Third Committee indicate that a common understanding was not reached, either on the scope or contents of the right to self-determination.[15] Articles 1 of both Covenants do not lead to an unambiguous reply to these questions. Faced with a layman's use or even with the abuse of the notion of 'self-determination' in the literature, it would be most difficult to invoke the doctrine to interpret Art 1 of both Covenants. Discussions on the interpretation of Art 1 usually focus on the question of whether self-determination is a human right or a principle and focus around the legal and political implications of the adoption of one or the other options.[16] In my opinion, the right to internal self-determination is formulated in Art 1, point 1 of both Covenants. The obligation of international law to safeguard rights and liberties in internal relations is imposed on states by the treaties concerning human rights. I am disregarding here the duty of international co-operation aimed at universal respect for and observance of human rights and fundamental freedoms, imposed by the United Nations Charter. The fact that the right to self-determination is proclaimed in the Preamble of the two Covenants and not in part three (in the listing of human rights) cannot be, in my opinion, a sufficient reason to consider that only the external aspect of self-determination was aimed at in this right. On the contrary, spelling out this right in an international instrument related to human rights implies, to my mind, that the 'right to internal self-determination' was also aimed at. The contents and the scope of that law are set by the list of human rights. At the same time, protecting human rights serves the purpose of the application of the right to self-determination.

Contents of both Covenants are the expression of a compromise between the Marxist doctrine and the modern liberal doctrine of human rights. The concept of self-determination of peoples is placed at the top in both doctrines. One can of course consider that the compromise provisions of the Covenants are based on different philosophical grounds and will be implemented under different political and economic systems. In relation to this Maritain wrote:

> ... il est possible d'établir une formulation commune de telles conclusions pratiques ... mais il serait très futile de chercher une commune justification rationelle de ces conclusions pratiques et de ces droits. La question soulevé ici est celle de l'accord pratique entre les hommes qui sont opposés les uns aux autres sur le plan théorique. Nous nous trouvons en présence du paradoxe suivant: les justifications rationelles sont indispensables et elles sont en même temps impuissantes à créer un accord entre les hommes.[17]

It seems that the quoted view is legitimate as far as the right of peoples to self-determination is concerned. Indeed, there are differences in the conceptions of morality and justice and there is also no unanimity on the notions of freedom and democracy. In my opinion, however, it is wrong to emphasise only differences of a doctrinal and philosophical nature. It is improper to consider every conflicting interpretation or application of a particular rule or principle as an expression of an ideological struggle. It seems to me that it is a shortcoming in the theoretical work of lawyers, philosophers and sociologists that they concentrate their attention mainly on differences, and neglect to emphasise the common human content of some notions and ideals.

I share the opinion that the achievement of practical goals rather than a consensus on ideological matters is the function of the United Nations Organisation and the substance of its activities.[18] What matters are practical conclusions: each partner to a common action is entitled to his own ideology and justification of his action.

Numerous human rights are interpreted and implemented in the same way, irrespective of socio-political systems. Yet, one must be aware that the entire list of human rights serves the purpose of the application of the right to self-determination, adopted by a given state. It would be difficult to discuss here which of the concepts of self-determination of peoples is 'better'. Especially as we have a tendency to evaluate one of the concepts critically against the standpoint of the other. It is only on rare occasions that an evaluation proceeds on account of concrete conditions. What I have in mind is not only socio-economic and political conditions but also conditions pertaining to civilisation, culture, religion and tradition. A given conception of human rights is created out of these conditions as well as shaping the ways of interpreting and implementing international instruments. The Covenants, which are the expression of a compromise between the doctrines of the East and the West do not take into account the African and Asian conceptions which are provided in Islam, Buddhism and in the ideals held by other cultures and traditions.

Human rights formulated in the universal instruments can undergo regional or sub-regional interpretation. This was the case with the African Charter. The list of human rights stated in the Charter is more inconspicuous than the one in the Covenants. But the Charter is not in contradiction with the Covenants: in both instruments the same rights can be found and some of them are worded identically. But the Preamble to the African Charter reads as follows: '*Taking into consideration* the virtues of their historical tradition and the values of African civilisation which should inspire and characterize their reflection on the concept of human and peoples' rights . . .'

I do not intend to examine the question of 'universalism vs. regionalism of human rights' or the problem of the interpretation of international instruments in particular states. These fragmentary remarks are made in order to justify my not attempting to give precise content and scope to the right of peoples to internal self-determination. Such an attempt would, in my judgement, be fallacious. The right to self-determination is formulated in the international instruments in a very general way and various concepts assign different meanings to it. One should recognise that there is a lack of a universal commonly accepted concept of internal self-determination. In concluding this section, I wish to stress the following:

1   A methodological difficulty can be encountered in discussing the contents and scope of the right of peoples to self-determination, both in its internal and external aspects. Some international instruments relate the principle of self-determination to interstate relations. In those instruments, the right of

peoples to self-determinaticn is set alongside the principle of the inviolability of frontiers, the territorial integrity of states and the principle of non-intervention in internal affairs. It is in that very context that the right of peoples to self-determination is developed in the *Declaration on Principles of International Law concerning Friendly Relations and Co-operation among States* and by the *Declaration on Principles Guiding Relations between Participating States* (Principle VIII) and in the Final Act of the Helsinki Conference.

Both Declarations repeat and reaffirm the right of peoples to self-determination formulated in the international instruments adopted before. But they neither enrich the contents of that right, nor introduce new elements to it that would exceed its scope. The states are obliged to respect that right in their relations. International instruments of this kind lead to relating self-determination to the principle of non-intervention or the principle of independence of states.[19] It would not be easy therefore, to ascertain in what way the term 'right to self-determination' is used in the doctrine of international law.

2   The question of specific contents of the right to internal self-determination is purposely disregarded in this paper. In my opinion, the right, declared in the international instruments and adopted by the United Nations has no universal commonly-agreed meaning nowadays and no universal contents. Moreover, the prospect of reaching such a universal interpretation seems to be fading today.

The concept of the right to internal self-determination must be analysed in close relation to the concept of human rights. The international instruments have probably led to some uniformity in interpretation and in implementation of human rights on the universal scale. The judicature of organs of international protection accounts for a lot in this respect. But such a uniform interpretation (or at least close to a uniform interpretation) is possible only in the case of certain particular rights and not in relation to all of them. It would seem that a universal concept of fundamental freedoms could be reached in a comparatively easier way. But today the odds are against a uniform interpretation of the whole body of civil and political, economic, social and cultural rights. Indeed, the interpretation and implementation of these rights have a basic implication for the definition of contents and scope to internal self-determination.

Contents of the right to internal self-determination are not stated with precision in international norms because a settlement of this aspect is not feasible and the matter is therefore left to the domestic law and practice of particular states.

Research Propositions

1   Rights of peoples appeared in international instruments even before the concept itself was elaborated. The notion 'people' is vague and leads to confusion. It is worth considering its replacement, in some cases, by such terms as rights of groups, rights of collectivities or rights of minorities.

2   Rights of peoples are recognised in the international instruments as human rights. Present thinking is, however, divided on this issue. Theoretical reflection on the modern concept of human rights and their scope is therefore necessary.

3   Rights of peoples are collective rights. Further research is therefore needed on the question of these rights, both at international and national levels.

NOTES

1   E Jouve, 'L'émergence d'un droit des peuples dans les relations internationales', in: *Pour un droit des peuples Essais sur la Déclaration d'Alger,* publié sous la direction de A Cassese et E Jouve, (Berger-Levrault, Paris, 1978), p 105, hereinafter quoted as *Essais . . .*

2   G Soulier, *Réalités du droit international contemporain* (Reims, 1977), p 230.

3   *Dictionnaire de la terminologie du droit international* (Sirey, Paris, 1959), p 233

4   F Rigaux, 'Remarques générales sur la Déclaration d'Alger', in *Essais . . . p 46.*

5   J Charpentier, 'Autodétermination et décolonisation', in, *Méthodes d'analyse du droit international,* Mélanges offerts à Charles Chaumont, A. Pédone (Paris, 1984), p 117.

6   K J Partsch, 'Fundamental principles of human rights: self-determination, equality and non-discrimination', in *The International Dimensions of Human rights* (Unesco, Paris, 1982), pp 63-4.

7   K J Partsch, op. cit., p 65.

8   See for instance: Report of the Human Rights Committee, General Assembly, Official Records: Thirty-Seventh Session, Supplement No 40/A/37/40: '. . . it was asked what steps the Netherlands had taken to help the peoples of South Africa, Namibia and Palestine seeking the right to exercise self-determination' (p 21); '. . . it was asked whether, in the particular cases of Namibia and Palestine, the Japanese Government had done all that it could have done in the international context to ensure that the peoples concerned enjoyed their right to self-determination; what steps it had taken to discourage South Africa from maintaining its domination over Namibia . . .' (p 12); '. . . the report contained no information on the self-determination of the territory known as Western Sahara . . .' (p 31).

9   J Charpentier, op. cit., pp 118-19.

10 A Cassese, 'La portée politico-juridique de la Déclaration d'Alger', in *Essais . . .,* p 63.

11 A Cassese, Political self-determination: old concept and new developments, in, *UN Law and Fundamental Rights* (Alphen aan den Rijn 1979, Sijthoff and Noordhoff), pp 137 *et seq.*

12 B Graefrath, 'A necessary dispute on the contents of the peoples' right to self-

determination', *GDR Committee for Human Rights Bulletin* No 1/1981, pp 11 *et seq.*

13   He wrote: 'The extensive interrelated norms of internal and external self-determination demand especially in our time that the peoples should have the liberty: to establish a socialist order of society, to overcome the imperialist limitations of the right to self-determination in a socialist revolution, and to free themselves from the fetters of the capitalist world market'.

14   A Verdoodt, *Naissance et signification de la Déclaration universelle des droits de l'homme* (Ed Nauwelaerts, Louvain, 1964) p 209.

15   Report of the Third Committee, UN Doc A/3077, General Assembly Official Records, Annexes X.

16   Compare with J C Fawcett, 'The role of the United Nations in the protection of human rights—Is it misconceived?', in *International Protection of Human Rights*, A Eide and A Schou, eds (Almqvist and Wiksell, Uppsala 1968), pp 95–102, and discussion on 'Self-determination and human rights', pp 282–8.

17   J Maritain, *L'homme et l'Etat* (Presses universitaires, Paris 1965), pp 69–70.

18   R Bystricky, 'The universality of human rights in a world of conflicting ideologies', in: *International Protection . . .*, op. cit., p 87.

19   F Capotorti, Discussion, in *International Protection . . .*, op. cit., p 284.

CHAPTER 8

The Right of Self-determination in International Law

R S Bhalla

This essay explores the nature and basis of the right of self-determination, and advances a radical proposal concerning the content and beneficiary of the right of self-determination as it ought to be acknowledged in international law. The starting-point is the thesis that the principle of self-determination is acceptable as a legal principle only in its application to the liberation of colonial territories. While there may be analogous moral rights ascribable to many sorts of national groupings, for example, where 'submerged' nations seek autonomy within or independence from larger states of which they have become part, these are by no means the same as the right to self-determination held by indigenous peoples against colonial powers. The case of indigenous peoples is, it will be argued, the appropriate one for application of self-determination as a legal principle. Moreover, it follows that the right vests only in indigenous peoples as such, not in whoever happens now to inhabit colonised territories alongside of the original indigenous population.

Self-Determination

Self-determination as it is generally understood in international law and relations refers to freedom from colonisation. It has never been taken or understood under international practice as applicable to self-determination for a part of a state.[1] That is a matter left to the domestic jurisdiction of the state itself and to the section of its people who want their status altered. In international law, the principle of self-determination is applied to people who have been deprived of it—deprived of the right to determine their own political, social and economic structure. What it provides for, therefore, is in reality a restoration of the status of which they were deprived by the colonial power. What is involved here is not secession from the colonial power, nor is it a case of granting some new right, for it is simply a restoration to the colonised people of a right of which they were forcibly deprived. In the domestic context, when a claim to self-determination amounts to a demand for secession, the nature and content of such a claim is quite incompatible with the notion of self-determination in international law. Self-determination does not involve secession. For this reason, the present paper is concerned with and is confined to the idea of self-determination as a concept of international law and it does not concede or conceive its application to national groups claiming secession from established states.[2]

Second, under international law any government, whatever its nature, dictatorial, democratic (western style), or military, so long as it is in effective control, is admitted in the international community. The question of determination of its nature is not raised. This is because the international community presumes (fiction) that an effective established, sovereign, independent government is a self-determined government. It is, therefore, fit to participate in international obligations. If the criterion of self-determination, in the sense of a free expression of popular choice, were applied to a dictatorial government, such a government would not be allowed to participate in international obligations and would thus be treated as unfit to take a place in the international community. This does not happen. Therefore, the problems of national governments, their mode of determination, their character are not raised at international forums. The function of international law is not precisely comparable to that of domestic law. Self-determination within an already self-determined state is a national determination rather than a continuing self-determination by the citizens of the nation.

Third, self-determination in its literal meaning or at a terminological level implies the right of the self to express itself, to organise itself in whatever way it wants. If this self-expression were taken to its extreme by granting every adult a right of personal self-determination[3] the existence of groups or associations as interdependent units would not be possible. The existence of groups or associations is possible only through interdependence. This implies restricting personal self-determination for the sake of living in a group, restricting one's self-satisfaction or sacrificing one's self-satisfaction to attain a greater satisfaction. But this greater satisfaction requires acknowledgement of one's own limitations. Here one can conclude that a merging of one's self with another self is the result of external pressure, the result of exterior agency rather than of one's own initial independent act of accession to a group. Thus if a group is satisfied in its unity with other groups and as a result a bigger group has come into existence, differences between sub-groups should be handled in the same spirit as that which brought about their unity in the first place. When new groups come into existence by association of pre-existing groups, the harmony within the groups is of paramount importance. This harmony is a natural growth within a community and is a condition of survival. Communities cannot come into existence as a result of simple aggregation.

They are like sea water which contains a natural harmony of chemicals which it is impossible to reproduce by analysing the sea water into chemical components and mixing them again. Such a communal fabric cannot be dismantled without destroying the entire nature of a group. Therefore, if secession is to be allowed it must again be on conditions determined within the larger group, and compatible with its character. The question of unity or secession is a question of national determination and not of self-determination. These problems of so-called self-determination can never gain perfection—mankind will always live in a state of imperfection, even though differences need not be considered irreconcilable.

These considerations show the defects in Dr Beran's approach to self-determination, for his approach reduces the concept of self-determination to the level of the cumulative personal determination in its implications. To allow the self-determination of individuals, and this proves too much,[4] making a mockery of self-determination of every individual, with iterative rights of secession, is to negate the concept of the state as a collection of groups. If the principle of self-determination is to be made productive, it must be given more restricted dimensions in space and in time. Secessionist movements within groups in a mother state cannot be cited as cases of self-determination, but must be handled as matters of national determination.[5]

The concept of self-determination refers to a process by which people determine their own sovereign status. It should, therefore, be accepted as fixing some of the terms of association within any state as a sovereign entity. No class of people can have a right to oppress others. Each cultural identity has a right to exist of its own. One can say that this is an imperative principle of action. This principle has come into existence because of various historical events such as the American War of Independence, the French Revolution, the Russian Revolution. These events established the idea of self-determination as an expression of the people to establish their identity. Crystallised through these events, the principle's social and political importance and existence cannot be denied.

Sometimes doubts are expressed about the status of the principle and arguments are advanced both for and against its existence in international law. Emerson[6] advocates that the principle of self-determination has no stable place in the international legal structure; it is essentially miscast in the role of a legal right as an operative part of either the domestic or the international system. Schwarzenberger[7] acknowledges the principle but denies its aptitude to become part and parcel of international law. On the other hand Starke[8] believes that the right of self-determination has achieved a wide recognition and acceptance in international law.

Starke's is the better view, for the principle of self-determination has become an accepted norm of modern international law. It is referred to in the UN Charter, and therefore imposes an obligation on the member states to facilitate the implementation of the principle. In fact, for the first time in history it is laid down in a comprehensive international document—being one of its basic tenets.

Nevertheless, the importance of the principle of self-determination as a legal principle seems to fluctuate considerably over time in the international community.[9] This confusion is due to the lack of clear-cut boundaries assigned to the principle. The principle has been accepted at peace conferences but often in obscure terms, so that its precise contents are always left somewhat in the dark. Its judicial applicability is always doubted, because it is made unamenable to generate any clear-cut rule of law. It is left in limbo because its political implications are such that different nations accept markedly varying versions of the principle. Some members of the international community want to apply the principle in the field of domestic politics of a sovereign nation; while others hold that the principle functions only as an instrument of decolonisation. They believe that in those cases where the issue is territorial disintegration of a sovereign independent nation because a certain group seeks separate territory, the issue does not fall within positive international law. Such an issue is a part of domestic conflict in which the international community should not interfere.[10] How such an issue of the group seeking independence from the mother state is to be settled, amicably or by force, is a problem of the mother state. These conflicting views have led to the unsettled nature of the principle of self-determination. But the view advocated here is, as stated, in favour of the more restricted interpretation of the principle, as applying to decolonisation only.

Self-Determination as a Legal Right

The current trend of juristic opinion recognises the principle of self-determination but abjures the recognition of any strict legal right to self-determination. Some even refuse to acknowledge that a 'right' of self-determination could ever attain legal status.[11] But if it is admitted that such a right could exist, its nature can be determined by considering whether it is recognised and whether it has a holder. If one could specify a determinate and recognised content and an identifiable right-holder, there would remain no doubt that it is an actual or potential legal right. As to the second of these, it has already been established that the right of self-determination can only be visualised in terms of a people and this raises the question of the precise definition of the people who are the right-holders.[12] The former of our questions concerns the recognition of the right. The existence of human associations implies the existence of civilised behaviour and civilised treatment of human beings. This general expectation is the very basis of human living as distinct from brute existence. Even a casual student of law realises that certain norms of behaviour, by virtue of their fundamental nature, have to be acknowledged as the first principles of civilised living. In the absence of respect for these norms of behaviour one cannot expect a human association, but Bentham's savage state.[13] Therefore it is quite safe to say that there has never existed and never will exist, a society that fails to recognise the basic principles of civilised behaviour.

One of these must be acknowledgement of the integrity of established human groups. Mere existence as a group must therefore be a 'vestitive fact', the title of the group to a right of existence. Salmond[14] states:

> . . . every right (using the word in a wide sense to include privileges, powers and immunities), involves a title or some source from which it is derived. The title is the de facto antecedent, of which the right is the de jure consequent.

The right of self-determination as a right of each group to have a meaningful living is, therefore, a part of the civilised norm. This principle is not new but it is born with the very existence of civilisation. In the interest of each group there is a tacit recognition that each group has a right to determine its own affairs. These norms have timeless existence. In the modern world they have been given institutional form. When groups fight, it is not that they do not recognise each other's right to exist, but that they presume their superiority over the other, either as a genuine belief or as a simple political expediency. If recognition is essential to qualify self-determination as a legal right, it has tacit recognition from time immemorial. It is tacit because there is no super-state-organisation which has a complete judicial system, like municipal law, to give it recognition. Its recognition is acknowledged through concrete manifestations when colonial territories are given the right to self-determination. It is, therefore, reasonable to accept the legal nature or give legal meaning to the right of self-determination. It is an original right (in the historical sense) and not a derivative right. At present it has been given institutional recognition.[15]

The right of self-determination remained dormant till the movement towards self-determination worked with elemental force against the colonial powers. This entire process could not have happened unless it was accepted that the right of self-determination existed and its relevance was realised only in issues of foreign dominance. The colonial powers trespassed on the right by aggression, by force. The aggression only made the right hibernate till the time came for its revival. It was merely in abeyance during colonisation. The right was there, the inability of colonised groups to enforce it did not extinguish the right. This is one reason why the international community recognises it, but is not in a position to enforce it except through political pressure.

The implementation of the right and the colonial powers' taking of decisions about granting it are political matters. These are not problems which are amenable to legal solutions. In this sense determination of the right inevitably becomes a political question, but this does not affect the right itself. The consequences of all these political questions are legal. It is a process regarding the revival of the right. Because of these political considerations, the extent and scope of the right is open to debate.[16] It is because of these problems that the right cannot be reduced to a rule of law. It is its application that creates problems, but this does not touch the authenticity of its existence and its legality.

Self-Determination as a Human Right

Humanity's greatest problem is how to preserve peace in a manner that can be accepted as just. To solve this problem, the right of self-determination is mooted in the international community as providing a part of the solution to the problem. No peace can be achieved unless all national aspirations are equally acknowledged. The basic object of the principle of self-determination is to guarantee that all people have a government of their choice that responds to their political and social needs through their common identity. These sentiments were given vivid expression by a Filipino senator[17] in the 1920s when he stated: 'We would prefer a government run like hell by Filipinos to one run like heaven by Americans'. Since under colonisation native peoples are not only deprived of their choice of government but are also subjected to racial discrimination and other inhuman treatment, the idea of self-determination has come to be linked with human rights.[18] Self-determination itself is regarded as a human right, since it is through the expression of the self that all other rights flow.[19] But such a conclusion is misleading. Suppose, for example, that a colonial power gives the native people some basic rights which it considers fundamental to their native identity like, for example, the right to worship, but refuses them the right of expression except in religious matters. Which of the rights to treat as basic human rights and which to withhold is a matter for the colonial power to decide. It depends on their effective control and their ability to govern the territory. The idea of human rights is so fluid that it cannot provide a basis for deciding which of the rights is more fundamental. Different persons will make a different list of human rights under different conditions and this will create not only quantitative differences but qualitative differences as well. There can be no coherence in the list of these rights because of their abstract nature. Nor can it be stated with certainty and clarity just which of the rights the colonial power should grant to the native people to keep up the momentum of human rights.

As a matter of fact the right of self-determination is allied to legal-political rights rather than to human rights. It is a right to the political governance of a territory which can take various forms, such as association with other groups, limited autonomy etc. It works on political options rather than on humanitarian grounds. Therefore one can conclude that human rights and self-determination need not be linked together. If they co-exist the result might be more fruitful, leading to more freedom and meaningful living, but their relation is not a logical necessity. The right of self-determination can exist without human rights. For example, the authoritarian regime of Idi Amin of Uganda was an inglorious regime for human rights in Uganda, but it was a self-determined regime of the indigenous people of Uganda. Since in self-determination it is the effective possession and not the continuity which is accepted, this regime was as representative as any other regime in the world. The questions of good government and bad government are questions of competing claims and not of self-determination.

The general view that self-determination involves the total participation of all the inhabitants living in the colony is based on respect for human rights. This is the pragmatic conviction that the majority counts, and is a political way out of the decolonisation process, but it is not a philosophy of human rights. The philosophy of human rights is a philosophy of each person's rights as a human being and has no necessary link with the common identity of the people as a people. The proposition that such a separation of human rights from self-determination will create diversity in human treatment is not a problem of human rights but more of political imbalance, which the colonial powers want to avoid. As Roy states:

> A strange irony of fate now compels those very members of the community of nations on the ebb tide of their imperial power to hold up principles of morality as shields against the liquidation of interests acquired and held by an abuse of international intercourse . . . To the extent to which the law . . . favours such rights and interests, it protects an unqualified status quo . . . and makes itself a handmaid of power in the preservation of spoils.[20]

The very rights which were inconsequential have suddenly aroused the conscience of the colonial power and have attained respectability in determining human societies. Self-determination is a political-legal question. Humanitarian considerations may constitute the inspirational basis in providing a solution to the question of self-determination, but they, by themselves, do not constitute the right of self-determination.

The techniques for bringing about self-determination are various, but human rights are only achieved by restoring human dignity. For example, the plebiscite is one of the techniques for restoring the right of self-determination (though it need not be identified with the whole population of the territory). Again, the concept of 'human right' is so foggy that its contents are always in doubt despite so much noise about human rights. Their political expression in terms of fundamental rights of individuals is nothing but a technique to put a leash around individuals to guide them towards state activities. Since these rights are granted within the unlimited interest of the state, their nature and tone is more political than humanitarian. As a matter of fact, within the political arena human rights only represent a practical makeshift arrangement and not a concern for real human aspirations. Political-legal morality and morality in itself, as can be expressed in Kant's categorical imperative, are skies apart. Therefore, self-determination and so-called human rights, apart from political expedience, are really not related.

The Determination of the 'Self'

Ever since the principle of self-determination entered the international arena, its basis has been shifting according to the whims of the political powers. Great expectations have not been fulfilled.[21] In view of such fluctuations, it might some day be abandoned. So, to keep it intact it needs to be repaired to fulfil the purpose it is designed to fulfil. It posits the concept of people as a unit qualifying for the right to deliberate upon their own interest in nationhood, to constitute a national identity, the identity of which the people in question has been deprived by colonisation either by force or by other means.[22]

As it is argued that the right of self-determination is a legal right and not simply a political right, to give it a persuasive legal significance it is essential to define the 'self' who is to exercise the right of self-determination. The expression 'self-determination' itself gives no clue as to the nature of the self that is to be allowed to determine. Therefore, the delimitation of the self is a first question if self-determination is to be accepted as a legal right. As Jennings[23] states, the people cannot decide until somebody decides who are the people. It is generally argued that the 'self' includes a total participation of all the inhabitants occupying a territory.[24] Such a view is misleading since it does not set a standard as to the self which is appropriate for the exercise of the right of self-determination. It undermines the very self which has the right of self-determination. It does not pinpoint the self which deserves special considera-tion on the ground of the diminution in identity suffered through colonisation; the very self which may be on the verge of losing identity.

It is the determination of this very self which is in question and not a determination of the territory. This argument refers to the self that was colonised in the first instance. It refers the indigenous people of the territory where self-determination is to be exercised. It is this indigenous criterion which is the sole criterion and no other *indicia* can be allowed in exercising self-determination. The right belongs to the people who were deprived of it.[25] Such an application of the right of self-determination needs a clearly-defined self. It is only then that the right of self-determination can be stated with reasonable precision and given an institutional expression.

The kind of self that legitimately invokes the right of self-determination is a preliminary question before the right can be applied. This self which is an indigenous self, is distinct from other selves. It is this distinctness which is the starting point in granting the right of self-determination. Under colonisation it is the indigenous self that suffered, the other selves are mere transplants to help the colonial power in advancing her interests and in suppressing the indigenous self. To include them in the process of self-determination is to grant them extra privileges over those accorded the indigenous people who were deprived of their rights at the time of colonisation. Again, the other selves have never considered themselves historically and culturally a part of the indigenous self. They have even failed before the attainment of self-determination to identify sufficiently with the aspirations of the indigenous people towards self-determination.

For example, in 1964 the Government of India raised in the UN the issue of South African treatment of people of Indian origin in that state. The Government of India felt that it had a moral and political obligation towards them because its predecessor had been responsible for the departure of the first Indian immigrants to South Africa.[26] If those people of Indian origin, who have left India to settle in South Africa, are a part of the self of South African people, the Government of India has no obligation towards them as part of the Indian selves. She has no right to raise objections even on moral grounds, because if morality is involved it cannot distinguish between people of Indian origin and other races who are also subject to repression. In the eyes of morality all human beings are equal under similar circumstances. Conversely, if it is argued that the acquisition of South African nationality by the people of Indian origin does not necessarily cause the loss of nationality of origin, it clearly leads to the conclusion that the people of Indian origin are not a part of the indigenous self. This leads to the conclusion that the right of self-determination belongs to the indigenous people.

Colonisation is an exercise of brute force. Its illegality lies in the very denial of civilised behaviour which both socially and morally implies that people are left to exercise their own free will in their own affairs. Therefore, colonisation is a trespass. It is a trespass against the selves who are trespassed upon. Until the trespass is vacated, it continues by analogy with the very simple principle of the tort of trespass. The people trespassed upon are the indigenous people and not the later transplants, that is, the selves who came after colonisation. It is this distinctness that immediately establishes the reasonable distinctness of the self who needs remedy against trespass, through self-determination. It is the fusion of this distinctness that is the cause of all problems in French New Caledonia, where the Kanaks want self-determination on the basis of their distinctness. France refuses to recognise this equitable and distinct principle because of its political repercussions. Social justice is sacrificed at the altar of political expediency.

Self-determination involves parochial sentiments.[27] It is based on the human desire to associate with one's immediate fellows. It is not a question of superior or inferior race but it is a question of common identity or consciousness of culture and historical community and continuity. The demand for self-determination is rooted in a wish to form a self-government to preserve cultural identity in the community of nations and to alleviate fears of dominance by alien values.[28] The question is: who is that self who has these fears? The answer immediately suggests itself, it is the indigenous self which has been subjugated. It is this self that wants to determine his identity, his common consciousness. Indigenous people are defined in a UN Report which states:

> indigenous communities, peoples and nations are those which, having a historical continuity with pre-invasion and pre-colonial societies that developed on their territories, consider themselves distinct from other sectors of the societies now prevailing in those territories or parts of them . . . are determined to preserve, develop and transmit to future generations their ancestral territories and their ethnic identity, as the basis of their continued existence as peoples, in accordance with their own cultural patterns, social institutions and legal systems.[29]

To ignore this distinctness and to attach importance to the sheer number and diversity of groups in the territory is to impair the gist of self-determination. Any diversion from this distinctness will negate the 'consciousness which constitutes a national identity . . . and allows for the continued flourishing of the cultural and historical community in question'.[30] If the whole population of the territory is included in the self-determination, it can lead to unpleasant results as in the case of Fiji where the indigenous population lost out to the outsiders. The granting of the right of self-determination to indigenous people by excluding others may appear intangible, ambiguous and problematic, but this does not make the principle of self-determination unnecessary nor invalid. Such an application of the right of self-determination is rational and unbiased, based on the colonial power's obligation towards those from whom the colony was seized and on a proper regard for their cultural identity. Such an application of the right of self-determination may not be comfortable to some, but it is certainly the most durable.

The nature and implementation of the right of self-determination has become complex not because of the complexity of the concept itself but due to the political implications involved. Its legal nature has been uncertain because of the lack of a judicial apparatus which would accept it and which would have the means to implement it, to enforce it. The concept has been given different meanings due to the ideological conflicts within the international communities. But it is submitted that one can construct out of the available materials a satisfactory and determinant conception of the right of self-determination, one which ought to be accepted by the international community.

NOTES

1   James Crawford, 'Outside the colonial context', in *Self-Determination in the Commonwealth*, Allan MacArtney, ed (Aberdeen, 1988) pp 1–2, 13–14; Gregory, 'The neutralization of the Aaland Islands' *AJIL*, 17, (1923), p 63.

2   For the opposing view see V P Nanda, 'Self-determination under international law: validity of claims to secede', *Case Western Reserve Journal of International Law*, 13 (1981), p 257. S P Sinha, 'Is self-determination passé?' *Columbia Journal of Transnational Law*, 12 (1973), p 260.

3   Harry Beran, 'A philosophical perspective', in *Self-Determination in the Commonwealth*, Macartney, ed, p 27.

4   Neil MacCormick, 'The determinancy of selves', ibid., p 113.

5   H Johnson, *Self-Determination Within the Community of Nations* (1967), p 50. S Kaur, 'Self-Determination in International Law' *Indian JIL*, 10 (1970), p 479.

6   R Emerson, *From Empire to Nations* (Cambridge, 1970), p 370.

7   G Schwarzenberger, *A Manual of International Law* (4th edn, London 1960), p 135. L C Green, *Report of the 47th Conference of the International Law Association* (1956), p 58.

8   J Starke, *An Introduction to International Law* (10th edn, London, 1989) p 116; I Brownlie *Principles of Public International Law* (3rd edn, Oxford, 1979) p 484; M Lachs, 'Some reflections on the problem of self-determination', *Rev of Contemporary Law* 2 (1957); Lenin, 'The principles of self-determination of nations in international law', *Soviet YBIL* 48 (1962); A Y Vyshinski, *The Law of the Soviet State* (trans H W Babb, New York, 1948), p 249.

9   Lee Gross, 'The right of self-determination in international law', in *New States in the Modern World*, M Kilson, ed (Cambridge, Mass, 1975), p 136.

10 Crawford, op. cit., pp 8–12, and see the authorities cited therein.

11 J Verzijl, *International Law in Historical Perspective*, 1, 324 (1968).

12 See Section 4 ('The Determination of the "Self"') below.

13 J Bentham, *Theory of Legislation* (4th edn, London, 1882), p 113.

14 J W Salmond, *Jurisprudence* (11th edn, London, 1957), p 378.

15 See UN Charter, Article 1 & 55; International Covenant on Civil and Political Rights, 1966, Art 1.

16 R Higgins, *The Development of International Law Through the Political Organs of the United Nations* (London, 1963), p 103.

17 Quoted in L C Buchheit, *Secession: The Legitimacy of Self-Determination* (New Haven, Conn, 1978), p 8.

18 *17 UN Monthly Chronicles* 52 (Nov 1980).

19 Crawford, op. cit., p 4. A Cassese, 'Political self-determination—old concepts and new developments', in A Cassese, ed *UN Law of Fundamental Rights*, (Alphen an den Rijn 1979), p 142.

20 Roy, 'Is the law of responsibility of states for injuries to aliens a part of universal international law', *AJIL*, 55 (1961), pp 863 and 866.

21 Austria was denied the right of self-determination when it decided to join Germany after the First World War.

22 Homestead by any means whatsoever cannot be bargained.

23 I Jennings, *The Approach to Self-Government* (Cambridge, 1956), p 56.

24 U Umozurike, *Self-Determination in International Law* 195 (1972).

25 Maureen Davies, 'Indigenous rights' in *Self-Determination in the Commonwealth* (MacArtney), p 45.

26 *Indian Council of World Affairs*, (India and the UN, 1975), pp 107–13.

27 Buchheit, op. cit., pp 1–2.

28 Neil MacCormick, op. cit., p 112.

29 UN Doc E/CN.4/Sub.2/1985/31.

30 Neil MacCormick, *Legal Right and Social Democracy* (Oxford, 1982), p 261.

CHAPTER 9

Biculturalism, Partnership and Parallel Systems: the Context of Maori Rights

Ian Macduff

The object of this paper is to provide a comment on the framework of Maori rights in New Zealand. That framework, as will be seen, is provided by the Treaty of Waitangi, dating from 1840. In exploring the rights implications of the Treaty, I will need to assume much of the philosophical and critical debate about rights. I will also need to pass over a great deal of the current constitutional discussion about the place that the Treaty had and has in the New Zealand legal framework. For the purposes of a discussion of indigenous rights, one main theme will be pursued, and that concerns the consequences, for the framing of substantive rights, of a politics of biculturalism and partnership.

Against an assumed backdrop of general and critical theories of rights, it is hoped that the following discussion of the special case of indigenous rights in New Zealand will illustrate several points. First, it has been a part of the discussion of rights to note the capacity of liberal legal systems to adapt to new demands for rights: the flexibility of liberalism is seen as either its virtue, because of the ability to meet new needs, or its vice, because of this apparent demonstration of normative vacillation. To the extent that there is growing recognition of the legitimacy of redistributive and rectification claims by the Maori, the New Zealand legal and political system illustrates that general capacity. But—secondly—that is not the full story. The demands for rights are not merely demands for specific and distinctive rights for the Maori; they are articulated as demands based less upon the promises and premises of liberal theory than on the unique status of the Maori as *tangata whenua*, as the original people of the land, and on the relationship of 'partnership' established by the signing of the Treaty of Waitangi in 1840. This lends a particular kind of texture and coherence to the contemporary debate in New Zealand. If, as is argued, liberalism is cast adrift from any firm moral moorings, thus allowing

102

a demand-driven response to rights, the emerging position in New Zealand is quite different in our having at least the current reassessment of the Treaty as a reference point for rights claims. Third, the nature of those Maori claims challenges the assumptions of universality and singularity of a legal system. If they were only claims based upon the promises of liberalism and law, they would be still difficult, but less of a challenge to the conventions of jurisprudence. But the direction which the debate has taken, not merely articulated by the Maori but now also in the Court of Appeal, has been towards recognition of a parallel jurisprudence which again affirms the distinct promises of the contract of partnership. Biculturalism is not merely a moral aspiration; it becomes a principle for the recognition of rights. Fourth, this 'rediscovery' of the meaning and implications of the Treaty is relatively recent, the Treaty having suffered either rejection or neglect during much of this century. In this period of the reinvention of the relationship of partnership, of a bicultural jurisprudence and of the rights which follow, it seems that rights are less settled than negotiable. While the founding 'principles of the Treaty of Waitangi' are affirmed in both recent legislation and judicial decision, the results are less a matter of a discovery of the one right(s) answer than of seeing those principles as the basis for renewed negotiation of the substance of the relationship between the Crown and the Maori.

To borrow and change an expression from a different setting, the contemporary discussion of Maori rights is largely a matter of 'bargaining in the shadow of the Treaty'.[1] The year 1990 marks the sesquicentennial year of the signing of the Treaty of Waitangi between a number of Maori chiefs and representatives of the British Crown in New Zealand. As that anniversary approaches, the questions being raised concern the manner in which the signing of the Treaty is to be marked, as a celebration of the foundation of nationhood, as a promise which has never been kept by the European settlers and their successors in power, as a fraud perpetrated on the indigenous people, or as the basis of a contract of partnership between the two equal parties, the Maori and the *pakeha*.

While the debate concerning the status of the Treaty develops in the media, in graffiti, in the number of recent publications on Treaty and related matters, it is also warming up in more formal settings, in the courts and in Parliament. The issues there include the claims to particular categories of Maori rights, to the institutional and distributional implications of the 'partnership' deal signed in the Treaty, and to the rectification of 150 years of injustice at the hands of a dominant and alien legal system. The debate is potentially divisive as references to the perceived demands of the Treaty challenge the conventions of liberal orthodoxy, European political and social hegemony, and the language of rights. At the very least, 'the Treaty' has become a symbol of the larger debate about the nature of the political relationship between the Maori and the *pakeha*.

What is clear at this stage is that the language of rights has not been abandoned because of the perceived limitations of that form of discourse. Perhaps because the language of rights is the most familiar and readily available, perhaps too because the issues are genuinely seen as those of clarifying questions of rights and rectification, we are stuck with that way of dealing with the relationship. It may, however, work in both directions: not only will this current debate sort out some of the ownership and distributive priorities, it will also give an expanded meaning to the notion of rights, especially to the extent that they are settled in this uniquely bicultural setting. In this sense, there may well be distinct non-individualistic and programmatic constructions of rights. As will be suggested later, the recognition of Maori claims, not merely in substantive terms but also in terms of the distinctive normative and cultural reference points, reinvests rights with spiritual as well as formal qualities. The liberal legal system is being required to make adjustments to accommodate a new range of claims and a new set of criteria. The challenge of rights in this sense is less the challenge of the multiplication of substantive claims than the multiplication of frames of reference.

If, too, this seems like a variation on the pluralism which liberalism is supposed to be able to accommodate, it is more than that. Pluralism, in the historical setting of the domination of one race by another colonising race, seems more like assimilation and the legitimation of that domination. The context of Maori rights is a political arrangement of equal partnership—the accommodation and recognition not merely of distinctive substantive claims but also of the distinctive normative and legal framework of the Maori as the foundation and justification of rights. This form of decolonisation involves the possibility of parallel legal systems.[2]

To talk of rights in New Zealand is necessarily to talk of the Treaty. While the Treaty is the distinctive reference point for the articulation of Maori claims to rights and recognition, it is also increasingly treated as the foundation of European, or *pakeha*, rights. The scope of rights that non-indigenous people have is similarly determined by this single document. This, of course, is not an uncontentious claim. While politicians, judges, perhaps the majority of the Maori, and an unassessed proportion of the non-Maori population might increasingly take the Treaty seriously as the foundation of a bicultural jurisprudence, there is also a distinctive voice that argues for the abandonment of the Treaty and the negotiation from scratch, of the terms of our social arrangment; or which insists on an ethic and jurisprudence of 'one culture—that is, New Zealander', which will frame similar rights for all. Because of the familiar appeal of the 'one people' and 'equality before the law' claims, it will have to be seen that the Treaty is the sort of document that justifies a leap beyond that principle in the framing of rights.

In a country which is also obviously multicultural it needs to be said at this stage that the arguments about biculturalism and the rights which follow from that are always sheeted home to the Treaty. The argument is, quite simply, that the Treaty was signed in 1840 between the representatives of the British Crown and a number of Maori chiefs. As successors to those two parties, the partners in the contemporary constitutional set-up are the Maori people, on the one hand, and the non-indigenous people of New Zealand, on the other. While there are people in significant numbers from perhaps the full range of other cultures in New Zealand, none of those other minority groups has the distinctive and historical arrangement—and rights—possessed by the Maori. Thus, as indicated earlier, the claims to Maori rights are not merely claims of a disadvantaged minority, though they may have that flavour in many substantive respects. They are the claims of the *tanagata whenua*, the people of Aotearoa, equal partners in the unique constitutional arrangement established by the Treaty.

The terminology most commonly heard in anticipation of the 1990 anniversary of the Treaty suggests that it in some way marks the foundation of nationhood. This concept needs to be treated cautiously at this stage, principally because of the implications of the civilising mission of the age of colonial expansion, the assimilation of indigenous people by an imposed culture, and the mark of 'nationhood' in a formal system of law and British justice. Nevertheless, the value in retaining this idea of nationhood is that it now requires a contemporary re-examination of the terms of that arrangement. If that is what we are celebrating, what is it that we are to celebrate? If the sole interpretation is that of the loss of tribal lands to the Crown through the subterfuge of law, the loss of the autonomy and dignity of a people through cultural domination, then one can understand the graffiti which assert that there is nothing to celebrate. On the other hand, an interpretation which now emerges in our political and legal language and which sees the Treaty as a source of principle for rights and constitutional partnership may point to a significant re-evaluation of the meaning of nationhood.

That the principles of Treaty partnership are already established in contemporary jurisprudence is indicated by the number of recent Acts of Parliament which carry an injunction to courts to give weight to the principles of the Treaty in applying the statutes or in the statutory assertion[3] that nothing in the legislation shall derogate from Maori rights. This recognition extends beyond the immediacy of legislation to the proposals, for example, of the Law Commission, in their 1989 Report on Maori Fisheries[4] and to the current review by the Ministry for the Environment of the body of resource law legislation. It receives still stronger recognition—at least as principle—in the Report of the Royal Commission on Social Policy[5] in their affirmation that the Treaty is a document which is to guide the future construction of social policy and is not merely an historical artefact. The same degree of recognition was accorded to the principles of the Treaty in the government's White Paper, *A Bill of Rights for New Zealand*. While that proposed Bill of Rights did not enact the Treaty or incorporate it into the municipal law of New Zealand, it did propose to enact the *rights* in the Treaty. Paragraph 4 of the preamble stated:

4(1) The rights of the Maori people under the Treaty of Waitangi are hereby recognised and affirmed.

(2) The Treaty of Waitangi shall be regarded as always speaking and shall be

applied to circumstances as they arise so that effect may be given to its spirit and true intent.

It has to be said that the Bill of Rights has moved no further than that White Paper and that little can be said to have come of the range of recommendations of the Royal Commission on Social Policy, but the point can at least be made that it has become increasingly part of the conventions of political and legal discourse to acknowledge the principles of partnership and biculturalism. One further example of this can be seen in the recent restatement of purpose by Victoria University which affirms the pursuit of the familiar academic and research goals, but in a manner consistent with the principles of partnership under the Treaty. It certainly cannot be said that we yet know fully what is meant by partnership and biculturalism, but what is being affirmed is that that is the language within which we will continue to work out the structure of rights within our political system. At the very least, it promises to add a distinctive voice to the discourse on rights.

Central to this reinterpretation of rights, both general and indigenous, is that interpretation of the Treaty which stresses the relationship of partnership between Crown and Maori. The importance of partnership is that it grounds not only the claims to the recognition of the rights of the Maori but also the claims to equal recognition of Maori values, spirituality, and law to *te ao Maori,* the Maori dimension. Further, this is not merely a pluralist acknowledgement of the cultural heritage of an indigenous people; it is, in the light of the Treaty, an affirmation of a bicultural polity.

The bicultural jurisprudence of rights that centres on the Treaty and on the concept of partnership has to be traced to the language of sovereignty used in the Treaty. In either positivist or normative terms, rights will have their foundation in a source of legitimacy. In New Zealand, the interpretation of the Treaty means that, in general terms, that Treaty is increasingly seen as the significant constitutional document and, more specifically, the legitimacy of Maori claims rests upon the distinct terms of sovereignty used in the Maori text of the Treaty.

There were a number of versions of the Treaty, in English and in Maori. It is not known how many drafts of the English version might have been prepared, and it is thought that it was not always the same version that was taken around the country for further signing following the initial signing at Waitangi.[6] It needs also to be noted that, despite the confident claims to British sovereignty based on cession dating from the 6 February 1840 signing, and despite the signatures added duing 1840, the representatives of the British Crown did not obtain the full consent of all the Maori people. Those difficulties aside, the main issue for present purposes is that there are significant differences between the two main versions in English and Maori. And it is in the Maori version, and specifically in the different words used to convey the concepts of sovereignty and authority, that the questions will arise concerning the sources of legitimacy of rights.

Two words are significant; both relate to forms of authority and sovereignty;

both appear in the Maori text of the Treaty. The first is *kawanatanga*, broadly used to convey the concept of sovereignty or civil government which the first article of the Treaty stated was being ceded to the Crown. In that article, or rather in its translation into Maori, the expression of cession without reservation is not a problem. But what has been the issue, and is now largely taken as the basis for the 'principles of partnership under the Treaty', has been the meaning of *kawanatanga*. It is not itself a Maori word but a construction derived from pronunciation and transliteration of 'governor' and hence 'governorship'. As such, it conveys something of the sense of civil authority, but none of the full complexity of sovereign authority which it might be assumed was being ceded.

If that were the only word at issue there would be still significant issues in drawing conclusions on the sources of indigenous rights within the framework of a liberal and monocultural system. But the sources of rights and the bases of a bicultural jurisprudence are complicated by the use of a different term for authority in the second article of the Treaty. Having apparently ceded civil authority to the Crown in the first, the second article reserves and guarantees to the Maori 'the full exclusive and undisturbed possession of their lands, estates, forests, fisheries and other properties . . .'. That is in the English version. In the Maori text, the concept of possession is omitted and in its place the word *rangatiratanga* is used (omitting also reference to forests and fisheries). *Rangatiratanga* clearly means far more than possession, for it implies chieftainship and authority. It is also unlike *kawanatanga*, a Maori word, thus more likely to be understood in its original sense.

Whatever the reason for using the two words in the separate articles, the effect is that Maori authority, a chiefly and spiritual authority, is taken to have been protected and preserved in the Treaty. One of the British objectives in pursuing the Treaty was to establish the basis of an ordered civil government in an increasingly unruly settlement, and thereby protect the interests of both the settlers and the Maori. In so doing, it was intended to protect Maori lands from settlers, and to ensure that any alienation of Maori land was to the Crown. The terms of the Treaty do this and more: the distinction between *kawanatanga* and *rangatiratanga* is sufficiently clear to lead to the contemporary conclusion that while civil authority was indeed ceded, the authority of the chiefs, the *rangatira*, was preserved. If this was intentional, it may be seen as an exercise in using the indigenous structures of authority to reinforce colonial rule.

Whatever the intention, the current effect of both judicial and statutory recognition is to affirm the importance of *rangatiratanga*. It has also to be noted that such *rangatiratanga* is not a creation of the Treaty and of the new sovereign, but is rather recognised and affirmed by the Treaty. But the legal and jurisprudential puzzles are only now being grappled with, for, if it is true that the Treaty cedes civil authority and affirms Maori traditional authority, there are now two sources of principles for the identification of rights. If as has been recently suggested, the Treaty is a 'profoundly moral document'[7] we still need to determine the implications of such a document in the affirmation of rights.

What is clear is that current claims, both substantive and political, cannot be heard within the framework of conventional jurisprudence. Quite apart from the substance of claims to lands, fisheries, the protection of *taonga* or treasures, there is the emerging recognition of a Maori jurisprudence which rests on and affirms the *wairua* or spirit of the Treaty. While the formalism of judicial interpretation may lead to the construction of the Treaty against the Crown in the case of doubt, this is not the same as the construction of a bicultural jurisprudence of rights which introduces potentially new canons of construction and interpretation.

Certainly it has not always been the case that the Treaty was seen as the foundation of a bicultural system of rights and jurisprudence. Recent findings of the Court of Appeal and of the Waitangi Tribunal take this view and lead the thinking in this direction. For example, The Tribunal denied that it was the intent—or at least the effect—of the Treaty to create 'one people', *he iwi tahi tatou*. Rather,

> The Treaty was an acknowledgement of Maori existence, of their prior occupation of the land and of an intent that the Maori presence would remain and be respected . . . It established the regime not for uniculturalism, but for biculturalism.[8]

This decade of the 1980s can be seen as a period in which a bicultural interpretation of rights is taken as a serious possibility and a plausible challenge to the conventions of liberal jurisprudence. It is interesting in this respect to note the fluctuations in the fate and reception of the Treaty, culminating in this current reassertion. Dr Claudia Orange identifies three main periods in the status of the Treaty:[9]

[i]   1840 to 1870: a period in which the Treaty served the European need for peaceful settlement and the Maori need for reassurance that certain rights would be respected;

[ii]   1870 to 1930: a period of European neglect, but continued Maori expectations of the Treaty;

[iii]   1930 to 1980s: a period of rediscovery of the Treaty by the pakeha.

Whatever reasons might be attributed to this rediscovery, the effect has been to begin to restate the conventions of race relations, rights and political organisation in New Zealand. It reflects, too, a shift from an early period in which there are pragmatic reasons for recognising indigenous rights under the Treaty, for the sake of settled government, through a period in which the inconvenience of recognising Maori rights leads to neglect (at best) or rejection (at worst) of the Treaty, through to the modern period in which the affirmation of Maori rights is seen as both necessary and possible through the framework of the Treaty. Certainly the current position is a far cry from the view expressed by Sir James Prendergast C.J. in *Wi Parata v The Bishop of Wellington and the Attorney-General* (1877)3 NZ Jur (N.S.)72, that

So far indeed as that instrument purported to cede the sovereignty . . . it must be regarded as a simple nullity. No body politic existed capable of making the cession of sovereignty, nor could the thing itself exist. So far as the proprietary rights of the natives are converned the so-called Treaty merely affirms the rights and obligations which, jure gentium, vested in and devolved upon the Crown under the circumstances of the case . . . The title of the Crown to the country was acquired, jure gentium, by discovery and priority of occupation, as a territory inhabited only by savages.

That case—and that view—effectively formed the precedent controlling Maori claims to redress through the Courts until *Te Weehi v Regional Fisheries Officer* [1986]1 NZLR 680. That case directly turned on the status of 'Maori fishing rights' in the face of legislation controlling fishing. The appellant was convicted under the Fisheries (Amateur Fishing) Regulations 1983 of taking undersized shellfish and under the Fisheries Act 1983 of behaving in a threatening manner towards a fisheries' officer. His unsuccessful defence at first instance and the grounds for appeal, were, on the first charge, that he was exercising a Maori fishing right, having been granted permission by the appropriate tribe to take shellfish for his own consumption and, on the second charge, that at the time of the appellant's alleged threat the fisheries' officer was not acting in execution of his duties. On appeal it was held that, as the customary fishing right had not been extinguished expressly by statute, it continued to exist. While the right was limited to the Ngai Tahu people and their relatives, it was one that nevertheless persisted and overrode the requirements of the statute. The conviction for taking undersized shellfish was, accordingly, quashed, though the conviction for threatening conduct was upheld.

On the face of it, this is simply a case about the persistence of customary rights notwithstanding the provisions of general legislation, and the case does not clearly turn on the implications of partnership under the Treaty. Rather, it might be taken as a case following a somewhat different tack and presenting the survival of Maori rights as a matter of 'aboriginal title'. Indeed, the cases and academic sources cited by Williamson J indicate that this is the line of reasoning. The general argument for aboriginal title is that such rights might be said to survive if they are not repugnant to common law, are not uncertain, or are not incompatible with prerogative rights.[10] Further, if those aboriginal or customary rights have not been expressly extinguished by statute, they can be said to persist. It is not at all clear, however, that such a line of reasoning is necessary in the case of Maori rights, given the interpretation of the Treaty and particularly the preservation of *rangatiratanga* in respect of lands, forests and fisheries. Indeed, the argument against using the principles of aboriginal title is that it is still potentially a formalist and monocultural defence of rights, deriving from a line of colonial law[11] And that cannot be an appropriate basis in the developing context of bicultural jurisprudence.

In the recent cases it has been unnecessary to determine the issues in terms of aboriginal or indigenous title at customary law as the questions of interpretation seem increasingly to turn on the place occupied in New Zealand's jurisprudence by the Treaty and by its principles of partnership.

What those principles are seen to require is, at the least, a practice of consultation between the 'Treaty partners' on the substance of rights. Further, they involve an increased recognition of the authority of the Waitangi Tribunal as the body most qualified to determine the validity of claims made under the Act. The Tribunal, established in 1975 by the Treaty of Waitangi Act, exercises its jurisdiction, extended by the 1985 amendment to the Act, in respect of claims made for the recovery of land alienated to the Crown and by the Crown to current holders of title and in respect of claims made to other rights assured by the Treaty. The Tribunal has been a significant force in interpreting the texts and implications of the Treaty, though its powers of redress are limited to those of making recommendations to the Crown. Its influence is likely to become greater as claims are tested in the courts and judicial reliance is placed both on the interpretation of rights under the Treaty and recommendations for settlement made by the Tribunal.

The most significant recent case, and one which confirms the recognition of the status of the Treaty as a source of rights, is *New Zealand Maori Council v Attorney-General* [1987] 1 NZLR 641. That case may be taken to mark the intention of both the judiciary and Parliament to take seriously the concept of partnership and the impact that may have on the capacity of the Crown to act in an unfettered manner.

In brief, the facts of the case are these. In order to give effect to the policy of corporatisation of some government departments and functions, the State-Owned Enterprises Act 1986 provided for the transfer of Crown land to enterprises such as the Forestry Corporation and the Land Corporation. Following the introduction of the Act, the Waitangi Tribunal made interim recommendations in respect of several claims made by Maori tribes. The basis for the action brought in the High Court and removed to the Court of Appeal was the concern of those claimants that, once Crown land passed from the Crown into the hands of the various State enterprises, the Crown might be unable or unwilling to negotiate with such enterprises for the return of the land. As some of the land which would pass to the State-Owned Enterprises was the subject of the interim recommendations of the Tribunal, the effect of the Act would have been to put that land out of the power of the Crown. This, it was argued, was contrary to the principles of the Treaty of Waitangi and expressly contrary to s.9 of the Act which provided that 'Nothing in this Act shall permit the Crown to act in a manner that is inconsistent with the principles of the Treaty of Waitangi'.

The nature of the action was an application for review of the Crown's proposed exercise of statutory power to transfer Crown land to a State enterprise. That was its formal nature. Far more than that, however, this was an action which would determine the status of the Treaty as a reference point for the settlement of rights and as a 'contractual' constraint upon the otherwise unfettered power of the Crown to act. At yet another level, the unanimous decision of the Court of Appeal confirmed the spirit of the Treaty as the foundation of partnership. In reaching the decision that s.9 of the State-Owned Enterprises Act bound the Crown not to act in any manner inconsistent with the principles of the Treaty and that it overrode the rest of the Act, the Court accepted that the Treaty was a document which related to fundamental rights, which should be interpreted widely and effectively and which was a living instrument taking account of the international human rights norms.

Above all, the judgements confirm a concept of partnership and, as a conse-quence, a requirement of consultation between the Treaty partners. The first part of that conclusion adds to the articulation of a bicultural jurisprudence of rights; the second part provides a framework for the ongoing negotiation of rights. What is important in this case is that it is not merely a matter of seeing the Treaty as a formal source of rights; it also confirms the possibility of seeing parallel sources of legitimacy and value within the legal system. Consistent with existing principles concerning the status of treaties, it is accepted that this Treaty cannot be the source of rights in domestic law, but it is to be taken as a source of more fundamental rights.

At the same time, the judgements affirm the significance and status of the Waitangi Tribunal in that, if the Tribunal were to find merit in a claim and recommend redress, the Crown should grant 'at least some form' of redress, though the nature of that redress might be the kind of matter left to negotiation between the Treaty partners.

In addition to the recognition of the Treaty as a source of principle for New Zealand law, this recent line of thinking begins to indicate an institutional reconstruction within the legal system: not only does partnership imply a parallel source of value in the Treaty and hence in *nga ture Maori*, it also implies a significance in the findings of the Tribunal, despite that body having only powers of recommendation. The effect of this decision was to rely on the findings and recommendations of the Waitangi Tribunal in respect of specific claims that might otherwise fall within the ambit of the s.9 proscription.

Again, both the substantive findings on the effect of the statute and the machinery of recommendation and negotiation are seen as consistent with the requirements of 'partnership' under the Treaty. It might be seen from the judgements in this case that there remains some vagueness about just what rights are involved. Possibly the most strongly stated requirement of biculturalism and partnership—to be translated into rights and duties—is that of acting with 'utmost good faith'[12] towards each other. This may still be a matter of aspiration and exhortation, not yet a clear jurisprudence of rights. But that seems less important than the political and legal indications of an intent to reconstruct rights in such a way that takes account of both the formality of law *and* the spirit of biculturalism. And if that seems too loose an interpretation of the position, the words of Cooke, R, in the *New Zealand Maori Council* case point to a willingness to struggle with the tension between form and spirit in the construction of rights. Having discussed the possible impact of the use of *kawanatanga* and *rangatiratanga* in the first two articles of the Treaty, Sir Robin went on to remark

> The differences between the texts and the shades of meaning do not matter for the purposes of this case. What matters is the spirit. This approach accords with the

oral character of Maori tradition and culture . . . The Treaty has to be seen as an embryo rather than a fully developed and integrated set of ideas. [663]

One matter remains after some of the dust of judicial interpretation has settled, and this is a matter less easily accepted within a conventional jurisprudence, but one which follows from both the cases and from the Maori articulation of concerns within the legal system. This is the question of the recognition of a parallel jurisprudence and methodology. Going beyond the recognition of specific rights and aspirations there is the increasingly stated view that, in a manner consistent with the meaning of the preservation of *rangatiratanga* over things that are Maori and as a consequence of the principles of partnership there is a need to give voice to *nga ture Maori* and *nga take Maori*, the distinctive norms and rules of the Maori. The implications of the principles of partnership are taken, by at least some Maori jurists, to mean more than affirmative action, equal employment and the granting of official status to the Maori language. Biculturalism, in a legal sense, may also mean the recognition of Maori cultural perspectives and norms in the substantive and procedural life of the law. This argument, rejected unanimously by both political parties in Parliament, is seen as a challenge to the core principles of the rule of law and the unity of the legal system. Yet the argument is that merely to employ Maori experts within the legal system, or to accord recognition to specific claims to rights, is to risk affirming the tolerance of the monocultural system and defeating the real purpose of biculturalism. While this issue goes well beyond the scope of this paper and can only be raised briefly, it is raised simply because it illustrates the struggle that is currently faced in working out the implications of partnership. It also illustrates one kind of answer to the issue which comes through much of critical legal studies in the sense that the urgent task is that of engaging in genuine discourse beyond the limitations of legal formalism on the terms of our social co-operation. To the extent that we choose to ignore the arguments about this aspect of biculturalism while recognising the legitimacy of particular minority rights, we may deal with only part of the discourse and agenda.[13]

Conclusion

The language used in this paper has been that of the founding of 'Maori rights' in the context of the Treaty of Waitangi and in the concept of partnership that is said to be the essence of that Treaty. It may still be argued that such rights suffer all of the limitations and disabilities of the rights that we deal with more conventionally in jurisprudence, and which attract the criticisms that rights are incoherent, individualistic, and non-programmatic. In using this language of rights there is a sense in which this is merely taking on board the popular and familiar uses. Yet it is also more that that and this is what lends the language of rights a texture which seems to suggest that there is a different kind of experiment and challenge to the jurisprudence of rights in New Zealand's post-colonial setting. In the first place, there is a kind of formalist irony in that it is the judiciary which has responded most readily, at least in the past two or three years, to the reconstruction of 'Treaty rights'. This of course may be taken too as an illustration of the vagaries of judicial politics, and the history of the reception of the Treaty suggests that this is yet another phase in its reception. The difference again is that the rights being recognised go beyond the expansion of substantive categories of rights or the recognition of new classes of rights-holders. While there are substantive rights being granted in respect of land, language, fisheries and so forth, this seems more than a liberal legal system adjusting its belt for a fuller body. The language in which those rights are affirmed is simply not the conventional language of a legal system adapting to new conditions. To talk, then, of the rights that arise as the result of the Treaty and of the relationship of partnership, is to talk of the necessity of reframing the conception, and not merely the substance of rights.

Secondly, the current challenges of rights are not easily received or assimilated in the consciousness of a country which has assumed the unity of law, the singularity of rights and the irrelevance of race in determining rights. For all the suggestion in the foregoing pages that we might be on the road to a new consensus on a bicultural jurisprudence, there is still a long way to go before the implications of that jurisprudence, and of partnership principles, are understood. This may well be the kind of setting in which there is a distinct task for jurisprudence to make accessible and comprehensible the implications of rights-talk in general, and bicultural rights-talk in particular.

Finally, even if the substance of all Maori rights is yet to be settled, that seems less important than the recognition of what might be seen as an overriding right, which is the right to have the Maori voice heard in the discourse on rights within law and social policy. In this respect, what matters more—in the context of a bicultural jurisprudence—than the positive identification and certainty of rights is the spirit of rights and partnership. It is for this reason that the challenge of Maori rights goes beyond the specific claims, to the aspirations of the Maori people to participate in the structures of choice in the legal and political system, to exercise authority in respect of things which are Maori, and to know that the Maori system of rules and values will also be granted recognition.

NOTES

1   Mnookin and Kornhauser, 'Bargaining in the shadow of the law: the case of divorce', *Yale L.J.* 88 (1979), p 950.

2   Since this paper was prepared for the Edinburgh Congress, the Government has released a document, *Principles for Crown Action on the Treaty of Waitangi* (Dept of Justice, Wellington, 1989) in which is spelled out the Government's interpretation of the meaning of 'partnership' under the Treaty. In part this document has to be seen as a response to the recent Court of Appeal decisions in which the moral and historical status of the Treaty has been affirmed and in which it has been

made clear that the Crown is bound by the 'principles of the Treaty'. In part, too, this is a response to the related calls for a parallel system of justice for the Maori (see, for example, Jackson, fn 13 below). In *Principles for Crown Action*, familiar legal principles of undivided sovereignty ('The Government has the right to govern and to make laws') and of the Rule of Law ('All New Zealanders are equal before the law') are matched by a recognition of the special status of the Maori (having a right '. . . to control their resources as their own') and by a diminished principle of partnership (the Government and the Maori being 'obliged to accord each other reasonable cooperation on major issues of common concern'). What partnership will mean in political and legal terms is clearly still to be settled, though for the Government it will not mean, at this stage, the recognition of parallel systems of dispute resolution if those are based on Maori principles.

3   E.g. Fish Protection Act 1877, s. 8: 'Nothing in this Act contained shall be deemed to repeal, alter, or affect any of the provisions of the Treaty of Waitangi, or to take away, annul, or abridge any of the rights of the aboriginal natives to any fishery secured to them thereunder'. And the Fisheries Act 1983, s. 88(2): 'Nothing in this Act shall affect any Maori fishing rights'.

4   Law Commission, *The Treaty of Waitangi and Maori Fisheries: Mataitai: Nga Tikanga Maori me te Tiriti o Waitangi,* Preliminary Paper No 9, Wellington, 1989.

5   Royal Commission on Social Policy, *The April Report,* 1988. And Royal Commission on Social Policy, *Towards a Fair and Just society,* ch 3. The Royal Commission observed, in the latter document, that though the 'principles of the Treaty of Waitangi' were in the Commission's terms of reference 'as one of the foundations of our society and economy, in fact the Treaty does not have a secure place in New Zealand's statutes and constitutional practices op. cit., p 14. The implications of the Treaty for social policy are also discussed extensively in M H Durie, 'The Treaty of Waitangi: perspectives on social policy, in *Waitangi: Maori and Pakeha Perspectives of the Treaty of Waitangi,* I H Kawharu, ed (OUP, Auckland, 1989), pp 280–99.

6   On the history of the Treaty, see the study by Claudia Orange, *The Treaty of Waitangi* (Allen & Unwin, Wellington, 1987).

7   Sir Peter Elworthy, 'Keynote Address' in New Zealand Planning Council, *Pakeha Perspectives on the Treaty* (Wellington, 1988) p 11.

8   Waitangi Tribunal, *Findings and Recommendations of the Waitangi Tribunal on an Application by Aila Taylor . . . in Relation to Fishing Grounds in the Waitara District,* Wai-6, 1983, p 61.

9   Claudia Orange, *The Treaty of Waitangi,* op. cit., p 15.

10   On aboriginal title, see for example, F Haskshaw, 'Nineteenth century notions of aboriginal title and their influence on the interpretation of the Treaty of Waitangi', in Kawharu, op. cit., pp 92–120.

11   D V Williams, 'Te Tiriti o Waitangi—unique relationship between Crown and Tangata whenua?', in Kasharu, op. cit., pp 64 and 84.

12   This might seem a stronger requirement than the obligation to accord each other 'reasonable co-operation' as is anticipated in the *Principles for Crown Action* (fn 2, *supra*).

13   For the most extensive, and contentious, discussion of the institutional implications of biculturalism, see Moana Jackson, *The Maori and the Criminal Justice System—He Whaipaanga Hou—a New Perspective,* Part 2, (Dept of Justice, Wellington, 1988).

CHAPTER 10

Self-determination and Decolonisation in the Society of the Modern Colonial Welfare State

Efrén Rivera-Ramos

The profound economic and political changes that led to the emergence of the welfare state in advanced capitalist societies eventually contributed to the transformation of late twentieth-century colonialism. A new type of social formation has developed under the tutelage of some of the more advanced Western democracies: the subsidised colony, or the society of the modern colonial welfare state. The mechanisms by which consent is reproduced (in a sociological sense) in such a society tend to generate a 'colonial consensus' that poses serious difficulties for the processes of self-determination and decolonisation In this paper we attempt to describe schematically such mechanisms and to raise some of the theoretical and practical problems encountered in the application of the concepts of 'self-determination' and 'decolonisation' to this new social reality. We will formulate a critique of a particular notion of self-determination prevalent among decision-makers in metropolitan states and among many Western commentators of international law. We will try to demonstrate the inadequacy of such a conception in the particular context of this new type of colonial arrangement.

The societies of the modern colonial welfare state are, typically, relatively small nations under the direct legal, political and military control of a great Western power. This characterisation may perhaps be applied to most of the still-existing colonial dependencies of the United States, France, the United Kingdom or the Netherlands. However, in order to avoid the risk of inappropriate generalisation, we will limit our assertions to some preliminary conclusions derived from the direct observation and study of one particular case: the Caribbean island of Puerto Rico. Some features of this particular social formation and of its relationship to its metropolitan society, the United

States of America, may find very close parallels in other small dependent territories. Others will be strictly specific to Puerto Rico. We hope that the theoretical insights gained from this case-study may serve to illuminate the dynamics of a type of colonialism that survived the post Second World War decolonisation wave.

Historical background

The Puerto Rican territory comprises several islands, the largest of which bears the name of Puerto Rico, located between the Caribbean Sea and the Atlantic Ocean. With an extension of slightly over 3,400 square miles and a population of 3.2 million (nearly 2 million more Puerto Ricans live in the United States mainland), Puerto Rico is presently the most important military outpost of the United States in the Caribbean region, a site for substantial investment for United States transnational corporations and one of the largest markets in the world for commodities produced in the United States or by American corporations.

Known as Boriken to the Taínos, its indigenous inhabitants in pre-Columbian days, the island became a Spanish colony after 1493, when Christopher Columbus disembarked on its shores during his second voyage to the 'New World'. The first settlement was established in the northern town of Caparra in 1508. The Taínos were virtually extinguished in a relatively short period of time, although some important imprints of their life and interaction in the island are still visible in Puerto Rican culture. Africans brought to work as slaves in the new colony were to provide the fundamental non-European element in the ethnic composition of the Puerto Rican population—which, historians agree, by the end of the nineteenth century had emerged as a distinct people. This 'new people' was a largely racially mixed (although racial differences were still socially relevant), class-structured, society whose socially dominant groups (creole landowners and a small, generally liberal, professional élite) had led several attempts to gain autonomic concessions from Spain during the nineteenth century. An armed uprising proclaiming political independence failed in 1868. But in 1897, mostly due to the instability and pressures caused by insurrection in nearby Cuba, Spain had granted a special Autonomic Charter to both islands, introducing reforms to colonial rule.

In 1898, as a result of the Spanish American War, Puerto Rico was ceded by Spain and became a colony of the United States of America. The development to this day of the formal political and legal relationship between Puerto Rico and the United States may be summarised as follows.

Upon occupying the island, the United States installed a military regime, which was replaced by a civilian government two years later, with the passage of the Foraker Act of 1900.[1] This law provided for a civilian Governor, an Executive Council, invested with legislative and executive functions, and a

House of Delegates, which would exercise legislative powers over vaguely defined local matters ('all matters of a legislative character not locally inapplicable'), including the power to modify and repeal any laws then in existence in Puerto Rico. The US Congress retained the power to annul the acts of the Puerto Rican legislature. The law vested the judicial power in the courts and tribunals already established by the military governors. The members of the House of Delegates would be elected by qualified voters residing in the island; but the Governor, the members of the Executive Council and the Justices of the Supreme Court were to be appointed by the President of the United States. Only five of the eleven members of the Executive Council had to be native inhabitants of Puerto Rico.

In 1899 a United States Provisional Court for the Department of Puerto Rico was established. Its three judges, all Americans, were appointed by the President. This body would later become the United States Court for the District of Puerto Rico, currently composed in its entirety by Puerto Ricans appointed to the bench by the President of the United States.

In 1917 the Jones Act[2] conferred United States citizenship on Puerto Ricans, restructured the Executive Council, abolishing its legislative functions, and established a bicameral legislature to be elected by popular vote. The latter was to exercise its powers over local matters, again somewhat vaguely defined. According to the relevant American constitutional doctrine, this legislative body, like those of the states of the Union, could not legislate on matters within the exclusive jurisdiction of the US Congress or pre-empted by 'federal' legislation.

In 1947 the US Congress permitted Puerto Ricans for the first time to elect their own Governor and in 1950 it passed legislation to allow the Puerto Rican population to draft its own Constitution, subject to certain limitations. The new Constitution became effective in 1952. It provided for the internal structure of the government of Puerto Rico and for a Bill of Rights. Although some have advanced arguments to the contrary, this Bill of Rights is generally regarded to limit only the actions of the Puerto Rican government, and not those of the government of the United States. Constitutional protection of individual rights of Puerto Ricans against the actions of the US government has been held by the US courts to be grounded on the fundamental provisions of the Bill of Rights of the United States Constitution.

The approval of the new Constitution in 1952 did not alter the basic legal and political relationship between the United States and Puerto Rico. Although bearing a new name, the 'Commonwealth of Puerto Rico' remains an 'unincorporated territory', which in American constitutional doctrine means that the island 'belongs to, but is not a part of, the United States'.[3]

The assertion made in this paper to the effect that Puerto Rico is still a colony of the United States—a notion that has gained increasing acceptance throughout the Puerto Rican political spectrum—is based on the following facts: (a) the United States Congress retains plenary powers over Puerto Rico in conformity with the 'territorial clause' (Article IV, Sec 3) of the US Constitution; (b) sovereignty resides in the United States, which exercises jurisdiction over the most basic aspects of life in the territory—communications, currency, labour relations, postal service, citizenship, the environment, etc—and controls all matters relating to foreign affairs and military defence; (c) Puerto Ricans do not participate directly in decisions taken on the above mentioned matters nor elect those responsible for those decisions.[4]

The reproduction of consent

As stated above, Puerto Rico became a colony of the United States in 1898, as a result of the Spanish American War. The oppressiveness of the Spanish colonial experience and the idealised view of the burgeoning American democracy held by most members of the Puerto Rican élite and even substantial sectors of the popular classes led to a warm welcome of the invading forces, which were regarded more as liberators than colonisers. This first ideological encounter with the future colonial master has profoundly affected the perception that most Puerto Ricans have since then entertained about the nature of their relationship to the metropolitan power. It, in fact, became the first important determinant of the reproduction of consent to colonial rule in that society.[5]

The several decades of unabashed economic exploitation, direct, even brutal, political domination and overt cultural imperialism that followed did produce diverse, at times violent, resistance movements. But since the mid 1940s an effective combination of repression and persuasion has been able to contain, though not totally suppress, resistance and, in general, a colonial consensus gradually emerged.

By a 'colonial consensus' we mean a generalised acquiescence among the population of the territory to the relationship with its metropolitan society. Its generative principles are economic, political and ideological. It is the result of the close interaction and cumulative effects of at least the following factors: (a) substantial access of the colonial population to the economic and political perquisites of the metropolitan society; (b) a significant degree of modernisation resulting from the extension to the colony of the metropolitan mode of production; (c) extreme economic dependence; (d) selective persecution of resistance movements (coupled with) (e) a generalised observance of the rule of law and the establishment of Western-type liberal democratic institutions for the internal governance of the territory; and (f) diverse ideological processes which, grounded on the material conditions of existence resulting from all of the above, help to generate a collective inability to conceive a non-colonial alternative.

All of these factors operate to reinforce each other in a complex, multi-dimensional process. It is most appropriate, therefore, to discuss them together. It must also be borne in mind that all of them impact the colonial society across class boundaries. The process may be described very schematically in the following manner.

Even though the colonial power and its ruling classes derive clear strategic and economic advantages from the relationship, Puerto Ricans have obtained some, even substantial, access to the economic and political entitlements, benefits and privileges abundant in the metropolitan society. Of course, the distribution and specific mode of access vary according to placement in the social, political and economic hierarchy. Local colonial élites benefit from their role as intermediaries of foreign capital (whose source is mainly the United States). A sizeable middle sector, largely the product of the modernising process—and mainly comprising persons in professional, executive and bureaucratic positions—tends to equate the conditions for its social survival with the permanence of the relationship with the colonial power. On the other hand, significant numbers of the working class and most of the unemployed and economically marginalised have come to depend directly upon considerable governmental benefits administered by the metropolitan state.[6] Much of the above was made possible by the economic and ideological transformations produced by the politics of the New Deal and, later, the social programmes of the War on Poverty of former President Lyndon B Johnson. Not even the so-called Reagan Revolution was able to dismantle the social, economic and political colonial machinery put in place by the metropolitan welfare state.

One obvious result of this process has been extreme economic dependence. The Puerto Rican economy has been characterised by a lack of self-sustained development, high rates of unemployment, a politically weakened working class—most of it unorganised—, a high degree of integration of local capital and local markets to the metropolitan economy and an extreme reliance on imports for access to consumer goods. Despite the structural deficiencies of such an economy, the relatively substantial degree of modernisation, to a great extent state-directed, and the transfer of monies from the metropolitan state— in some cases in the form of direct cheque payments to the population—allow ample sectors of the people in the territory to enjoy an economic standard of living superior, in many respects, to that available to the populations of many neighbouring formally independent states.[7]

Coupled with the dissemination, by colonial élites, of the belief that any other political condition is not economically viable, these material conditions of existence reinforce the perception in large segments of the population that this is the best possible world and that any other, though desirable at heart (for cultural or other reasons), would only spell catastrophe. Even more than in the metropolitan society itself, social programmes perform a crucial stabilising function within the colony. As a student of these processes has perceptively noted:

> The astronomical quantities of metropolitan [fund] transfers, together with other artificial measures, constitute *a new strategy to legitimize and perpetuate the colonial regime* by a great power in a small dependent society.[8]

An extremely important ideological element in the historical process of the reproduction of consent in this particular social formation has been the granting of United States citizenship to the people of the territory. This legal concept—with some undeniable attendant material consequences—has been a crucial ingredient in the complex relationship that has developed between the metropolitan state and its colonial subjects. On the one hand, it has tended to attenuate the relative weight of historically significant factors like ethnicity, language and culture in the process of formation of the identity of the 'self'. On the other, it has served as an important discursive instrument to formulate demands. Many demands for access to the social and economic programmes administered by the US government are justified on the basis that Puerto Ricans are US citizens and, therefore, are entitled to non-discriminatory treatment. This justification is offered even by those who favour some sort of autonomous status for the island. The response to and satisfaction of those demands on those grounds—which is not always the case—has contributed to a tendency to integrate the colonial society into the metropolis. In fact, one important demand formulated on the basis of citizenship has been the request made by an important sector of the population that Puerto Rico be admitted as the fifty-first state of the Union. As recent events in the island have demonstrated, even political independence is inconceivable to many without retention of the citizenship of the former colonial power.

The economic and political entitlements and benefits extended to the population at large have been conjoined with periods of intense repression or persecution against selected liberation or popular movements. Pro-independence activity has been criminalised in various ways, equating its advocacy with 'lack of patriotism', 'communism' and 'subversion'. The result has been a pervasive fear and rejection among significant sectors of the population of anything that hints at separation from the United States.

Although many aspects of life in the colony are directly controlled by the organs of government of the metropolitan state, internal governing processes—'in the limited sphere to which they apply—have been organised according to the principles of liberal representative democracies, so that officials of the colonial government are elected by popular vote. Despite the selective persecution of advocates of independence or members of popular movements perceived as 'subversive' or destabilising forces, a relatively general acceptance of the rule of law and the development of legal institutions typical of Western liberal legal systems guarantee a certain degree of respect for individual rights, such as freedom of speech and assembly. The situation described above has had two general effects: (a) it has led many people to attribute such 'conditions of freedom' to the colonial relationship itself and (b) it has helped to generate the belief that the relationship with the metropolis—though subordinate, therefore colonial, in nature—has been established by, and ultimately depends on, the will of the people in the colonial territory.

That will must always be expressed within the limits of colonial legality. But the latter imposes strictures on ways of transforming the very social and economic conditions that operate to reinforce dependence, acceptance, 'consent'. 'Consent' is thus continually reproduced. The will of the people in the colony is conditioned, through the effect of heteronomously-determined needs, by the colonial situation. Therefore, that 'will' (as expressed through colonial legality) is usually to reaffirm the relationship.[9] Acquiescence becomes the justificatory principle of the relationship of domination. It is colonialism by consent in its most elaborate and sophisticated version.

Another aspect of the complex and intricate relationship that develops among the economic, the political and the ideological realms in this type of social formation is the process by which the colonial power becomes an 'exemplary center' for the colony.[10] Economic practices, political processes, legal forms, educational policies, communication techniques, knowledge systems (including specific ways of problematising reality and providing solutions to social and personal conflicts), and, not least of all, the very style of life of the metropolitan society become paradigms to be adopted or simply imitated by the colonial people. That wholesale mimesis as a mode of constituting one's own social existence—especially, but not exclusively, among the upper and middle classes—has the gradual effect of incorporating the world view prevailing in the metropolitan society to the daily life of the colony. That incorporation slowly produces a largely unquestioned acceptance of the fundamental premises of the political, economic and social patterns of behaviour of the dominant society.

Thus, it is through what Abercrombie, Hill and Turner have described as 'the massive and constraining quality of everyday life' that ideology has its most devastating effects.[11] To paraphrase the French sociologist Pierre Bourdieu: colonial structures create a *habitus* that produces practices which tend to reproduce the regularities immanent in the objective conditions of the production of their generative principle.[12] In a colonial context this phenomenon may be considered the reverse (or negative) version of that 'daily plebiscite' to which Ernest Renan referred more than a century ago.[13]

The 'acceptance' of the regime as 'natural', through this process, leads to a widespread inability to imagine a non-colonial alternative. For a substantial number of people the only conceivable 'alternative' is that of complete integration into the metropolis—what a prominent Puerto Rican anti-colonialist leader of this century referred to as the culmination of colonialism.

The processes we have been describing may also be explained in terms of the Gramscian concept of 'hegemony'.[14] Gramsci used this category to refer to the inducement of consent to class-based rule largely, though not exclusively, by means of persuasion procured, again mainly, through the practices and institutions of what he called 'civil society'. We are referring here to the generation of 'consent' to colonial rule, that is, rule by an alien power over an entire population. Yet it is our contention that in the type of social formation we are describing, many of the mechanisms that help produce 'consent' operate in the same or similar manner as the processes by which the hegemony of the ruling classes is secured inside the metropolitan society itself. Perhaps the main difference is the extent of the intervention of the state in the process. This difference is produced to a large degree by the unequal development of the colonial economy with respect to that of the metropolitan society, a condition which requires a much more active intervention of the state apparatus to compensate for the disequilibriums produced by the market, by capital-intensive patterns of investment and by the structural deficiencies of a highly dependent economy. State intervention, however, is not exclusively, nor even mainly, in the repressive mode. It is directed at persuasion as much as it ultimately relies on the use of force, if necessary, to contain dissent. And even the use of force has its limits, for it must be buttressed by the belief that it is a 'legitimate' use of force. The similarities between the ways in which legitimation and hegemony are reproduced in the colony and in the metropolitan society result from the fact that the economic and political institutional framework and the social life processes of the colonial territory have been structured in accordance with the organising principles of the metropolitan society. Of course, the colonial condition adds another dimension which provides its own specificity to the process. Throughout this paper we have been describing that specificity. But what is most interesting here is how the means by which acquiescence is obtained—and legitimation produced—in the colony draw heavily on the mechanisms by which mass loyalty is reproduced in advanced capitalist societies.[15] This is perhaps one of the fundamental characteristics of what we have been calling the society of the modern colonial welfare state.

The situation described does not preclude, of course, the possibility of a collapse of what we have called the 'colonial consensus'. Every system of domination produces within itself 'objective potentialities' for change.[16] There is always the possibility of a crisis of legitimation of the colonial model produced by the breakdown of the economic, political and ideological mechanisms by which the hegemony of the metropolitan power is maintained in the colony. Furthermore, subordinated groups and peoples have historically demonstrated a capacity to resist total ideological incorporation and permanent political and economic subordination.[17]

In fact, resistance movements and transformative struggles have occurred and still take place in Puerto Rico. They include social, economic, ecological, political and cultural demands. Some are directly linked to the system of colonial domination. In other cases the connection is not consciously or overtly established. Those struggles, acting on the objective conditions auspicious to change inherent in the situation, may reverse the direction of the process.

Self-Determination: Two Divergent Views

What are the implications of the processes described above for concepts like 'self-determination' and 'decolonisation'? Without purporting to exhaust all the dimensions of the question, we now turn to some of the pertinent problems.

The concept of 'self-determination' is part of the legacy of the Enlightenment. Its conceptual lineage may, arguably, be traced as far back as Greek classical philosophy. Certainly it is germane to some of the most basic ideas of seventeenth- and eighteenth-century European continental and

Anglo-American philosophical and political thought. But it is in late eighteenth- and nineteenth-century German philosophy that the term 'self-determination' seems to have been first used.[18] It referred, primarily, to individual self-determination. For Kant, Hegel and Marx human beings were essentially beings capable of self-decision. As a contemporary philosopher of the Hegelian-Marxist tradition has aptly explained it: from the historically-demonstrated capacity of human beings to act in a free, purposeful and autonomous manner, the normative conclusion can be derived that they must be equally treated as self-determining beings.[19]

The Aristotelian notion of 'political man'—expanded in Marxist thought to that of the 'social', 'communal being'—coalesced with nineteenth-century nationalist ideology to produce the idea that certain human groups, constituted on the basis of specific objective and subjective characteristics, should be treated as collective 'selves' not only capable of, but normatively entitled to, self-determination.[20]

Socialist writers commonly referred to the 'self-determination of peoples' by the beginning of this century. Lenin, for example, decried annexation of colonial territories as a violation of the principle.[21]

Proceeding from a different philosophical and political tradition, at the close of the First World War President Woodrow Wilson—reacting to 'both Bolshevik initiatives and wartime exigencies'—proclaimed the principle of self-determination as a central element of the peace.[22] He based his conception on the liberal notions of self-government, consent of the governed and democracy, excluding, of course, any reference to economic self-determination.[23]

After the Second World War, the principle became the moral justification and legal rationale for the world-wide decolonisation movement that erupted largely as a result of that global conflict.[24]

Throughout, however, the content of the concept, as a political principle of international relations and as a rule of international law, has been determined less by theoretical system than by political expediency and the actual outcomes of political struggles. Its historical development, in this respect, has been similar to that of the related concepts of 'democracy' and 'freedom'.[25]

Today by the self-determination of peoples is usually meant the right of a people to shape its own political destiny and to provide for its economic, social and cultural development.[26] Of course, there is ample controversy as to who are the 'selves' who may claim the right. However, there is agreement among most commentators that, as a rule of international law, at a minimum the right may be claimed by the peoples of colonial territories. Another considerable source of controversy is the content and scope of the right. But again, there is wide consensus that it includes, if anything, the right of a colonial people to rid itself of the political control of its colonial masters.[27] At the very least, then, self-determination is equated with the right to political decolonisation.

Many authors argue that the right to self-determination may be claimed also by collectivities other than colonial peoples.[28] We will not address the issue here fully because it is not necessary for the purposes of our argument, since we are dealing with the people of a colonial territory. But it will become evident from our discussion of the nature of the right, below, that we proceed from the premise that the right to self-determination extends beyond the colonial context. It is also unnecessary to discuss whether the content and scope of the right may vary according to the subjects who claim it (whether colonial peoples or national minorities or other groups within a sovereign state). It is a well-established rule of international law that, in the case of colonial territories, in its 'external' dimension the right includes the right to full political independence, that is, the right to form a separate sovereign state.

Historically the claim to self-determination has been made effective either through peaceful means, or violently, including civil disobedience or various other forms of political resistance. As the metropolitan powers came to grips with the realities of their disintegrating empires, the vehicles for self-determination for colonial peoples, under the supervision of the international community of states, have increasingly become associated with electoral mechanisms of various types. The referendum and the plebiscite have been typical instruments to 'allow' the population of a colonial territory to express its 'will' regarding its future relationship with other peoples, including the former metropolitan state. Not infrequently metropolitan states limit their understanding of the concept of self-determination to this strictly electoral version of democracy, in which the important thing is that the colonial people be given the 'opportunity to exercise their right to choose'.

That version of self-determination, particularly favoured by some Western commentators of international law, reduces the right to a question of method. It is the method of choice, and not a particular outcome, that is crucial.[29] This view is based on the procedural notion of justice typical of traditional liberalism. It makes unwarranted abstraction of the substantive effects of material inequality and relative positions of power. Although not explicitly stated, one can easily perceive the undue weight placed on the voluntaristic, highly formalistic, principle of autonomy of the will—applied here to collective action—with its almost exclusive reliance on the outward manifestations of consent as the basis for the assessment of the validity of choices.

This limited view has another basic flaw. It tends to reduce self-determination to a single, one-time act. A contrary perspective—implicit in the definitions contained in the two international covenants on human rights—holds that self-determination must be understood as a continuing capacity, and, therefore, as an inexhaustible right. A people has a right to determine continuously, free from external interference, not only its external relations, but also its internal organisation, its governing structures and processes and the normative order most adequately attuned to its particular historical circumstances and needs. This is precisely where the question of outcomes becomes crucial. For any outcome—no matter the alleged fairness of the election process—that has as its principal effect the continued subjugation of the colonial territory to the metropolis is a contradiction of the very notion of self-determination. The question is whether nations may 'self-determine themselves out of self-determination'.[30] If self-determination is to have any substantive meaning at all, that question must be answered in the negative. The criteria to solve the normative problem whether a specific colonial territory is truly exercising its right to self-determination when it chooses among different political status alternatives must be: (a) whether the outcome is not a reaffirmation, under whatever guise, of the subordinate status of the colonial people and (b) whether the people making the decision retain the continuing capacity for self-determination in their everyday experience.

This raises the question whether alternatives other than full independence are valid choices for the solution of the colonial problem. Of course, any people, in the exercise of its right to self-determination, may decide to establish different kinds of political arrangements with other peoples or states. But, first of all, those decisions must be made freely. Secondly, the specific arrangements must be premised on the principle of equality of peoples and must not result in the impairment of the capacity of the peoples involved to exercise continuously their right to self-determination, that is, to re-examine those arrangements, propose their modification and, in certain circumstances, opt for their dissolution. In the case of arrangements between a former colony and its former metropolitan power a special scrutiny is required because of the imbalance of power that usually prevails in the relationship between the two entities. Moreover, they must be preceded by a recognition of the sovereignty of the people of the colonial territory. In short, only those alternatives freely chosen and premised on the principles of sovereignty, equality and respect for the continuous exercise of the right to self-determination embodied in the criteria advanced above should be considered legitimate options.

Failure to take account of the effects of the inequality of power and to address the question of substantive content, or outcomes, is not the only limitation of the proceduralist version of self-determination. A still more serious defect is its total disregard of the material and ideological conditions under which some modern colonial societies must determine their future political status. Less susceptible of measurement, more controversial in nature, those conditions, amounting frequently to very severe constraints, may prove to be, ultimately, the true determinants of a people's future.

The capacity for self-determination, like freedom, of which it is but a manifestation, may exist only in potential. Under historically unfavourable circumstances the majority of a population subjected to colonial rule, may, in a given conjuncture, 'choose' a relationship with its metropolis that is ultimately a denial of self-determination. The formal act of election may result only in the legal masking of a colonial relationship that remains colonial regardless of the juridicial appellation with which the 'new' status comes to be known.

Extreme economic dependence, lack of self-sustained development, and heteronomously-determined needs may become staunch material hindrances to the exercise of collective freedom. On the other hand, diminished national self-reliance, poor collective self-esteem, fear, insecurity, attitudes of self-deprecation and self-subestimation, and the incapacity to conceive a different world, that is, a non-colonial existence, may prove formidable psychological and ideological constraints.[31] A realistic appraisal of a people's true condition of liberty must, therefore, take those circumstances into account.

Normatively, the question of the material and ideological conditions under which the people of a colonial territory come to decide their future relationship with the metropolitan power becomes of crucial importance when assessing the validity of options other than independence. From a moral, political and jurisprudential point of view the legitimacy of such choices—especially when claimed by the metropolitan power itself—can only be determined on the basis of an evaluation of the totality of the circumstances leading to the decision. Not only the method of choice, but the outcome itself must be closely scrutinised; not only formal procedures, but the conditions underlying the process must be examined. Only a thorough historical evaluation may serve the purpose.[32]

Let us suppose, for example, that at some point in the colonial past there prevailed, among the people of a given territory, a strong sentiment for independence which was not only unheeded, but in fact actively discouraged or repressed by the colonial power. Let us further assume that the latter has delayed for many years the granting of independence or the final resolution of the political status question, without providing the people of the territory the opportunity to opt effectively for a decolonising solution. Let us imagine, additionally, that during that long period of external control, through deliberate policy, neglect or for whatever reason largely imputable to the colonial power, the territory has evolved into an extremely dependent society without an adequate self-sustaining economic structure, so that opting for political independence or a status very close to it is perceived not to be viable. These and other factors may lead to the conclusion that, in such a case, opting for a 'solution' short of independence has not only not been a truly free exercise of self-determination, but, in effect, a result of the violation of the principle. The question is not purely academic. Its resolution may involve very high stakes, including the validity claims for particular forms of struggle conducted by those unsatisfied by the results.

From the above discussion it is easy to see why the mechanisms that serve to reproduce consent in the society of the modern colonial welfare state present formidable obstacles to the application of the concept of self-determination. The strictly procedural notion of self-determination, in making abstraction of the dynamics of power in advanced capitalist societies, and of the particular effects of those dynamics in the colony-metropolis relationship, obviates the fundamental question of substantive content. It brushes aside the perennial question of the conditions of freedom. It purports to do away—by not looking—with the constraining effects of material dependence and ideology.

On the other hand, the 'broader', 'substantive' version, requires for its application a more complex set of processes—having little to do with procedures—that would in effect require the decolonisation—at least to a substantial degree—of the people of the territory (that is, their ideological and substantial material independence or the clear perception and conviction that the latter is possible) before they come to a situation that permits them to determine freely their political condition.

This brings us fully to the relationship between self-determination and decolonisation, a relationship which, although evident is hardly unproblematic.

Self-determination and Decolonisation

Colonialism is a denial of self-determination. Yet self-determination and decolonisation are not identical. As we have defined it, in its 'broader' version, self-determination refers to the capacity, and consequent right, of a people freely, and continually, to determine their internal processes and their external relations. It is a day-to-day endeavour. Decolonisation, on the other hand, is the process by which a colonial people liberates itself from the juridical, political, economic and ideological control exerted upon it by an alien power. Self-determination is broader than independence. For it must continue to be exercised after independence. It does not end with decolonisation. For the very purpose of decolonisation is to allow the former colonial people to pursue their own development free from external constraints.

Thus defined, is decolonisation the result of, or a precondition for, the effective exercise of self-determination? To regard it as a precondition implies that under colonial circumstances a people cannot effectively exercise its full capacity for self-decision. Therefore, decolonisation must precede self-determination. On the other hand—a voluntary relinquishment of power or third-party interventions apart—how is a people to liberate itself from foreign control if not through the process of affirming its capacity to assume control of its own destiny?

If only juridical and political decolonisation occurs—for example, the attaining of sovereignty—it is not unlikely that the lasting economic and ideological effects of the colonising process continue seriously to impair the capacity for self-determination of the former colonial peoples, as historical experience has demonstrated in the African and Latin American contexts.[33] Yet, these partially decolonising processes may, at the same time, boost the capacity of a people for full self-determination, in the continuous exercise of which that people may proceed to complete its process of liberation or to advance to a higher level of enjoyment of collective freedom. It must be concluded, then, that the relationship between self-determination and decolonisation is not unidirectional, but dialectical. They are reciprocally conditioned. By virtue of the former the latter may be put into motion. But until the decolonising process is completed—to the extent possible under contemporary conditions—the self-determining capacity will remain limited, a potential in the process of being realised, and becoming realised to the extent that it is being exercised to bring to its full extent the process of decolonisation.

But again we run into the wall of the consent-reproducing processes that characterise the modern colonial welfare state of advanced capitalism. Only a breakdown of those processes, caused by externally- or internally-generated crises, or both, may effectively set in motion the factors that could produce a collective decision to proceed along the decolonisation path.

An analysis of the possibilities, probabilities and characteristics of those crises is well beyond the limits of this paper. However, theoretically, we think it is safe to propose that the process may begin when the colonial people, especially its most subordinated and oppressed members, begin to define autonomously needs and demands. If from a certain point in history, in the type of social formation we are examining, significant sectors began to identify their material and spiritual well-being with the colonial relationship,[34] starting to locate the source of their dissatisfaction in that very same relationship is to step into the track of decolonisation. For as Dov Ronen has argued, it is when a ruler (in this case a colonial power) is perceived as the *obstacle* to the attainment of material or spiritual goals that the drive for self-determination is activated.[35] Needs and demands must be autonomously defined and articulated in terms of a project for a superior social existence. Only when those needs and demands, so defined and articulated, enter into contradiction with colonial structures and practices, will the colonial consensus start to crumble. And only then may we truly speak of self-determination and decolonisation.

On law and theory

Two final notes are warranted. One refers to law. The other to theory and transformative struggles.

If law—including the international legal order—is to come out on the side of liberation, it must transcend the formalistic perspective. It must take cognisance of results and conditions.

An important normative question that arises from the above discussion and which the 'law' must address is the following: does the metropolitan power have an affirmative duty to collaborate actively in the removal of the material and ideological constraints to self-determination and decolonisation in the type of social formation we have described?

The factual basis on which to ground such an obligation may include: (a) the past conduct of the colonial master; (b) the relative positions of power of the peoples involved and (c) the benefits historically derived by the metropolitan power from the colonial relationship. As David Gosling argues in his discussion on 'Obligations of Affluent Nations to the Poor in the Situation of "Radical Inequality"', historical injustices and past wrongs should become the basis for claims that impose a duty on a former colonial power to contribute to the self-sufficient development of a new nation.[36]

The normative grounds may be provided, among other considerations by: (a) the notion that past inequities may not serve as a basis to perpetuate a situation of subordination by granting merely formal rights of choice at some late time in the colonisation process and (b) the principle of 'maximization of community values'.[37] By virtue of this principle the metropolitan power must act in such a manner as to promote, not thwart, the values furthered by the principle of self-determination. As the latter has emerged in this period of history in the collective conscience of humankind—through the struggles of colonial peoples throughout the world—those values include: (a) the abolition of colonial subjugation and domination and (b) the maximisation of opportunities for equal participation in world processes.

As has been already argued, the colonial relationship itself is a continuous denial of self-determination. It is not sufficient that a colonial people be provided with formal guarantees of adequate procedure when faced with the selection of alternative political futures. The colonial master, as a matter of principle, must contribute to undo, or at least minimise—to the extent that it is historically possible—the constraining effects of a long process of colonial domination. Particular measures would depend on the specific historical and contemporary conditions of the peoples involved. They may, theoretically, include strategies designed to bolster material and ideological self-sustenance and self-reliance as well as provisions for specific guarantees of viability for the options of full sovereignty and independence throughout a transition period.[38] The international community, acting through its legal organs, must be the enforcer of such a duty.

Finally, a brief comment about theory is apposite. For many, theory is only a matter of abstract speculation. For others, it is a necessary moment of *praxis*, that is, an essential part of that reflexive activity the ultimate aim of which is the transformation of social conditions.[39] For those who hold the latter view, the identification of the 'objective potentialities' for change inherent in the system of modern colonial domination—as in every situation of domination—becomes a theoretical and practical imperative. For it is in the capacity of struggling anticolonialist forces to make the most of those 'potentialities'—not in expectations of 'co-operation' from reluctant colonial powers—that there lies the hope for final emancipation from colonialism in all its forms and guises.

NOTES

1 31 (US) Stat. at L. 77 (1900), 48 USCA 731.
2 39 (US) Stat. at L. 951 (1917), 8 USCA 731.
3 See *Balzac v Porto Rico,* 258 US 298 (1922).
4 Commonwealth residents do not vote for the President of the United States nor elect representatives to the US Senate or House of Representatives, except for a non-voting Resident Commissioner for the Commonwealth of Puerto Rico who sits in the latter body.
5 See W Mattos Cintrón, 'La formación de la hegemonía de Estados Unidos en Puerto Rico y el independentismo, los derechos civiles y la cuestión nacional', *El Caribe Contemporáneo,* 16 (Enero-junio, 1988), pp 22–4.
6 In 1987 direct payments to individuals by the US federal government amounted to 23 per cent of personal income in Puerto Rico. J Dietz, *Historia Económica de*

Puerto Rico (Río Piedras, Huracán, 1989), p 232. (Published originally in English under the title *Economic History of Puerto Rico: Institutional Change and Capitalist Development* (Princeton, 1986). Since the mid 1970s roughly 50 per cent of the Puerto Rican population has consistently qualified for and received Nutritional Assistance vouchers or cheques from the US government. See C Gautier Mayoral, 'El efecto de los problemas sociales y de las estructuras económicas sobre la política en Puerto Rico', in *Seminario: Puerto Rico en la era de la descolonización* (Universidad de Puerto Rico, 1987), pp 14–22.

7   We will not discuss here the enormous social costs of these processes (increasing crime rates, drug consumption, mental disorders, etc). Suffice it to say that they form a painful side effect of unequal development and dependence and are, perhaps, one of the potential driving forces leading to a re-evaluation of an economic and political model that is taking its toll on the quality of life in the colony, despite the claimed economic 'successes'.

8   Gautier Mayoral, op. cit., *supra* note 6, p 17 (translation supplied; emphasis in the original).

9   In another context, De Sousa Santos has sustained the view that the exercise of power in advanced capitalist societies will be characterised more and more by 'repressive consensus', that is, consensus obtained in conditions of inequality. B de Sousa Santos, 'Law and community: the changing nature of state power in late capitalism', *International Journal of the Sociology of Law*, 8 (1980), pp 379, 390.

10 For a discussion and application of the concept of the 'exemplary center' in recent anthropological work, see C Geertz, *Negara: The Theatre State in Nineteenth-Century Bali* (Princeton, 1980).

11 N Abercrombie, S Hill, B S Turner, *The Dominant Ideology Thesis* (London, 1980), p 166, quoted in G Therborn, 'The new questions of subjectivity', *New Left Review* (Jan/Feb 1984), pp 97, 105.

12 See P Bourdieu, *Outline of a Theory of Practice* (1977), Ch 2, 'Structures and the habitus', pp 72–95.

13 E Renan, *¿Qué es una nación?* (Madrid, Instituto de Estudios Políticos, 1957), p 107, quoted in J A de Obieta Chalbaud, *El derecho humano de la auto-determinación de los pueblos* (Madrid, Tecnos, 1985), p 36.

14 See, generally, A Gramsci, *Selections from the Prison Notes* (London, 1971).

15 See J Habermas, *Legitimation Crisis* (Cambridge and Oxford, Polity Press, 1988).

16 Bourdieu, op. cit., *supra* note 12, pp 72–95.

17 Abercrombie, *et al.*, 'Determinacy and indeterminacy in the theory of ideology', *New Left Review*, 143 (Nov–Dec, 1983), pp 55–64; G Therborn, op. cit., *supra* note 11, pp 97–107.

18 See M Pomerance, 'The United States and self-determination: Perspectives on the Wilsonian conception', *American Journal of International Law* 70, no 1 (Jan 1976), pp 1–2.

19 Mihailo Markovic, 'The principle of self-determination as a basis for jurisprudence'', *Archiv für Rechts-und Sozialphilosophie (Beiheft Neue Folge)*, 13 (1980), pp 181, 187.

20 For an analysis, within the liberal tradition, of the relationship between individual and collective self-determination, see N MacCormick, 'Is nationalism philo-sophically credible?', in this volume, Chapter 2. See also D Ronen, *The Quest for Self-Determination* (New Haven and London, Yale Univ Press, 1979). For a rejection of the notion that the right to collective self-determination may be derived from the individual right to self-determination, see R T De George, 'The myth of the right of collective self-determination', in this volume, Chapter 2.

21 V I Lenin, *Imperialism: the Highest Stage of Capitalism* (New York, International Publishers, 1977), pp 120–1.

22 Pomerance, op. cit., *supra* note 18, p 2.

23 Idem., pp 15–19.

24 R A Friedlander, 'Self-determination: a legal-political inquiry', in *Self-Determination: National, Regional, and Global Dimensions,* Y Alexander and R Friedlander, eds (Westview, 1980), p 319.

25 The fact that the principle has been inconsistently applied thorughout this century has led Professor De George to refer to the right of self-determination as a 'myth'. See De George, op. cit., *supra* note 20. To the extent that all rights in liberal political ideology operate as 'myths', that is, as clusters of beliefs whose mere formulation is no guarantee of their actual enjoyment, Professor De George is essentially correct. (See S Scheingold, *The Politics of Rights,* [1974]). But if he means to imply that the right does not 'exist' in international law, that is, that it cannot form the basis of a valid claim because of its ambiguities and inconsistency in application, he is, of course, mistaken. I am sure that the 'ambiguity' of such 'rights' as the right to 'the due process of law' or to 'equal protection' or of 'freedom of speech' in American Constitutional law (not to say anything of their hazardous history in American political and legal practice) does not preclude Professor De George from accepting the 'existence' of such rights in the American Constitutional system.

26 See, for example, the definitions contained in the International Covenants on Civil and Political Rights and on Social, Economic and Cultural Rights and in the 1970 Declaration of Principles of International Law concerning Friendly Relations and Co-operation among States in Accordance with the Charter of the United Nations (UNGA Res 2625/XXV).

27 See, generally, Alexander and Friedlander, eds, op. cit., *supra* note 24; de Obieta Chalbaud, op. cit., *supra* note 13, p 178; and the excellent discussion by A Michalska, 'Rights of peoples to self-determination', in this volume, Chapter 7.

28 In this volume see, for example, Ramose, MacCormick, Bengoetxea and Shivji. See also De Obieta Chalbaud, op. cit., *supra* note 13; and Ronen, op. cit., *supra* note 20.

29 Cf. for example, M Pomerance, 'Self-determination today: the metamorphosis of an ideal', *Israel Law Review* 19 (1984), pp 327–30.

30 R Berríos Martínez, 'Self-determination and independence: the case of Puerto Rico', *Am Soc of International Law, Proceedings* 67 (1973), pp 16–17.

31 Cf. C Mojekwu, 'Self-determination: the African perspective', in Alexander and Friedlander, eds, op. cit., *supra* note 24, p 234; M Amador, *Política Internacional,* (Buenos Aires, 1970), quoted in N Lerner, 'Self-determination: the Latin American Perspective', in Alexander and Friedlander, op. cit., pp 69–70.

32 The need to contextualise any discussion about rights, particularly group rights, is forcefully brought forth in Ian Macduff's discussion of Maori rights in this volume. See Macduff, 'Biculturalism, partnership and parallel systems: the context of Maori rights', Chapter 9. The need arises from the fact that the conditions of existence of various groups—which give rise to claims that are to be recognised as 'rights'—are generally the product of significantly different historical processes. The 'meaning' of a right—especially one like that of collective self-determination—cannot be determined in the abstract, but in relation to history and specific contemporary context.

33 See M B Ramose, 'Self-determination in decolonisation', in this volume, Chapter 4.

34   See J Rodríguez Beruff, 'Puerto Rico en el plano internacional. Intereses metropolitanos y reconsolidación del colonialismo', *El Caribe Contemporáneo*, 17 (Julio-Diciembre 1988), p 35.

35   D Ronen, op. cit., *supra* note 20, pp 46–47.

36   D Gosling, 'Obligations of Affluent Nations to the Poor in the Situation of "Radical Inequality"' this volume, Chapter 6.

37   This principle has been suggested by Ved P Nanda to assess the validity of claims for territorial separation in non-colonial contexts. See V P Nanda, 'Self-determination outside the colonial context: the birth of Bangladesh in retrospect', in Alexander and Friedlander, eds, op. cit., *supra* note 24, pp 193–220. We believe that, *mutatis mutandis*, the principle may also serve to judge the validity of claims by a colonial power that a given territory under its jurisdiction has exercised its right to self-determination by choosing a particular political status in a plebiscite or a similar process.

38   For a suggestion that under the umbrella of human rights principles contained in the UN Charter a norm may be developing that small ex-dependencies are *entitled* to continued assistance from the former colonial power or from the international community, see R Clark, 'The trust territory of the Pacific Islands: some perspectives', *Am Soc of International Law, Proceedings*, 67 (1973), pp 19–20. Ramose, in his discussion about the relationship between former colonial masters and new states, refers to an 'imperative of restoration and restitution', while Gosling makes the point that compensatory justice may impose a duty to institute a positive policy to bring about structural change. See, this volume, p 30 and Chapter 6, respectively.

39   Cf. G Petrovic, 'Praxis', in *A Dictionary of Marxist Thought*, T Bottomore, *et al.*, eds (Cambridge, Harvard, 1983), pp 384–9; A Sánchez Vázquez, *Ensayos marxistas sobre filosofía e ideología*, (Barcelona, Oceano, 1983), pp 35–46.

(I am grateful to E Vicente, M Godreau, A García-Padilla, A Matanzo, D Nina and A Fortier, who read a first draft of this paper and made valuable suggestions. Also to Professors M D A Freeman and W Twining, of University College London, whose comments on further drafts definitely helped to improve the paper).

CHAPTER 11

Nationalism and Self-determination: the Basque Case

Joxerramon Bengoetxea

Discourses about nationalism can be of different types. A provisional classification would distinguish between descriptive-explanatory discourses and normative-justificatory discourses on nationalism. The present essay adopts a normative-justificatory discourse. It does not try to describe or explain Basque nationalism. This is already being done by historians, political scientists, sociologists, anthropologists and social psychologists. This essay argues for a certain version of nationalism and tries to justify it in practical-philosophical terms (Part One), and participates in the debate on Basque nationalism (Part Two). Needless to say that any justificatory discourse is conducted upon certain epistemic and axiological presuppositions, and many of these originate in descriptive or explanatory accounts of nationalism and *ethnicism*. As regards my own moral stance, I find it useful to say that I locate myself within a liberal, non-cognitivist framework.

My discourse falls into practical philosophy and is primarily addressed to moral, political and legal philosophers in the understanding that a philosophical (and this also means analytical!) approach to nationalism is not only possible but also desirable. The debate on nationalism, as carried out by politicians, has suffered from the tendency to avoid certain fundamental questions such as: how can (if at all) nationalism be justified? What are the relations between positive legal rights and claims based on a moral-political right? Upon which subjects is the right to self-determination predicated? How can one distinguish between different versions of nationalism? What are the relations between the right to self-determination and the claim for independence?

A Philosophical Approach to Nationalism

1   I start by distinguishing two forms of nationalism: *sub-state nationalism* (the nationalism of nations without a state) and *established-state nationalism* (the nationalism of the nation state). Basque or Scottish nationalism is different from Spanish, French or British nationalism. Where lies the difference? The Basque Country and Scotland are parts of already established states (Spain and France in one case, the UK in the other) and what Basque and Scottish nationalists claim is the right to determine by themselves what sort of relationship they wish to hold with the larger states of which they are presently an integrating part. Established-state nationalism raises no such claims. A Spanish, French or British nationalist does not question the status of their respective states and usually considers them as nation states. They wish to maintain the integrity of their own state and claim that sovereignty lies therein.

2   Nationalism has a bad press among philosophers. Both forms of nationalism are partly responsible for this. Some sub-state nationalists have resorted to political violence in support of their claims and violence, which amounts to a denial of discourse, is very hard to justify especially in situations where nationalist claims can be defended by engaging in democratic discourse. Other sub-state nationalists have supported their claims only by mere negation of a postulated enemy: some Basques and Scots have defended their nationalism by simply negating most things Castilian or English. This is not a very constructive way to defend one's nationalism. Nationalism is all too often associated with bigotry and prejudice, and sub-state nationalists are partly to blame for this: it is indeed very easy to define oneself by opposition to others. But established-state nationalism deserves much of the credit for the bad reputation nationalism has as a philosophical concept. Chauvinism, zealous or extreme patriotism and militarism are very readily connected to established-state nationalism. Obsession with territorial integrity, with the creation of national sentiments amongst the population of the state, with the need for uniformity of the population and an accentuated dislike for pluralism, be it cultural, linguistic, social, religious or even racial, are features of the extreme forms of established-state nationalism i.e. totalitarian nationalisms such as those which Nazism, Fascism or Francoism (so-called National-Catholicism) represented.

Philosophers who have denied nationalism any credibility have probably had such extreme patriotic nationalisms in mind. Indeed, extreme *patriotism* hardly seems a tenable philosophical position: such patriotism postulates that loyalty to one's nation is an overriding value, not just a *prima facie* value, but a value 'all things considered' to which other axiological considerations yield. In its extreme versions, patriotism pretends to justify violence to others and a negation of human rights if this is 'necessary' to defend the 'Patrie', to keep it pure and secure. (Some time ago one could hear or read the motto *Aberria ala hil!*—the Nation, or death—in some Basque streets or even today bastions of zealous Spanish patriotism such as the armed forces and police still cry *Todo por la Patria!*) There are, of course, different theories as to what exactly counts as necessity in that case. The *raison d'Etat* could be considered a case of necessity for most versions of patriotism with which I am acquainted.

The claim for a moderate patriotism as a moral virtue has been recently advanced by MacIntyre (1984):

> What the patriot is committed to is a particular way of linking a past which has conferred a distinctive moral and political identity upon him or her with a future for the project which is his or her nation which it is his or her responsibility to bring into being (p 14). . . . A central contention of the morality of patriotism is that I will obliterate and lose a central dimension of the moral life if I do not understand the enacted narrative of my own individual life as embedded in the history of my country (p 16).

How then can nationalism be distinguished from zealous or extreme patriotism? In the case of sub-state nationalism one can attempt a distinction between the two in the following manner: a nationalist who would cease being a nationalist—though not necessarily cease being a moderate patriot—once his/her nation achieved the desired degree of sovereignty or exercised its sovereignty in an acceptable way would not count as a zealous patriot. A nationalist who would be willing to maintain the principle of self-determination within the nation once it had achieved the desired status would not count as one either. A nationalist can perfectly negate extreme patriotism, i.e. negate that the nation is the most important moral-political value. A nationalist, and a moderate patriot need not exclude any institution, practice or loyalty from being put in question and perhaps, upon consideration, rejected. In my opinion, the moment one sets limitations upon the criticism of the social *status quo* one's patriotic virtue turns into a vice. Patriotism would then constitute a virtue as long as it remained self-critical or liberal. (Therefore, I slightly disagree with MacIntyre's suggestion that the morality of patriotism and the morality of liberalism are incommensurable.)

Chauvinism is a type of zealous patriotism at a cognitive-evaluative level. It consists in believing that one's own culture, life-style and traditions are superior to—and not just different from—those of other nations. The 'little Englander' attitude is a type of chauvinism. Chauvinism is the other face of bigotry. A bigoted person holds prejudices against people that are different just because they belong to a different culture, religion, social or ethnic group, or because they speak a different language. Chauvinism is a prejudice in one's own favour; a prejudice to the effect that one's cultural and national features are to be favourably evaluated and of course are immune to criticism just because they are one's own. In other words, whatever is characteristic of one's nation is, merely for that fact, good.

Zealous patriotism, chauvinism and bigotry are not inherent in nationalism, but they are positions into which it is very easy to slide from some versions of sub-state or established-state nationalism.

3   What form of nationalism would I support and how would I ground my nationalism? I support sub-state nationalism i.e. the right of nations without a state to constitute a sovereign state or to exercise their sovereignty in the way they consider acceptable. The justification of sub-state nationalism thus lies in the right to self-determination. Sub-state nationalism affirms the right to self-determination whereas established-state nationalism tends to negate this right to those nations within established states which wish to exercise such a right.

The extent to which the right to self-determination is affirmed is an important (though not always conclusive) criterion to distinguish sub-state nationalism from established-state nationalism. This does not mean that established states deny the right to self-determination altogether, but rather that they will limit its scope and will restrict its implementation conditions by imposing strict requirements regarding the subjects of this right (e.g. being under colonial rule). It is precisely this established-state nationalist approach to self-determination which has inspired both the positivisation of this right in public international law and the practice of the international community (international relations). Since the present international order is built upon the established-state model it comes as no surprise that it should favour the status quo i.e. the maintenance of territorial integrity and the principle of non-interference with the 'internal' affairs of established states.

4

> The right of self-determination, a representative right of peoples, has an essential feature common to natural rights of man: it is a right existing prior to the establishment of a state. That it is a positive right under international law does not mean that it is *created* by international law. Rather international legal instruments providing for the rights of self-determination are to be construed as *confirming* it. In this sense, there clearly exists a parallel between the positivisation of human rights in domestic constitutions and that of the right of self-determination in international law. That the right of self-determination is a human right should be understood in this context (Onuma, 1989, pp 144–5).

There are two ways of looking at the right to self-determination: (1) as a right prior to the establishment of a state—in this sense it would be a kind of natural right similar to human rights—(2) as confirmed by positive international law. (1) and (2) do not necessarily coincide. As a result, the status of 'self-determination' as a right is quite fuzzy. Can it be a legal right prior to the establishment of a state? Is it merely a moral-political right i.e. a right according to some normative system different from law? If one holds it is a legal right prior to the state then one is presupposing a theory of law which does not accept the state-dogma of classical legal positivism: law as ontologically dependent on and subsequent to the state. This dogma either leads to the proposition that the state constitutes the law but is not constituted by the law or else it becomes circular. If the right to self-determination is not created or constituted by the states, and it is still a legal right, whence comes its recognition as being law? It could be customary law or it could be a general principle of law. In the second case the principle would have to be distinguishable from whichever formulations it took in international legal instruments and this requires an ontology of law committed to accepting the existence of legal principles not yet incorporated into legal documents, or not following from these as logical or interpretative consequences (Peczenik–Wróblewski, 1985, *passim*).

Even if one adopts the theory of law which is most removed from state-oriented dogmas, the institutional theory of law (MacCormick-Weinberger, 1986 and Bengoetxea, unpublished), one will still recognise that it is the states' institutions (or those of international organisations formed by states) which determine the practice of recognition of certain norms as being 'legal' and that the *opinio iuris vel necessitatis* required for customary law is still an opinion determined by the international community as constituted by the states.

Rights belong in normative systems. Law is not the only normative system. It is just the most institutionalised and controllable one, but there are other normative systems, like for example, morality or politics. The right to self-determination would be one such moral-political right. The statement that there exists a right of self-determination is always a statement relative to a normative system. That there is a legal right of self-determination is a statement the truth-conditions of which can be checked (or verified or falsified!) by reference to a certain (conception of the) legal order (international law or domestic-constitutional law). The statement that there is a moral-political right of self-determination will be a relative statement dependent on a given axiological system. Largely because non-legal normative systems lack a certain degree of institutionalisation it is harder to control system-relative statements referring to them or to their components. Such statements have lesser decidability.

To derive a statement about the moral-political right to self-determination from a statement about the legal right to self-determination or vice versa is to commit a kind of category mistake. The Basque Country, Scotland and other European nations without a state would have a hard case arguing for their legal right to self-determination. Present European Constitutions do not recognise them as having such a right and public international law recognises the right only in the case of former colonies (although a wider interpretation could, arguably, be obtained from the common Article 1 of the International Covenants on Human Rights 1966). Yet, one can plausibly argue that the Basque Country and other European nations without a state have a moral-political right to self-determination. That this statement is system relative, i.e. that it depends on a given axiology, does not make it less tenable. Can there be system-independent moral statements? Saying that according to our axiology, there is a moral-political right of self-determination does not save us from supporting or justifying our claim.

The right to self-determination is thus defined in wide terms as covering the moral-political right that every nation or ethnic group (and other social entities) have to decide about their own institutional organisation. By contrast, a leading Catalan constitutionalist has defined the right in such a narrow way that it almost loses reference: 'the right to self-determination means the right to liberty and independence of peoples as against the superpowers which try to control the world following their own interests' (Solé Tura, 1985, p 146, my translation). This is not a workable definition; it is even more restrictive than most legal definitions of the right and the definition confuses two notions that are only contingently related: self-determination and independence.

5   How, then would I support the moral-political right to self-determination? Self-determination is a democratic principle which extends the principle of personal moral autonomy to a collective level. Just as the individual is sovereign to decide on moral beliefs and moral conduct, so are communities free and sovereign to decide how they organise themselves. The Kantian principle of moral autonomy is a regulative ideal. The principle of self-determination is also a regulative ideal. It does not pretend to have descriptive import. Its function is twofold: justificatory and action-guiding.

The right to self-determination of peoples as such is only a manifestation of the wider principle of self-determination which applies to social (communal) entities with different degrees of generality or inclusiveness, from the workplace to the nation. The main idea is that each human grouping has the right freely to organise itself for the aims and purposes which that grouping characteristically pursues. The nation is free to decide which institutions it wishes to establish and foster and how it wishes to exercise its sovereignty. Of course, practical constraints cannot be ignored, but this is not an argument against self-determination as a regulative ideal. Some authors have elevated such practical constraints to the logically prior moment of defining the status of the principle which then becomes dependant upon contingent circumstances. Thus Solé Tura says,

> in a country like ours [he refers to Spain], at this time of the twentieth century, I think that one can no longer talk about the right of self-determination as a mere ideological principle, that is, without clearly explaining its political implications and therefore, without relating it to our historical process, taking into account the model of State we have inherited and which is defined in the Constitution, the dominating social values, and the role which Spain plays in the European and world contexts (1985, 146, my translation).

The moral-political right of self-determination, in Solé Tura's axiology, is diluted into tradition, constitutional borders and a certain interpretation of history (practical constraints).

The subjects of the right to self-determination can, in my submission, be peoples (nations, ethnic groups), workers, students, families, and other forms of association. Self-determination in the workplace, for instance, would be the right of workers freely to organise themselves and have a say in the running of the workplace and decide on their participation in the product of their work. This, again, is a regulative ideal which can find various practical instantiations. My conception of the right to self-determination is conceptually related to the principles of liberty, equality, and autonomy-sovereignty. The fact that there are other considerations (legal institutional constraints, socio-political constraints, viability, efficiency, etc) which one ought to weigh along with these in any practical deliberation about how to organise the workplace or the political principles of the nation does not amount to a denial of the regulative ideal of self-determination of social entities.

There will be problems in further defining the subject of the right to self-determination in relation to nations. One can ask: what constitutes a nation? This is a fundamental question. There are two main approaches to the question. One approach stresses 'objective' factors such as a distinctive language and culture, a distinctive history and territory, population (ethnic groupings) etc. The 'subjectivist' approach focuses the attention on the way people see and explain themselves to themselves and to others; in other words, it looks at the way ethnic and national identities are constructed and negotiated. As Smith has pointed out (1986, pp 212–14),

> nations are long term historical processes, continually re-enacted and reconstructed but within definite limits . . . nations require ethnic cores, homelands, historic territories . . . they need myths and pasts if they are to have a future. Throughout this essay, by nations I mean ethnic groups established within a territory, its members having some consciousness of themselves as forming a distinctive group and wishing to continue being different; nations not only raise the claim that they are different, they also claim they want to be different. Nationalism is both backward-looking and forward-looking.

6   There is a danger in requiring this or that nation to have certain qualities in order to have a right to self-determination. This is the danger of *paternalism*. Paternalism, in this connection, amounts to imposing on the community the conditions it should fulfil in order to determine itself or even imposing the way the community should determine itself or define itself. This imposition comes from outwith the community and violates the principle of autonomy.

In my opinion the subjective element (the will of the community) is extremely important, but it is not unrelated to 'objective' factors. People will construct and negotiate their national identity by drawing on certain elements: language, culture, religion, history, etc, or a combination of these. It will be up to the nations themselves to construct their own identities.

A further paternalistic danger is constituted by the argument that only those nations which would be viable as independent states should hold the right to self-determination. Apart from being paternalistic, this argument suffers from two other faults. It is self-defeating and confused. Nations can reply that they have the right to be wrong and to make their own mistakes. Besides, the argument is concerned with only one of the possible outcomes of self-determination—independence—rather than with the principle of self-determination itself.

This infelicitous identification of self-determination and independence is not rare, even among nationalists. Yet, independence is not the logical consequence of self-determination, contrary to what MacCormick seems to think:

> the evident need that the nation be free to express its will leads logically to the view that there must be self-determination of nations and that, since the sovereign state

is the supreme form of political-legal order [we agree up to this point] each nation must be or become a sovereign state (1982, p 255).

Non sequitur. In my submission, it is perfectly possible to consider oneself a nationalist while remaining critical of the classical nationalist creed that to each nation there should correspond a state; a creed which, not surprisingly, as MacCormick himself explains, finds its converse in the fact that wherever there are sovereign states they seek to legitimate themselves by adopting the rhetoric of nationhood portraying the state as the institutional embodiment of a postulated nation.

Self-determination is the right each nation (and other social entities) has to determine or pronounce itself on the status it wishes to have as a nation. A nation can decide to constitute an independent state, or to associate with other nations in a federal arrangement, or to have a special autonomous status within a larger plurinational state i.e. to share its sovereignty with other nations. Different institutional and governmental arrangements are possible; unshared sovereignty is just one of them. This standpoint presupposes that sovereignty resides within the nation and that it is the nation which should decide on how to exercise such sovereignty. The acceptance of this principle is, in my opinion, the minimum and sufficient requirement of nationalism. The difference between a sub-state and an established-state nationalist is not that one defends this idea while the other contests it. The difference is rather that one considers that sovereignty resides within one's nation (although it, as yet, is not organised as a state) and the other considers that the basic unit enjoying sovereignty is the established state which (s)he will usually call nation state. A sub-state nationalist will use a non-legal or political notion of sovereignty whereas the established-state nationalist uses a political notion of sovereignty which happens to coincide with the legal notion (international law again favouring the state).

7   Classical nationalism postulated the creed that every nation should become a sovereign state, independent from larger political units. The French Revolution brought along an imposed unification of the different *ethnie* (the term is borrowed from Smith, op. cit.) that made up France and attempted to eliminate cultural (as well as legal) diversity. To the unitary state that was being formed there should correspond one and only one *Nation Française*. The state-nation thus set up culminated and re-enacted a process of political and administrative centralisation. What sub-state nationalism did was simply to reverse the claim: to each nation there should correspond one state. In both cases the nation was seen as a unitary (monolithic) phenomenon which tolerated no cultural pluralism or national diversity:

> State elites employ the tactic of 'bureaucratic nationalism': they claim that their state constitutes a nation and the nation is sovereign and therefore integral and alone legitimate. Inevitably the result of turning nationalism into an 'official' state ideology is to deny the validity of claims by any community which cannot be

equated with an existing state within the regional system of states . . . Even in well established states like France and Spain, Bretons and Basques [of both sides, and one could add Corsicans and Catalans] have resisted the imposition of an official nationalism based on dominant French–Parisian and Castillian ethnic myth-ologies and symbolisms (Smith, 1986, pp 221–3).

In contrast with those extreme versions of nationalism which imply ascribing an absolute force to the claims of the nation and which have so often led to the suppression of cultural and national diversity, I wish to argue for a version of nationalism which embraces and fosters cultural pluralism and to reject reductionist homogenisations. I call myself a nationalist because I believe the Basque nation, a heterogeneous and culturally pluralistic ethnic community, itself distinguishable from other ethnic communities by virtue of certain historical and cultural (mainly linguistic) factors, has a moral-political right—and should have a legal right—freely to determine how it wishes to organise itself politically and institutionally and what type of relationships it wishes to enter into with other nations.

8 States are all too often taken for granted, as if they were natural and irremediable entities, as if the international order could not possibly be organised on a basis different from that of contemporary established states. One gets the impression that whoever wishes to criticise this state of affairs bears the burden of proof. The *status quo* favours the present-day context of nation states. They embody the scope of legality. Sub-state nations contesting the established order have the law against them, on the side of established states. Yet, classical sub-state nationalists have clung on to the idea of the state as the desirable end subsequent to the exercise of the right to self-determination. How desirable is the model of the state?

Without going so far as to predict or desire the withering away of the state, there are several factors which point to the idea that the state may no longer be the idol Hegel thought it to be i.e. the culmination and embodiment of reason. The fact that states still are the main units that integrate the international com-munity does not mean that any attempt to organise the international com-munity and international law on the basis of alternative (not necessarily mutually exclusive) institutions is doomed to fail, nor that any hope for the transformation of the classical Hegelian model of the state should be abandoned. There are some signs that point to the idea that precisely such a transformation may already be taking place: the growing *polymorphism* in international law and the transformation of modern (especially Western European) states in two directions arguably inspired by sub-state nationalism and *supranationalism* respectively: decentralisation or devolution and the sharing of sovereignty in certain spheres of traditional state competence. It is not exaggerated to say that this transformation amounts to a silent revolution

States are no longer the sole subjects of public international law, the sole holders of legal personality in international law: international organisations, arguably liberation organisations (such as the PLO), peoples (at least colonies, but, according to a wide interpretation of Article 1 of both International Covenants on Human Rights, also nations) and even human beings (at least as holders of rights, especially in the European context) could be counted as subjects of international law. Needless to say, the whole structure of international law would have to undergo a thorough transformation (a revolution) until it is generally accepted that the main objective of international activity is not the states but rather human beings in their twofold dimension: as individuals holding liberal and social rights and as members of social entities which hold the right to self-determination in the political and economic spheres.

The second factor concerns the gradual transformation of the state, at least in Western Europe. The processes of decentralisation, federalisation or regionalisation of the state in many cases have implied more than just a managerial or bureaucratic deconcentration. Many formerly centralist-unitary states have devolved powers to the regions or nations that make them up. This has led to the idea that administrative competences within one state can be shared among different institutional units.

An even more significant factor has been Jean Monnet's revolutionary idea of giving up certain spheres of traditional state sovereignty to larger institutional arrangements of an inter-state nature (namely to the European Communities). This idea of jointly pooling out state competences and resources into larger institutions is contributing to the recognition that sovereignty is a matter of degree, that it can be shared. The traditional requisite of absolute sovereignty as the salient feature of the state no longer holds. The establishment of the European Communities has constituted a real revolution in legal-political thought. The establishment of the European Commission and Court of Human Rights (within the Council of Europe) can be mentioned as a further revolutionary example.

Still, this interesting development of European supranational institutions should not lead sub-state nationalists to become over optimistic. Even though in order 'to lay the foundations of an ever closer union among the *peoples of Europe*' (in the words of the Preamble of the Treaty establishing the European Economic Community, stress added), member states have had to give up some traditional spheres of sovereignty, it can be argued that the Communities have, at the same time, strengthened the states' position because the Community does not question actual member state configurations and because states are still the institutional units upon which the Communities are built and operate.

9   As a result of this momentous transformation of the state (especially of the member states of the European Community, which are also parties to the European Convention for the Protection of Human Rights and Fundamental Freedoms) it makes sense to pause and think about the desirability for sub-state nationalists to stick to the classical programme of organising their nations as a state. The discussion will differ in each nation, and I can only conduct mine from my own perspective, Basque nationalism. All I can hope for is to encourage other European sub-state nationalists to conduct similar discussions and advocate a deep co-operation and co-ordination of our struggles especially in the context of Community Europe.

The Basque Contribution to the Debate on Nationalism

1   The Basque Country (Euskal Herria) is formed by seven historical territories: to the north of the Pyrenees (North Euskadi) there are Labourd, Lower Navarre, and Soule (Zuberoa) which are part of the French Département des Pyrenées Atlantiques; to the south of the Pyrenees (South Euskadi) there are Upper Navarre (a Spanish Autonomous Community) and the Basque Autonomous Community formed by Araba, Biscay and Gipuzkoa (which the Constitution and Basque Autonomy Statute call Euskadi or Pais Vasco). There are several Basque nationalist parties on both sides of the Pyrenees. All of them see Euskal Herria as a nation and aspire, at least in the long run, to the unification of the seven territories. Basque nationalism is strongest in Gipuzkoa, stronger in the Basque Autonomous Community than in Navarre, and it is weakest in North Euskadi or Pays Basque. There is a direct relation between Basque-speaking areas and Basque nationalist areas. After the totalitarian regime of General Franco, Spain underwent a process of democratisation which led to the 1978 Constitution. The Constitución Española is based on democratic principles, human rights and the rule of law. As regards the organisation of the Spanish state, the Constitution, which was really a compromise between the main Spanish political parties of the time and Catalan nationalists, provides for a process of decentralisation and limited devolution of powers to the 'historic nationalities' and to the other Spanish regions which would form 'Autonomous Communities'. When the Constitution was submitted for referendum it was approved by a clear majority in Spain as a whole, but the majority of Basques abstained. In clear contrast to this plebiscite, the Basque Statute of Autonomy was approved by a clear majority in the Basque Country. This poses and reflects a problem regarding the acceptance and legitimacy of the Spanish state in the Basque Country.

At the moment there are four main Basque nationalist parties in South Euskadi or Euskal Herria: (by order of vote-importance) the moderate nationalist-centre/right Basque Nationalist Party, the radical nationalist Herri Batasuna, the strongly nationalist-social democratic Eusko Alkartasuna and the moderate nationalist-left Euskadiko Ezkerra. None of these manages to represent more than one-fourth of the Basque electorate, but they jointly represent almost three-fourths of the electorate. Each of these parties offers a different nationalist agenda. All except Herri Batasuna accept the present institutional configuration of Euskadi as a working frame in which to carry out political action. Herri Batasuna does not accept the present state of affairs as a workable starting point, but so far they have failed to provide an alternative. Eusko Alkartasuna is actively vindicating the right to self-determination and the creation of a Europe of the Peoples, ideals which most nationalists share.

Herri Batasuna concentrates its activity in calling for negotiations between the Spanish state institutions and the military organisation ETA.

The situation in Navarre is more complicated. Basque nationalism is much weaker there and almost dominated by Herri Batasuna (followed by Eusko Alkartasuna). Basque nationalism is strongest in those areas of Navarre where Euskera (the Basque language) is still spoken. The moderate Basque Nationalist Party has been almost wiped out of Navarre, and Euskadiko Ezkerra seems to be attracting some urban votes. The main problem in Navarre is that there is a very strong anti-Basque feeling on the part of the major parties (the right-wing, traditionalist Union of Navarrese People UPN and the Spanish Socialist Party PSOE).

2   Basque nationalists' stance regarding the Spanish Constitution is the first interesting point for discussion. Whereas the majority of the Basques support the Basque Statute of Autonomy (the legality of which stems from the 1978 Constitution) the Constitution itself was not supported by a majority of the Basques. Many, especially Spanish parties, regard this as a contradiction. In my opinion it is only an interesting paradox, and one which I shall make no attempt to resolve or 'deparadoxify' (to use a term dear to Luhmannites). From the point of view of the Spanish legal system, the Constitution is the highest norm (the top of the pyramid). Statutes of Autonomy are hierarchically inferior. On the other hand, some Basque nationalists see the Basque Statute as a Covenant between the Baque Country and the Spanish state and they allege that this view is coherent with Basque political history. Behind these different views there lie intricate preconceptions about sovereignty and legitimacy, into which I shall not delve now.

There are two possible readings of the Spanish Constitution. It can be seen as a working framework for democratic action and practical political discourse, as a way to organise political debate. But it can also be seen as the consolidation of the Spanish nation as a state. On its first reading, the Constitution could be acceptable to Basque nationalists since it recognises the principles of parliamentary democracy, human rights, formal equality and the rule of law. Yet, at the same time as the Constitution consecrates the indissoluble unity of the Spanish 'nation', it does not recognise the right of self-determination and it solemnly proclaims that Spain is the common, indivisible homeland (*Patria*) of all Spaniards (Article 2). It only recognises historic nations under the ambiguous term 'nationalities'. It comes as no surprise that these Spanish nationalist tones are hard to swallow for most Basque nationalists; recognising them would amount to giving up the claim that the Basque nation is sovereign.

3   Another interesting feature about the Basque Country, which is taken up in the nationalist debate, is cultural pluralism. Most nationalist movements have concerned themselves with the construction and reconstruction of national identity. Since Basque nationalists postulate the existence of the Basque nation, we usually refer to an *ethnie* (ethnic group) which forms this

nation. Although the Basque ethnic community can be easily recognisable from a distance, its uniformity seems to dissolve the closer we look at the Basque community and the more we attempt to pin it down. The political fragmentation of Euskal Herria into two (even three) different political communities in Spain and France is only the most visible sign of that diversity. But there are other signs, like the linguistic situation. Euskera is spoken in only some parts of Euskal Herria, and in those parts, not by all the population. There is a very considerable presence of immigrants, especially in Biscay and Gipuzkoa, and, for several reasons, these immigrants are not integrated into Basque culture. The immigrant question has always been present in the nationalist debate. Contemporary nationalism has come to terms with the question and has generally recognised cultural diversity in Euskal Herria. Most nationalists no longer consider such diversity as a threat to the Basque nation, and ideas of 'purity' have fortunately been forgotten. Perhaps it could be argued that only Basque nationalists have assumed the idea of pluralism seriously, incorporating it into their agenda: real bilingualism is generally advocated by Basque nationalists whereas non-nationalists and Spanish nationalists in the Basque Country do not seriously advocate real bilingualism (making sure that everyone in the Basque Country speaks Euskera and Castilian and has real opportunities to speak them in all Euskal Herria). Similar considerations hold as regards the Pays Basque.

4   There is also a paradox in self-determination. The moral-political right of self-determination is widely recognised and advocated by Basque nationalists. Even moderate (wrongly called 'pragmatic') nationalists accept it in principle, if not always as a matter of pressing policy. There is wide recognition of the principle as inspiring social entities in general, not just the Basque nation. Thus the importance of workers' co-operatives in Euskadi is considerable, and students' participation in the running of universities is also advocated. Of course the principle is not always instantiated but many regard it as a regulative ideal. Yet there is a question where some of those who support self-determination stumble. This is the Navarrese question. Some Basque nationalists have adopted the view the Navarre is not negotiable, that without Navarre there is no Basque Country. Yet, perhaps the majority of Basque nationalists hold that Navarre too has a right to determine what status it wishes to have regarding the rest of the (peninsular) Basque Country. Spanish nationalists in Navarre also adopt an extreme view: they say that Navarre cannot and should not join the Basque Country, that Navarre cannot be negotiated. There is a point where the principle of self-determination seems to disintegrate: can we meaningfully vindicate the Basque nation's right to self-determination but at the same time deny it to the historic territories that make up the Basque nation? Most probably not.

One of the most delicate issues Basque nationalists have to address is how to achieve the unification of the seven Basque territories. This is a problem shared with Catalonia, but not with other Western European nations without a state. Are we willing to compromise over institutional arrangements that fall short of the ideal even although they can contribute to co-operation between all Basque territories on important matters like language and culture? This is a crucial question. I think that we should.

5 The other paradox about self-determination is that, being an expression of sovereignty, it is a right which cannot be exhausted by use. The right is not wasted once exercised. It can be exercised again and again, it is not a once and for all right. This characteristic of the right could lead to very unstable situations in theory. In practice the right will be exercised whenever a considerable proportion of the population of a territory (e.g. Navarre) demands that their right be exercised. This can be measured in the elections. If there is a Basque nationalist majority in Navarre, there is a high probability that the right will be exercised (and, as regards Navarre, this is legally possible).

This point brings us close to an idea that has recently been put forward by some moderate Basque nationalists: the idea that in each election the Basque Country is exercising its right of self-determination, that it is determining itself from election to election. This is a very confusing and defeatist idea. It has the practical effect of avoiding any final pronouncement on the exercise of the right. What is the mandate and what are the implied terms of an election? The election of representatives who will defend different political options in the different institutions. The elections held in the Basque Country are held with the implied mandate to form the Basque Parliament, the chambers of historic territories and the local councils, or to send a certain number of representatives to the Spanish Parliament, or send representatives to the European Parliament (in this last case, since Spain forms a single constituency Basque parties have to contend against Spain-level parties). In none of these elections is there a mandate for the Basque Country to decide what status it wishes to have. This is simply out of the question. Further proof that this idea is very confusing is constituted by the fact that 70 per cent of the Basques vote nationalist and yet this has never led to any satisfaction on our part that we have exercised the right to determine ourselves.

6 Perhaps the most pervasive problem in the present debate on Basque nationalism is the question of violence. By violence I mean especially the military actions of ETA but also the violence which, on several occasions, the Spanish Governments have, directly through the police forces and indirectly by setting up para-military groups, exerted in the Basque Country. The term 'terrorism' is not the most adequate. The majority of Basques do not feel terrorised by ETA. Basques are fed up and tired of ETA. ETA is like a nightmare from which it is very difficult to awaken. Perhaps it started out as a dream at a time when it was clear that Franco (or his followers like Carrero Blanco) would continue to govern Spain despotically suppressing any manifestation of things Basque, and that something had to be done. But once there was the possibility of fighting for Basque rights in a democracy most Basques have anxiously waited for the day when ETA would decide to dissolve itself. Perhaps it is naive to say that Spain suddenly became a democracy when Franco died.

It did not. And even today the process of democratisation and decentralisation is incomplete (the Senate does not reflect the Autonomous Communities and the Armed Forces and the Police still need to undergo democratic changes and to reflect the Autonomous Communities). But still, the Constitution has made it possible for the Basques to defend their claims within existing state institutions. The dream gradually turned to a nightmare. Most of the Spanish Governments' responses to ETA's violence, treating it as a purely criminal phenomenon, have only made this nightmare even more unbearable adding up to the *action-repression-action* spiral.

Our position regarding ETA's violence in the 1980s is clear: it must stop, it is of no use and it cannot be justified. The Basque nationalist debate can be carried out in open, public *fora* (in the *agora*, to use Habermas' term) respecting the basic rules and principles of rational practical discourse. ETA is a military organisation; and militarism is the negation of discourse. At the present time discourse is possible. The basic rules and principles of discourse require that there be no limits to what can be discussed. This means that all options are discursively possible or open, including self-determination and the recognition of sovereignty to the Basque nation.

It might be interesting to point out that ETA has lost support as its members have progressively tried to secure their own personal integrity and have distanced themselves from their military objectives (using tactics such as car-bombs and parcel-bombs that have killed a few postmen) and as they have lost any sense of discrimination regarding their targets: the so-called mistaken targets, the killing of civilians and even of former ETA members who had opted for peaceful struggle.

7   The point that any option can be defended (except those options which themselves negate discourse) brings us back to the debate on the Spanish Constitution. If the Constitution is the frame for an institutionalisation of general practical discourse (à la Habermas-Alexy) then it could be accepted by Basque nationalists, at least as a working framework, not as an end state. But if the Constitution sets substantive limitation to what can be discussed, if the unity of Spain or the recognition of the right of self-determination is beyond discussion, then we will find ourselves at a standstill and we will not accept the Constitution. This does not mean that we will justify ETA's violence, but rather that we will condemn those who stick to that reading of the Constitution as being negligent in not trying to do anything to solve the Basque problem. The main political forces in Spain thus have a great political responsibility in trying to make sure that all positions are viable. Recognising the sovereignty of the Basque nation is probably the starting point. Options then will range from full independence to maintaining the present situation. I would personally opt for maximum degrees of autonomy and recognition of a special status within the European Communities as a transitory stage towards the creation of a Europe of the peoples where the Basques would share their sovereignty with other European nations under the guiding principle of solidarity. But the main question now becomes: are we willing to make

compromises that fall short of the unification of the Basque Country? Are we willing to make compromises that fall short of the Europe of the Peoples? Are we going to take the risk that 'the best' become an enemy of 'the good'? I cannot answer these questions. I can only hope that all sub-state nationalists will start addressing them.

Postscript

On 29 October 1989 General Elections were held in Spain. The results in the Basque Country do not differ, essentially, from the percentages produced in this paper. However, a recent development in Basque politics needs mentioning. In the aftermath of the elections, the radical Basque Nationalist party, HB, decided that it would take up its four seats in the Cortes. On the night of 20 November the day before the new Parliament was to be constituted, and exactly fourteen years after the death of the dictator Franco, the four elected Herri Batasuna MPs and the three elected Senators were sitting down to a meal in a Madrid restaurant when two masked men stormed in and shot one MP dead and gravely wounded another. Still HB quickly made it clear it would go to Parliament despite the attack and press for negotiations between ETA and Madrid.

Note: the words right *of* self-determination and right *to* self-determination are used interchangeably. I wish to thank Neil MacCormick for his valuable comments on a draft of this paper and Drs Barrere, Ezquiaga and Igartua for the friendly discussion which led to some of the ideas defended in this essay.

BIBLIOGRAPHY

Joxerramon Bengoetxea, *Interpretation and Justification: the Jurisprudence of the European Court of Justice,* PhD Thesis, University of Edinburgh 1989, and 'An Institutional Theory of EC Law?', forthcoming.

Neil MacCormick, *Legal Right and Social Democracy* (Oxford, 1982).

Neil MacCormick and Ota Weinberger, *An Institutional Theory of Law* (Dordrecht, 1986).

Alasdair MacIntyre, 'Is patriotism a virtue?', *The Lindley Lecture,* University of Kansas, 1984.

Yasuaki Onuma, 'Between natural rights of man and fundamental rights of states', in *Enlightment, Rights and Revolutions,* Neil MacCormick and Zenon Bankowski, eds (Aberdeen, 1989)

Aleksander Peczenik and Jerzy Wróblewski, 'Fuzziness and transformation. Towards explaining legal reasoning', *Theoria,* LI, 1985.

Anthony D Smith, *The Ethnic Origins of Nations* (Oxford, 1986).

Jordi Solé Tura, *Nacionalidades y Nacionalismos en España* (Madrid, 1985).

CHAPTER 12

Perestroika in the Western Wing— Nationalism and National Rights within the European Community

Huw Thomas

Since the 1960s many of the old 'certainties' have collapsed and clattered to the ground like ninepins. Before that fateful decade the world legal order was made up of nation states and everyone knew what that meant and what they did. Since then much has happened to unsettle that familiar frame of reference. Supranationalism on the one hand and decentralisation in response to 'sub-state nationalism'[1] on the other have emerged as new realities. They have imposed themselves on the political agenda.

All, however, was not as clear as that 'Old Modality' might have suggested. When seeking the profounder insights into the human condition one turns, instinctively of course, to the world of sports commentary. From the early days of radio and television, we, in the United Kingdom—as if any Kingdom would declare itself to be disunited!—have grappled with concepts such as 'home countries' and 'home internationals'. These terms, presumably, indicate that such countries, internationals and the 'national' teams comprising them amount to something less than 'proper' national representation and do not involve 'foreigners'.

Debate on 'National Rights' tends to take the form of a discussion on terms including: nation; nation state; nationalism; independence; self-determination. As a form of sub-text, concepts of 'autonomy' and/or 'home rule' also appear.

Nationalism has suffered, hitherto, from an uncritical advocacy which tends to lack both intellectual coherence and integrity. Similarly, this has bred an uncritical and dismissive rejection of nationalism by those who would regard themselves as 'progressive' in political terms.

Nationalism has been likened to 'religion'—a dogmatic influence which

149

attempts to curtail or distort the contents of a political agenda which a rational, secular democratic society would draft for itself. MacCormick deals with these aspects.[2]

> A part of the odium philosiphicum attaching to nationalism . . . lies precisely in its failure to universalise and treat essentially like claims in like manner . . .

> Since the French Revolution, there was until a few years ago an insistence both on the exclusiveness and the absoluteness of national rights . . . There was a parallel doctrine of unity.

MacCormick then responds with a twofold argument. First, he denies that nations are chimerical objects and, secondly, he advocates 'a moderate form of nationalism shorn of some of the more absolutist claims which in my opinion have been the source of the acutest problems about nationalism' (MacCormick, op. cit., p 16).

Bengoetxea criticises MacCormick for asserting that independence is 'the logical consequence of self-determination' (Bengoetxea op. cit., pp 139–40). This comment of MacCormick's however, appeared (as Bengoetxea indicates) in 1982.[3] By 1989, however, MacCormick states:

> That future need not be one that replicates the errors of the past. There are signs in the European Community that we are slowly learning how to transcend the sovereign state without dissolving the nation. In such a setting, the ancient nationalities of Europe can perhaps again come into their own, in conditions of mutual security, mutual respect and a whole variety of interlocking levels of non-sovereign government. (MacCormick, op. cit., p 18).

Bengoetxea's frame of reference is as follows:

> Self-determination is the right each nation (and other social entities) has to determine or pronounce itself on the status it wishes to have as a nation. A nation can decide to constitute an independent state, or to associate with other nations in a federal arrangement, or to have a special autonomous status within a larger plurinational state i.e. to share its sovereignty with other nations. Different institutional and governmental arrangements are possible; unshared sovereignty is just one of them. (Bengoetxea, op. cit., p 140).

The Celtic countries of the British Isles comprise Ireland, Scotland, The Isle of Man, Wales and Cornwall. Ireland gained the status of a British dominion in 1922; independence, as 'Eire', in 1937 and, finally, in 1949 became the Republic of Ireland. The Republic of Ireland acceded to full EC Membership in 1973 along with Denmark and the UK. The Isle of Man is not a part of the UK. In 1290 it became a protectorate of the English Crown. The English Crown appoints a Lieutenant-Governor and the UK Parliament legislates for non-domestic matters. The UK Parliament is responsible for foreign affairs. Internal matters are the preserve of the 'Tynwald', the Isle of Man's legislature. Cornwall has been integrated into England, has the status of a county, and exercises, therefore, only the appropriate English local government functions.

There is a Cornish Nationalist movement—Mebyon Kernow (Sons of Cornwall)—but this seems to have made little progress or impact.

In 1603, James VI, King of Scotland succeeded to the throne of England also in succession to Queen Elizabeth I who died without heir. After the execution of Charles I, Scotland was incorporated into the Commonwealth (later Protectorate) by Oliver Cromwell, the English ruler. Following the restoration of the Monarchy, under Charles II, Scotland regained its legislature. In 1707, however, in the midst of great controversy, Acts of Union were passed in both the Edinburgh and London Parliaments. Scotland nonetheless retained its distinctive legal system and institutions, for example, a separate, Presbyterian, established church.

Wales was conquered by military action in 1282. A rebellion in the early fifteenth century saw the brief reassertion of Welsh unity and kingship. An 'Act of Union' with England was promulgated in 1535. Thereafter the English Crown administered Wales from Ludlow through The Council of Wales and the Marches (border country) under a President. This Council, in abeyance during the Commonwealth and Protectorate, was restored under Charles II but eventually abolished in 1689.

The later seventeenth and eighteenth centuries witnessed the gradual assimilation of Wales into English politics. During the nineteenth century, however, the cause of Welsh nationalism was espoused, initially from within the Liberal Party and, to some extent, thereafter, the Labour Party. Various national institutions were inaugurated, including a National Museum and Library together with a (federal) University of Wales. Cardiff was declared the capital city of Wales in the early 1950s.

Plaid Cymru (The Party of Wales) holds three Parliamentary seats in the UK legislature at the time of writing. Neither Plaid Cymru nor the Scottish National Party—both of whom co-operate to form a Parliamentary pact—has yet attained its primary objective of legislative autonomy or 'Home Rule' for its respective country. However, every major UK party—except the Conservatives, who hold power—are committed, in one way or another, to such a development. Government affairs for Wales and Scotland are conducted through Welsh and Scottish offices headed by cabinet ministers designated Secretary of State for Wales/Scotland.

Efrén Rivera-Ramos[4] in his paper on the status of Puerto Rico, and its relationship with the United States of America, draws attention to the salient features of modern 'welfare-state' colonialism and domination many of which represent remarkable parallels with the recent historical experiences of Wales and Scotland:

> Even though the colonial power and its ruling classes derive clear strategic and economic advantages from the relationship, Puerto Ricans have obtained some, even substantial access to the economic and political entitlements, benefits and privileges abundant in the metropolitan society . . . Local colonial élites benefit from their role as intermediaries of foreign capital whose source is mainly the United States. A sizeable middle sector, largely the product of the modernising process and mainly integrated by persons in professional, executive and bureau-

cratic positions—tends to equate the conditions for its social survival with the permanence of the relationship with the colonial power. On the other hand, significant numbers of the working class and most of the unemployed and economically marginalised have come to depend directly upon considerable govermental benefits administered by the metropolitan state.

The Puerto Rican economy has been characterised by a lack of self-sustained economic development, high rates of unemployment . . . a high degree of integration of local capital and local markets to the metropolitan economy and an extreme reliance on imports for access to consumer goods . . .

Coupled with the dissemination, by colonial élites, of the belief that any other political condition is not economically viable, these material conditions of existence reinforce the perception . . . that this is the best possible world and that any other, though desirable at heart (for cultural or other reasons) would only spell catastrophe. (Rivera-Ramos, op. cit., p 119).

Colonialism, therefore, is nothing 'new'. It is significant that the first serious English attempt at subjugating Scotland was in 1286—a mere four years after the final Welsh military defeat. Crude expansionism and exploitation was there for all to see well before a coherent critique became available to reveal it for what it was. The fact that Welsh and Scottish independence was lost *before* the Industrial and Technological Revolutions merely disguised the exploitative economic effects of English rule. There was no inherent inevitability in the peripheralism and regionalised marginalisation of Welsh and Scottish economic development—economic dependence was *caused* because of the fact of military conquest and subsequent attempts at political incorporation.

With the advent of the European Community, an opportunity arises for a restructuring of the politico-economic order. Against the background of a more rational deployment of basic economic factors across the European region my aim is to sketch out a legal/normative framework within which the current national and state systems within the EC can develop in response to the cultural, in addition to the economic, demands of the late twentieth century. An internal restructuring of the EC can be facilitated through legal change. Such a change, I would argue, is necessary if both the standard of material existence and the quality of life of the citizens of the Community are to be improved even-handedly in the context of a rapidly changing Europe.[5]

Why is a restructuring necessary? Nationalism is, of course, a potent force in politics. The lengths to which established nation states go to lay claim to being the 'authentic' expression of nationalism is proof of that. Conventional wisdom has it that states such as Poland and Hungary, today, can more readily endure Eastern Europe's more radical restructuring because they are 'genuine' nations in contrast to the predicament facing the political institutions of the German Democratic Republic. In a somewhat different context, this applies, too, to the USSR where—to Western eyes—the nationalities are espousing nationhood and statehood and laying less emphasis on 'Union'.

On the day the Berlin Wall was breached, West German Chancellor Helmut Kohl said that West and East Germany, 'are and will remain one nation and we belong (sic) together'.[6] The concept of 'belonging' with all its clarity and opacity is at the heart of nationalism.

Prof MacCormick addresses the dual—and sometimes conflicting—concepts of civil and national liberty or independence. He does this by considering the phrase—all too often a throw-away remark— 'it's a free country'. (MacCormick, op. cit., p 9).

It is true that civil liberty and national independence may seem to be at odds with each other. Fascism in Europe and elsewhere in recent history together with the 'growing pains' of many newly independent countries have exhibited such a conflict very clearly. Such conflicts can, however, I would argue, be resolved through a dialectical framework involving the unifying principle of *freedom of expression*. Nationalism is an aspect of freedom of expression.

It is a well-worn tenet of both radical Marxists and Anarchists that

> . . . the most imperfect republic is a thousand times better than the most enlightened monarchy. . . the democratic system gradually educates the masses to public life.[7]

However imperfect, therefore, the political system of a newly emergent 'independent' nation may be, the fact of independence itself enhances the quality of life of the people. No role in society is barred to a citizen merely because of *who* he or she *is*. The whole panoply of institutions of the body politic becomes accessible to the citizenry without preconditions such as yielding primacy to a language other than one's mother tongue; concepts of family and community obligations other than those acquired through birth and 'indigenous' socialisation. The list is endless and obvious. We are concerned with values and culture.

In general terms, it is accepted that cultural diversity and pluralism is desirable—every culture has something to offer in the development of the human race. Nationalism is the traditional mechanism (although not the only one) whereby cultural diversity and identity find expression in the world politico-legal order.

A well-known aspect of the critique of colonialism is that of its internal aspect—the distortion of the human self, through an alien ideology backed by a subtle combination of conditioning and force.[8] The cause of female emancipation is an example of this concept. Women (man's first colonial exploit) will never be thoroughly free—it is argued—until women themselves can see through the ideological concept of themselves imposed upon them by men. To paraphrase a Marxist maxim—the criticism of self is the beginning of all criticism.

Self-knowledge and insight are fundamental preconditions for social harmony and political cohesiveness. Hegel's concept of *Aneignung* is significant here.[9] Similarly, human beings, as social animals, relate collectively with other groups. Healthy, candid, critical and constructive interpersonal behaviour is desirable both on an intra-group and inter-group level. Perhaps the greatest virtue of freedom of expression is that it allows a human being to confront and accept the truth about himself/herself. The conventional attitude, of course, that 'progress' depends upon freedom to criticise and reform the external phenomena of political, economic and social structures may be only part of the picture.

The expression of national identity is, therefore, both a reflection of and a logical outcome of the expression of individual identity. A legal regime which facilitates the expression of identity frees human and economic resources for the ordinary processes of partisan or ideological politics. The political process is not therefore 'distorted'—yes, an ideology upon an ideology!—by the need to assert a national identity in the face of a countervailing, hitherto dominant nationalism which is implacably opposed to it.

Much of the odium with which nationalism has been invested has resulted from competing, expansionist nationalism coupled to the concept of a nation state. When nationalism is seen to be an end in itself it degenerates—all too easily—into a brutal, oppressive, tyrannical system trampling any notions of freedom of expression—individual or civil—into the ground. Ultimately, of course, the 'means corrupt the ends' and the whole enterprise becomes a self-destructive spiral into which hapless individuals are drawn, dehumanised and, all too often, killed.

Nationalism, as a means to an end, decoupled from the traditional 'sovereign' state, produces a healthier outcome. Where nationalism is accommodated, its expression welcomed and its cultural contribution valued, the community as a whole benefits. Social, economic and political dialogue can take place against a secure background of identity in a mutually supportive, pluralist, multi-cultural community based on diversity and consensus rather than uniformity and authority.

An insecure nationalism (threatened or threatening) resorts to wildly irrational concepts such as exclusivity by or through birth; race and blood purity; language and social stereotyping. A secure nationalism is 'open textured', welcomes new members and regards change without trepidation. Nationalism is about values, culture and community—it is not about race. Racial or ethnic elements may have contributed to its historical origins but it is only one of a number of elements in a communual lineage comprising, for example, language, learning, politics, descent, history or institutions. Almost invariably, the racial element is a 'blend' from interaction with earlier peoples and such a blend need not be 'freeze-dried' for the future of, or future well-being of, the nation.

That, I would argue is *why* the EEC legal order should facilitate the expression of nationalism. The next question is *how* the legal order should achieve this aim. The European Community evinces three levels of political activity in general terms.

supranational
national
sub-state national

These components of the EC 'body politic' are informed—to a greater or lesser extent—by concepts of sovereignty and self-determination. Such an amalgam of concepts marks off nationalism from regionalism. The latter tends to concentrate on the *redistribution* of political power and decision-making *within* agreed national and state entities.

This also explains why many states prefer to articulate the recognition of sub-state nationalities within their borders and the consequent political concessions in terms of 'devolution' or 'decentralisation'. By opting for the semantics of regionalism they hope to douse the flames of a countervailing nationalism, avoid further demands and preserve the myth that the seat of the established state enshrines the residual source of nationhood and sovereignty.

Bengoetxea starts by distinguishing '*sub-state nationalism* . . . the nationalism of nations without a state' from '*established-state nationalism*'. He says

> Basque or Scottish nationalism is different from Spanish, French or British nationalism . . . The Basque Country and Scotland are parts of already established states . . . and what Basque and Scottish nationalists claim is the right to determine by themselves what sort of relationship they wish to hold with the larger states of which they are presently an integrating part . . . (Bengoetxea, above, p 134)

Welsh nationalism, like Scottish nationalism, espouses these aims. However, both nationalist movements claim much more. Both are committed to securing 'independence, self-determination and sovereignty'. Plaid Cymru (The Party of Wales) aims

a   To secure self-government for Wales and a democratic Welsh State based on socialist principles.

b   To safeguard and promote the culture, language, traditions, environment and economic life of Wales through democratic socialist principles.

c   To secure for Wales the right to become a member of the United Nations Organisation.[10]

Just as current moves in the EEC towards a single market and proposals for economic and monetary union have provoked a crisis for many who espouse existing national sovereignty (i.e. the member states), these trends have provoked a reassessment of aims amongst Welsh and Scottish Nationalists. It is recognised that the increasingly supranational politico-legal order of the European Community may well render redundant and anachronistic the very prize of national state sovereignty before it can be achieved.

The phrase 'Equal Partnership in Europe' has come to the fore as an interpretation of 'independence' in a more contemporary context.

By implication, therefore, both Welsh and Scottish Nations—having reclaimed their sovereignty and self-determination—would not *need* to *exercise* their right of membership of the United Nations. As the signatory member states of the European Community would pull back from unilateral action at the level of public international law, the rising profile of the emerging nationalities would meet and be approximated in a general pooling of sovereignty pledged to the cause of European Union.

The implicit premise for such a development is of course the federalist (or confederalist) scenario—a stage at which the neo-functionalist logic of the present era becomes explicit. Ultimately the chief actor on the international law level would be the European Community—not the member (signatory) states—and one seat would be occupied at the United Nations. By pooling their sovereignty all the nations of the Community would invest in and derive benefit from the enhanced power and influence of a single voice for whatever proportion of the continent was included in the EC by that time. As a corollary, of course, all political, diplomatic and military activities with regard to foreign affairs and external security would—by this time—have been merged.

By furthering development at the supranational and sub-state national levels we can foresee a gradual weakening in the pre-eminence of the national level in the workings of the EC sub-state nations who aspire to full statehood should not be forced to *secede* both from their existing state systems and, therefore, from the Community only to have to negotiate accession as if their recent past had suddenly ceased to exist. Bengoetxea comments:

> A sub-state nationalist will use a non-legal or political notion of sovereignty whereas the established-state nationalist uses a political notion of sovereignty which happens to coincide with the legal notion (international law again favouring the state). (Bengoetxea, above, p 140)

The EC legal order, however, is a discrete legal order—not merely the creature of an International Treaty or Convention. By creating a community of unlimited duration, with its own institutions, personality and legal capacity the member/signatory states have irreversibly yielded the 'absoluteness' of their sovereignty. They have created a new legal order which takes precedence over national (municipal) law. The creation of new legal rights at Community level is not subject to veto by the *legal systems* of member states—it is not conditional.[11] Moreover, through Jean Monnet and the European neo-functionalists we have come to see that, in Bengoetxea's words, 'sovereignty is a matter of degree, that it can be shared' (above, p 142).

To this end national entities within the EC should be allowed to move up from the 'sub-state' to the 'state' level of membership should they so wish. This should be seen as a matter for the *internal* legal order of the EC. This would not be something which could shake the firmament of international law and be achievable only at the cost of some violence—real or institutional.

Hitherto sub-state nationalism has been the exclusive preserve of the national legal order. Relations between, for example, the Federal German Government and the Government of Bavaria have been regarded as an internal German issue. Similarly, relations between Madrid and the Basque Government in Spain, or between Brussels and the various linguistic communities in Belgium have been outwith the apparent remit of the EC legal order.[12]

That, however, need not always be so. The EC Commission maintains an office and representation in both Cardiff (Wales) and in Edinburgh (Scotland) in addition to its main UK presence in London. This signifies that political activity in Wales and Scotland—although integrated into UK structures—is nonetheless distinct and the problems of those countries are as discrete as their histories.[13] However obliquely, therefore, sub-state nationalism has had an effect on EC political discourse and dialogue can already be seen on the three levels to which I allude.

Where sub-state national entities are represented by elected governments, of course, they can wield considerable influence—indirectly and by way of lobbying activities—with both the European Parliament and Commission. Herman and Lodge[14] have described the less than ideal nature of Community law-making—in particular the 'bicephalous' executive element comprising Council and Commission. The signatory member states have resisted any federalist tendencies within the EC institutional framework and have attained a crude, functionalist, inter-governmental system with regard to executive government. One way out of that impasse would be to encourage the growth of the Council into an 'upper chamber' of the Parliament with a remit, *inter alia*, to protect the residual interests of the member states.

By raising the various nationalities of the European Community to a status similar to that of the member states the EC could ensure a far more equitable sharing of sovereignty. Historically, there would remain to a signatory member state a certain primacy or *kudos* but, as a corollary, there would be a duty to *encourage* developments leading to a more equal partnership between the nationalities. Many of the smaller nations would be content, no doubt, with a measure of devolution and autonomy on a sub-state basis. On the other hand, the distinction between the signatory member states and the 'maturing' nations should be approximated as the Community moves to subsume, supranationally, the personalities of its component parts in international law.

Practical interim steps in such a scheme could include allowing other nationalities to join the Committee of Permanent Representatives; the European Council and Council of Ministers for example. The membership of the Court of Justice, Court of First Instance and Commission would also have to be reviewed.[15] Steps such as these within the parameters of a coherent strategy would satisfy the desire for sovereignty within the re-emerging nations without forcing a sub-state national entity to pursue a political outcome which would no longer be practicable and, in the process, cause disruption and conflict.

Such a reform of the Community's internal order is not altogether unprecedented:

> At its meeting on November 29 1983 the Council of Foreign Ministers of the EC decided to negotiate expediently on the terms and conditions for both Greenland's withdrawal from the EEC and its transformation into one of the overseas countries and territories (OCT) by January 1985.[16]

Greenland had been discovered by Norsemen and, from the sixteenth century, claimed by Denmark. In 1953, however, Greenland—under the Constitution of that year—became integrated into the Danish Realm. This was one of the permissible respones to the United Nations General Assembly Resolution 1514 (XV) on the Declaration on the Granting of Independence to Colonial Countries and Peoples.

In 1972, following a referendum, Denmark negotiated membership of the EC. Denmark acceded to the EC on 1 January 1973 together with the Republic of Ireland and the United Kingdom. The results of the referendum in Denmark, however, showed the inhabitants of Greenland and the Faroe Islands to have rejected EC Membership.[17] The Faroe Islands enjoyed a measure of autonomy from Denmark in the form of Home Rule. As a result the EC Treaties were not made applicable to them. Greenland—as an integral part of the Danish realm—was treated according to its legal status and acceded to EC membership, subject to a protocol containing a number of favourable conditions.

Under the Home Rule Act of 1979 Denmark granted Greenland a measure of autonomy by way of 'limited decentralization'.[18] In 1982, the Greenland authorities instituted a referendum which again rejected EC membership. The Greenland government then requested the Danish authorities to negotiate Greenland's withdrawal from the Community and transition to OCT status.[19]

In presenting its opinion to the Council in 1983,[20] the Commission proposed acquiescing to the request from the Danish government on behalf of the Greenlanders.

In addressing the legal questions the Commission studiously avoided any wide-ranging examination and merely analysed OCT Status and the question of Greenland's conformity with OCT criteria.

Kevin Mason, writing in 1983, states:

> . . . the Commission has demonstrated a pragmatic approach . . . of adapting EC legal theory to the . . . economic realities of Greenland rather than rigidly applying various treaty provisions . . . (and) appeal to the OCT status, even with the proposed modifications, obviates the necessity for the Commission to invent new law.[21]

In summing up the Greenland issue, Mason adds

> . . . the present situation is theoretically as though a portion of a Member State (Denmark) were attempting to withdraw from the Community . . . the pragmatic approach (of the Commission) . . . draws attention away from the theoretical but important problem of how a political entity . . . which entered the Community as something less than a Member State but as something more than a colony goes about leaving the Community.

Weiss states the 'basic legal issues' thus

> (i) The EEC treaty established a new legal order as a constitution of a nascent European Federation . . .

(ii) Amendments, according to Article 236 EEC, are subject to the consent by individual Member States who, in that respect remain the 'Masters of the treaty' . . .[22]

And, of course, 'there's the rub'. It is indeed ironic that a case such as Greenland's can do such violence to the Community legal order and yet go through, as it were, 'on the nod'. If it came, however, to a matter of raising a nationality to 'equal partnership' *within* the EC, to integrating it more directly in the fate of the Community in response to the aspirations of its people— legally, a far less traumatic event than withdrawal—it would, no doubt, be opposed vehemently and obdurately by more than one 'master of the treaty'.

If we are, in MacCormick's words[23] to 'transcend the sovereign state without dissolving the nation' we must show how a practical normative/legal philosophy can be constructed *within* the internal legal order of the European Community to realise such a goal. Thus, we may be able to allow the full expression of nationalism, self-determination and cultural diversity within the European Community yet contribute, through the maturing supranationalism of that Community to the goal of a stable, consistent and coherent international legal order.

NOTES

1   J Bengoetxea, (this volume, Ch 3) distinguishes two forms of nationalism: sub-state nationalism (the nationalism of nations without a state) and established-state nationalism (the nationalism of the nation state).
2   Neil MacCormick, (this volume, Ch 2, pp 17–18).
3   Neil MacCormick, *Legal Right and Social Democracy* (Oxford, 1982).
4   E Rivera-Ramos, (this volume, Ch 10).
5   Although written from an Euro—and ethnocentric perspective, I hope that this paper addresses issues of relevance to any proposed supranational grouping of states established in pursuit of aims similar to that of the EEC. Regional security or military arrangements are, of course, outside the remit of this paper but issues of biculturalism, multiculturism and plurality, however, are of interest although they appear not to raise such an obvious or overt challenge to the established, external, institutional political structure of state or federal models. See Ian Macduff, (this volume, Ch 9).
6   *Financial Times*—11/12 November 1989.
7   Bakunin—cited in Daniel Guerin, *Anarchism* (Monthly Review Press, 1970), p 20.
8   See, for example, Frantz Fannon, *The Wretched of the Earth* (especially the classic preface by Jean-Paul Sartre) (Penguin, 1967).
9   See, for example Alasdair MacIntyre, *Marxism and Christianity* (Pelican, 1971) pp 14–15:

> Man has to overcome his self-estrangement. He is already on the way to doing this when he recognises that he is alienated . . . The path back to self-knowledge and to being at one with one's self is what Hegel calls 'appropriation' or 'coming to one's own'.

10 Extract from Constitution of Plaid Cymru (The Party of Wales)—cited in membership card for 1989–90.

11 See on this, for example—43–75 *Defrenne v Sabena* (1976) ECR 455; 26/62 *Van Gend en Loos v Nederlandse Administrie der Belastingen* (1963) ECR 1; 6/64 *Costa v ENEL* (1964) ECR 585. P Pescatore, 'International Law and Community Law—a cumulative analysis', *Common Market Law Review,* 7 (1970), pp 167–85. J-P Warner, The relationship between European Community Law and The national law of member states, *Law Quarterly Review,* (1977), pp 369–86.

12 But see *infra* at p 157 *et seq*—Greenland.

13 A more flexible approach to National representation at EC level should go some way towards accommodating Richard De George's criticism:

> The myth reveals a widespread liberal belief in the autonomy of persons and in the right of peoples to be free of foreign domination and of tyrannous rule. But the myth hides the fact that the right . . . is simply not thought appropriate for many groups, or for many minorities within established states. (op. cit., *supra*, p 2).

14 V Herman and J Lodge, *The European Parliament and the E.C.* (MacMillan, 1978); and see also Hermann and Van Schendelen, *The European Parliament and the National Parliaments* (Saxon House, 1979).

15 At present the Court of Justice (and, now, the Court of First Instance) together with the Commission comprise appointees from the member states.

16 Friedel Weiss, 'Greenland's withdrawal from the European Communities', *European Law Review,* 173 (1985), pp 173–85.

17 Idem., p 176.

18 Idem., p 175.

19 Association as Overseas Country or Territory TREATY OF ROME (EC) 1957 (Arts. 131–6). In effect a measure to cater for the remaining colonies and dependent territories of France and the UK and the Netherlands. Territories must be *non-European* and must possess *special relations* with Member States.

20 Commission opinion on the Status of Greenland, *Bulletin of the European Communities,* Supplement 1/83

21 Kevin Mason, 'Greenland—withdrawal from the EEC' *Georgia Journal of International and Comparative Law,* 13 (1983), pp 856–76.

22 Weiss, op. cit., no 17, p 176–7.

23 MacCormick, this volume, Ch 2.

Index of names